POP CULTURE AND THE DARK SIDE
OF THE AMERICAN DREAM

POP CULTURE
AND THE DARK SIDE OF THE AMERICAN DREAM

CON MEN, GANGSTERS, DRUG LORDS, AND ZOMBIES

PAUL A. CANTOR

 UNIVERSITY PRESS OF KENTUCKY

Scholarly publisher for the Commonwealth,
serving Bellarmine University, Berea College, Centre
College of Kentucky, Eastern Kentucky University,
The Filson Historical Society, Georgetown College,
Kentucky Historical Society, Kentucky State University,
Morehead State University, Murray State University,
Northern Kentucky University, Transylvania University,
University of Kentucky, University of Louisville,
and Western Kentucky University.
All rights reserved.

Editorial and Sales Offices: The University Press of Kentucky
663 South Limestone Street, Lexington, Kentucky 40508-4008
www.kentuckypress.com

Cataloging-in-Publication data available from the Library of Congress

ISBN 978-0-8131-7730-4 (cloth : alk. paper)
ISBN 978-0-8131-7732-8 (pdf)
ISBN 978-0-8131-7733-5 (epub)

This book is printed on acid-free paper meeting
the requirements of the American National Standard
for Permanence in Paper for Printed Library Materials.

Manufactured in the United States of America.

Member of the Association
of University Presses

We're a big rough rich wild people and crime is the price we pay for it, and organized crime is the price we pay for organization. We'll have it with us a long time. Organized crime is just the dirty side of the sharp dollar.

Raymond Chandler, *The Long Goodbye*

CONTENTS

PREFACE

With this book I am continuing the exploration of American popular culture that I began in *Gilligan Unbound: Pop Culture in the Age of Globalization* (2001) and carried forward in *The Invisible Hand in Popular Culture: Liberty vs. Authority in American Film and TV* (2012). In these books I have already analyzed examples of several of the most important genres of popular culture: the Western, science fiction, the horror movie, and film noir. In this book I return to some of these genres, but for the first time I take up the gangster story, which allows me to discuss some of my all-time favorite works, the *Godfather* films and *Breaking Bad*.

As in my previous books, I do not claim to offer a systematic survey of my topic, in this case the dark side of the American dream. I am a literary critic, not a historian or a sociologist. I discuss representative examples of a significant strain in popular culture. Each of the works I analyze tells us something important about my central subject, but I do not claim that they tell the whole story. I show that a set of themes runs throughout these works, but that does not mean that other works do not have something significant to add to a full treatment of the dark side of the American dream. My readers will no doubt think of many works that they wish I had included in this book. If I had the time and space, I would have added several chapters, for example, one on F. Scott Fitzgerald's *The Great Gatsby* or one on Orson Welles's *Citizen Kane*. To mention a lesser-known work but one that I particularly like and that would have fit perfectly in this book, I wish I could have written a chapter on Albert Brooks's hilarious film *Lost in America,* which offers brilliant variations on my central theme, dealing as it does with several classic components of the American dream: the road trip, the mobile home, the nest egg, gambling, and Las Vegas. But there is just so much one can do in a single book, and I admit that I have sacrificed breadth for depth. I would rather analyze a few works thoroughly than to survey a wide range of works superficially.

Even though I have narrowed my focus to a handful of works, this book still covers a lot of ground. We will move from *Huckleberry Finn* in 1884 to *The Walking Dead* in the present day, from comic treatments of my subject to tragic treatments, and from a novel to films to television shows (with W. C. Fields's juggling act thrown in for good measure). And we will do all this while ranging over the map of America—from New York to California, with many stops in between, including Atlanta, Albuquerque, and Arlington, Virginia (just to mention the *A*s).

Chapters 1, 2, and 5 have been published previously in various forms, but all three have been rewritten and substantially expanded for this book. Chapters 3 and 4 appear in print for the first time. Analyzing popular culture raises all sorts of difficult issues of interpretation, which academics tend to obsess over but which general readers might find boring. I have tried to keep such so-called hermeneutical questions to a minimum in the book proper. For those who want to learn my stand on such issues—for example, why I speak of Francis Ford Coppola as the "author" of the *Godfather* films when so many others had a hand in their creation—please turn to the appendix of chapter 3, where I briefly discuss these matters and also provide citations to more extensive treatments in my two earlier books and elsewhere.

I have generally confined to the notes material that would be of interest mainly to specialists and scholars, but not to general readers. I have also worked to keep the individual chapters relatively self-contained, even at the price of some repetition, for the sake of readers who are particularly interested in one of the works I discuss. But I believe that these works benefit from being discussed together. I do not attempt to tell a single continuous narrative in this book, but the chapters keep coming back to a set of common motifs and thereby build on one another.

INTRODUCTION

The [American] dream is a vision of a better, deeper, richer life for every individual, regardless of the position in society which he or she may occupy by the accident of birth. It has been a dream of a chance to rise in the economic scale, but quite as much, or more than that, of a chance to develop our capacities to the full, unhampered by unjust restrictions of caste or custom. With this has gone the hope of bettering the physical conditions of living, of lessening the toil and anxieties of daily life.

John Truslow Adams

Sharks and Sponges

Americans love success stories. Accordingly, American popular culture is filled with them—stirring tales of ordinary people achieving what is known as the American dream. With their rags-to-riches plots, Horatio Alger's novels were bestsellers in the nineteenth century, and they have been re-created ever since in films and television shows. Over the years, Americans have been bombarded with stories that teach a simple lesson: if you work hard and remain true to your vision, you will be rewarded and get to live the American dream.[1]

One peculiar home of the success story in American popular culture is the game show and, more recently, reality TV. The titles of game shows, from *Queen for a Day* to *Who Wants to Be a Millionaire?*, make their aspirational nature clear. These shows compress achieving the American dream into a conveniently compact time frame. Through varying combinations of skill and luck, the contestants get to realize their dreams almost instantaneously and right before our eyes on the television screen, thus providing an uplifting spectacle. As for reality TV, one of its most successful incarnations is ABC's *Shark Tank,* a show in which ordinary Americans pursuing their dreams appear before a panel of already successful businessmen and businesswomen.[2] These "wantrepreneurs," as they are known, seek to get the savvy sharks to invest in their fledging ventures, asking for, say, $100,000 for a 10 percent stake in their businesses. Although a lot happens behind the scenes that we do not get to see on *Shark Tank,* the deals made are basically for real. The sharks are genuinely wealthy investors, who do put up their own money. Some of the business plans pitched have gone on to become big winners, most notably the Scrub Daddy sponge brought to market by shark Lori Greiner with help from the QVC channel, which quickly reached revenues of over $100 million per year. *Shark Tank* is living testimony to the reality of the American dream. For all the show-biz hype involved, in the end the financial figures do not lie, and both the contestants and the sharks frequently refer with good cause to the way that they are living the American dream.

I confess to being a big fan of *Shark Tank*. So why am I writing about popular culture and the *dark* side of the American dream? Why don't I act like a good American and look at the bright side of things? The answer is suggested by the famous opening sentence of Tolstoy's *Anna Karenina*: "Happy families are all alike; every unhappy family is unhappy in its own way" (Constance Garnett's translation). Success stories can be edifying, but after a while they all begin to sound alike and they can become boring. If only for the sake of variety, one begins to long for a story of someone who *failed* to achieve the American dream. Such stories are more dramatic and, frankly, more interesting; they may reveal something about the American dream that an endless parade of success stories would conceal. From F. Scott Fitzgerald's novel *The Great Gatsby* to Orson Welles's film *Citizen Kane,* some of the great American classics have told the stories of people who pursued the American dream, but with disastrous results. In the core of this book, chapters 3 and 4, I discuss perhaps the greatest achievement in American cinema, Francis Ford Coppola's *Godfather* films, as well as perhaps the greatest achievement in American television, Vince Gilligan's *Breaking Bad.* One of the reasons these achievements are so great is that Coppola and Gilligan do not follow the crowd by simply buying into the American dream; rather they raise profound doubts about its validity and viability, and in the process reveal something important about America.

One can acknowledge the historical reality of the American dream—the United States has indeed proved to be a land of opportunity for millions of people—while still admitting that the American dream is not an unproblematic concept. It is in fact very much to the credit of American popular culture that, even in the face of general celebration of the American dream, it has at times been willing to raise doubts about this widely cherished ideal. One has to admire the artists who have had the courage to ask tough questions about the American dream, but we should also admire those segments of the American public who have embraced these dark visions. The contempt many intellectuals have expressed for the taste of the American public needs to be reconsidered in light of the way that narratives as dark and complex as the *Godfather* films and *Breaking Bad* have become commercial successes. This book explores the question of why portrayals of the dark side of the American dream have resonated with and appealed to broad segments of an American public normally thought to be naively optimistic in its vision of itself.

All the works I discuss in this book—from *Adventures of Huckleberry Finn* to *The Walking Dead*—expose the inner tensions in the American dream. It turns out that there is no single conception of the American dream, and the different versions can be at odds with one another. In one traditional version of the American dream, a man is supposed to work hard to earn enough money to support his family and to keep them supplied with all the amenities of life. But the man's work inevitably takes him away from his family, and it may ultimately threaten to subvert the very family values he set out to promote. As we will see, the conflict between "business" and "family" is at the heart of both the *Godfather* films and *Breaking Bad,* works that show that in his efforts to protect his family, a man may end up destroying it. Americans like to think that they can have it all—that all their values are fundamentally compatible. The *Godfather* films and *Breaking Bad* are deeply disturbing because they force us to think about the difficult choices that human beings sometimes have to make between one set of values and another, choices that in traditional literature are regarded as tragic.

An Overview

I begin this book with Mark Twain and his *Adventures of Huckleberry Finn.* Twain provides a good starting point for someone who, like me, wants to claim that the line between elite culture and popular culture is often drawn arbitrarily and keeps changing over time. Twain is today regarded as a classic American author, and *Huckleberry Finn* has become part of the canon of great works of American literature. But in his own day Twain was highly successful commercially and regarded as a popular author, barely one step above a journalist. *Huckleberry Finn* was initially condemned by many cultural gatekeepers as a vulgar novel, especially for its broad humor and its use of American vernacular language. *Huckleberry Finn* is a perfect illustration of the way that the elite culture of today is often the popular culture of an earlier time period. I predict that a hundred years from now the *Godfather* films and *Breaking Bad* will still be remembered and taken seriously as American classics, and for many of the same reasons that elevated *Huckleberry Finn* into the literary canon. Indeed the canonization of the *Godfather* films is virtually complete, and that of *Breaking Bad* is already well under way.

Mark Twain also provides a good place to begin examining the American dream. Like several of the creative figures I discuss (including Coppola, Gilligan, and W. C. Fields), Twain himself is a living embodiment of the American dream, providing a classic American success story, as he rose from humble beginnings to fame and fortune. Moreover, like W. C. Fields, who began life as William Claude Dukenfield, Mark Twain renamed himself; born Samuel Clemens, he reinvented himself as a literary celebrity after not doing as well as he had hoped in earlier, nonartistic careers. Twain thus illustrates in his own life an important component of the American dream—the ability to refashion one's identity to get ahead in the world. The fluidity of identity in democratic America turns out to be a central theme in *Huckleberry Finn* and gives us our first glimpse of both the bright side and the dark side of the American dream. Released from the shackles of aristocratic society in Europe, with its fixed social hierarchy, Americans are free to become the best that they can be and to rise in social and economic position. Twain associates this social mobility with frontier existence—*Huckleberry Finn* deals with an era when the Mississippi was the beginning of the Wild West. Like many nineteenth-century writers, Twain celebrates the frontier for giving Americans a chance at a fresh start in life.

But the dark side of the American dream surfaces once one realizes that a fresh start may easily become a false start. The freedom to reinvent oneself that Americans cherish is also a license for imposture. In *Huckleberry Finn* the American ideal of the self-made man is shadowed by the specter of the con man. As a result, a book that celebrates democratic freedom also chronicles the many ways that freedom can be abused. In a pattern that we will find repeated in subsequent chapters, in *Huckleberry Finn* the entrepreneurial spirit of America, embodied in many a get-rich-quick scheme, shades over imperceptibly into various forms of criminality. In the misadventures of the charlatan king and duke, Twain identifies a problem in the new democracy—its need to find new forms of nobility and thus its nostalgia for traditional European aristocratic poses—attitudes that have made Americans peculiarly susceptible to Old World impostors.

Chapter 2, on W. C. Fields, is something new for me, almost a biographical essay. With my background as a literary critic, in my work on popular culture I generally choose to discuss a single film or television show and analyze it with the care I would exercise in interpreting a work of literature. In my Fields chapter, I do discuss at some length what is probably his best film, *The Bank Dick*, but I also survey his whole show-business career, which took him from vaudeville to the Broadway stage to Hollywood and stardom in both movies and radio. The stage persona he painstakingly crafted over his long career is his most lasting achievement and has allowed him to pass into the realm of show-business legend. Like Twain, Fields lived the American dream, but he struggled enough to do so that he became acutely aware of its dark side. In an almost postmodern fashion, Fields was extremely self-conscious in his art and delighted in exposing its artificiality. His favorite role in films was as a con man. Indeed he thought of himself as conning his audience with the cinematic power of illusion that Hollywood placed at his disposal. His films generally deal with men in uncomfortable domestic situations who turn to get-rich-quick schemes in a desperate attempt to escape the suffocating atmosphere of their homes. In one of his best films, *It's a Gift*, Fields takes up a specific variant of the American dream—"California Dreamin'"—the compulsion to go to the West Coast to make one's fortune. As a comedian, Fields necessarily gives his films happy endings, but they usually occur as a result of improbable turns in the plots, thus raising doubts about how realistic the successful resolutions truly are. Fields offers the paradox of an artist who provides lighthearted portrayals of the dark side of the American dream.

With chapter 3, on the *Godfather* films, I pivot from the comic works of Twain and Fields to Coppola's more serious—and even darker—treatment of the American dream. Coppola created an American classic by dwelling on the classic American experience—immigration. The American dream has perennially drawn immigrants to the United States, and their fate has been its toughest test. Does America live up to its claim to be a land of opportunity for foreigners, or is it all an empty dream? In the story of the Corleone family, Coppola portrays Sicilian immigrants struggling to create a new and better life in the United States. They must navigate the difficult transition from the Old World to the New, and also from the past to the present, from a quasi-feudal way of life in Sicily, rooted in antiquated customs, to a modern America characterized by impersonal economic relations and corporate organization. For Coppola, the American dream even at its best extracts a cost by forcing people to abandon their traditional communal way of life. For immigrants, chasing the American dream becomes even more difficult. Because of various forms of prejudice and government restrictions, they are barred from many of the usual paths to making a fortune, and that may tempt them into a life of crime.

Twain and Fields treat comically the thin line between legitimate business and criminality in America. Coppola takes this issue very seriously; the identification between organized crime and capitalism is central to the *Godfather* films. The Corleones *are* criminals, but they exhibit many of the virtues that are celebrated in the annals of famous American entrepreneurs. In some ways, Vito Corleone does achieve the American dream by succeeding in business and providing for his family. But he never fully enjoys his status; he remains entangled with organized crime forces, and he lives to see the dashing of his hopes for his sons to become prominent members of legitimate social circles. In his son Michael's efforts to complete his father's dreams, he follows the familiar American pattern of moving west and hopes to reinvent the Corleone family in a setting right out of a Western, a frontier casino. Michael manages to triumph over all his enemies and even to stymie the federal government's efforts to bring him down, but in the process he destroys the one thing he claimed to value more than anything else—his family. In the immigrant experience, Coppola sees the American dream as a source of tragedy, and I analyze both Vito and Michael Corleone as tragic heroes.

In my ongoing attempt to show that film and television should be taken seriously, one of the aims of this book is to introduce the concept of tragedy and the tragic hero into the study of popular culture, an effort that culminates in chapter 4 on *Breaking Bad*. Having devoted much of my career to studying Shakespeare, I have often used his plays as reference points in interpreting films and television shows. Chapter 4 fulfills a long-held dream of mine—to offer a systematic comparison of a Shakespeare play with a work of popular culture. I use *Macbeth* to help us understand *Breaking Bad*. I expect that this will be the most controversial chapter of my book. Many will be horrified that I speak of the murderous drug lord Walter White as any kind of hero, let alone a Shakespearean hero. For many, including, as we will see, the creator of the show, Vince Gilligan, White is the *villain* of *Breaking Bad*. They view him as a moral monster, responsible for the deaths of women and children. That he is, *but so is Macbeth,* as witness the way he has Macduff's wife and babes slaughtered. Many refer to Macbeth as a villain, but as the title of the play shows, he is the hero of the play, albeit a tragic hero.

Shakespeare's tragic heroes are morally complex figures and not simply good guys or bad guys (Othello strangles his innocent wife to death, and yet we come to think of him as "one that loved not wisely but too well"). We have grown too accustomed to Shakespeare's plays. Having become almost foundational documents of our culture, they are assumed to be conventional, morally and otherwise. In fact, Shakespeare's tragedies are intellectually daring and raise disturbing questions about human existence. Are all forms of human excellence compatible? Can a man admirable in certain respects nevertheless commit terrible deeds under extreme circumstances? Because he was troubled by such perplexing questions, Shakespeare wrote tragedies. You do not write genuine tragedies if you are comfortable with the world, if you think that the world order is simple and unconflicted and that all ethical issues can be easily and unequivocally resolved. Whatever else they do, Shakespeare's tragedies should make us shudder at the way that the world order refuses to follow any simple moral calculus. I am not claiming that Vince Gilligan is the equal of Shakespeare—no one is—but I do believe that *Breaking Bad* comes as close as American popular culture can to the level of Shakespeare's dramas (which we should remember were the popular culture of their day). And one reason for my judgment is that the show poses the same kind of difficult and unnerving ethical questions that are raised by *Macbeth*.

I realize how odd it must sound to speak of Shakespearean tragedy in relation to a mere television show, especially one dealing with a crystal meth manufacturer. We are not used to thinking of television shows as tragedies. Genuinely tragic narratives rarely appear in American popular culture because, generally speaking, Americans do not have a tragic view of life. As we have seen, Americans love success stories, and that is another way of saying that they love happy endings. We speak of "Hollywood endings" because American popular culture has a way of making stories end happily, even when they may momentarily flirt with tragedy. American popular culture usually tells morally simplistic stories, with clear-cut distinctions between the good guys and the bad guys. This kind of melodrama is the opposite of tragedy. It is hardly surprising, then, that the concepts of "tragedy" and "tragic hero" do not often appear in discourse about American popular culture. I will argue that these concepts can in fact be very helpful in analyzing contemporary television, especially the kind of complex and dark protagonist that has emerged in American television since its quantum leap in sophistication as a result of the new opportunities created by the development of cable TV and streaming services. People just do not know what to call a character like Walter White. Hero? Villain? Antihero? I hope to show that a great deal falls into place once one begins to think of Walter White as a tragic hero (spoiler alert: I will ultimately concede in chapter 4 that White is a very peculiar kind of tragic hero).

Breaking Bad could be viewed as a kind of sequel to the *Godfather* films. The series contains several references to the films, showing that the characters themselves are aware of their precursors in popular culture. More to the point, *Breaking Bad* continues the history of organized crime in America that the *Godfather* films initiate. The War on Drugs replaces Prohibition; Mexican drug cartels replace the Mafia; organized crime, which does not reach the national level until well into *The Godfather Part One* and makes its first steps toward going international only in *The Godfather Part Two,* reaches the global level in *Breaking Bad,* infiltrating deep into the structures of multinational corporations. The penetration of organized crime into corporate America that Michael Corleone can only dream of seems to be an accomplished fact in *Breaking Bad.*

Thus *Breaking Bad* builds on the themes we will see developed in the earlier works I discuss in chapters 1 through 3. In the hallowed American tradition of the self-made man, the mild-mannered Walter White reinvents himself as the fearsome drug lord Heisenberg. The thin line between legitimate business and crime in Twain, Fields, and Coppola becomes even thinner in *Breaking Bad,* as the art of money laundering is carried to new heights, and drug profits spill over into such fixtures of our daily lives as a car wash, a laundry facility, and a fast-food chain named Los Pollos Hermanos. The tension between business and family highlighted in the *Godfather* films appears once again in *Breaking Bad.* Like Michael Corleone, Walter White ends up destroying the family he claimed to be protecting. And the westward movement in quest of the American dream in the works of Twain, Fields, and Coppola culminates in the New Mexico of *Breaking Bad,* a latter-day Wild West, perilously set on the borderland between civilization and barbarism. The show is filled with shoot-outs and even stages its own Great Train Robbery. Beginning with the tamest version of the American dream—a middle-class home in the suburbs—*Breaking Bad* veers off in a more exciting and dangerous direction, as Walter White goes on a bizarre and perverse journey of self-realization and self-fulfillment that goes tragically awry and comes close to destroying all that he holds dearest in his life. *Breaking Bad* offers the most disturbing glimpse into the dark side of the American dream that we will see in this book.

Enter the zombies in chapter 5. As if *Breaking Bad* were not depressing enough, I have chosen to conclude this book by analyzing the "end-of-the-world-as-we-know-it" scenarios that have sprung up seemingly everywhere in the landscape of popular culture in the past decade or so. I concentrate on probably the best and certainly the most successful of these shows, *The Walking Dead,* but I also bring up *Falling Skies, Revolution,* and a few other examples of this genre. These shows presented me with a real challenge as an analyst of popular culture. Their popularity seems hard to explain. Why would audiences be attracted to such grim and gruesome narratives? Why would people enjoy stories of the utter destruction of everything that normally makes life worthwhile? My previous book on popular culture, *The Invisible Hand in Popular Culture,* was published in the fall of 2012, and I found myself searching for something new to analyze in television. I kept hearing about AMC's new hit *The Walking Dead* and decided to give it a try to see if I could find something interesting in it. At that time, zombies were decidedly not my cup of tea. I had always liked Val Lewton's classic 1943 horror movie *I Walked with a Zombie,* but I had never warmed up to George Romero's modern reboot of the zombie genre in *Night of the Living Dead* and its sequels. Quite frankly, I was repulsed by the low opinion of humanity Romero's films embody. So I can honestly say that I approached *The Walking Dead* with no preconceptions and no high expectations. By winter break of 2012, when I decided to check out *The Walking Dead,* I had already missed two seasons of the show, but what are DVDs for if not such situations?

I would not place *The Walking Dead* on the artistic level of *Breaking Bad* or the *Godfather* films. It is a well-cast and well-written show, with a lot of solid production values, but I would never call it Shakespearean. I did, however, immediately like the show, precisely because it rejects Romero's misanthropic view of humanity. There are many bad guys in *The Walking Dead* and some really choice villains like the Governor and Negan, but the core characters are by and large admirable, especially for the courageous and even heroic way that they respond to the crisis brought on by the zombie plague. The show is American in spirit because it celebrates the independence and self-reliance of ordinary people who are forced to fend for themselves in the absence of all the authorities and institutions that traditionally had protected and taken care of them. Like other postapocalyptic narratives, *The Walking Dead* provides a kind of thought experiment: what would happen if some disaster brought civilization to its knees and people had to survive on their own? Would the result be complete anarchy and the utter destruction of humanity? Or would people be able to find ways of reorganizing themselves and restoring some limited form of order?

The Walking Dead is reassuring in the way that it shows ordinary people working together to fight the zombies and the fellow human beings who threaten them, and to rebuild their lives. In a variation of the traditional American dream, several of the good characters reinvent themselves, going from the weak and meek roles that they played in pre-apocalyptic times to strong and assertive characters who know how to take care of themselves (this is especially true of a number of women in the series, including Andrea, Carol, and Maggie). The more I thought about *The Walking Dead,* the more I realized that it reflects widespread anxieties about social and political developments in the wake of the economic downturn that began in 2008 (as we will see, *Breaking Bad* embodies the same anxieties). Many Americans felt betrayed by the elites who had claimed to have the expertise to make the country run smoothly and to see to its citizens' welfare. Some Americans lost their sense of their own agency as human beings. They no longer believed that they were in control of their lives and felt buffeted around by unseen and alien forces. By the time *The Walking Dead* debuted in 2010, more and more Americans were feeling that the traditional American dream—especially of secure home ownership—was beyond their reach.

Amid the ruins of that version of the American dream, an older version reemerged—a vision of the pioneer spirit that had built America in the first place. Instead of relying on remote and uncaring elites, Americans began to think that they had better relearn how to rely on themselves. Maybe an apocalypse would give them the opportunity by returning them to a more basic existence. Like the other works I discuss in this book, *The Walking Dead* offers in its own way an almost nostalgic tribute to the American West and frontier existence. That explains why the show's most iconic moment is an image of a sheriff's deputy riding into Atlanta alone on a horse. As we will see, disillusionment with cultural, scientific, and political elites runs throughout *The Walking Dead,* and it returns to an older, more basic American conception of heroism. The show reflects a fear that, in their quest for middle-class security, Americans lost sight of the frontier virtues that they once identified as their core values, above all self-reliance and independence.

The Western as the Flagship American Genre

The way I reached the conclusion—to be documented in chapter 5—that *The Walking Dead* is a Western in disguise was facilitated by my work on my book *The Invisible Hand in Popular Culture*. There I began to understand that the Western is, as many have suggested, the archetypal genre in American popular culture, perhaps America's most distinctive and important contribution to world culture. The Western is the prime example of American popular culture as thought experiment, a test of the nature and value of law and order. Whatever its reality may have been, the Wild West is imaged in popular culture as a lawless land, or at best a land in which law and order are just beginning to emerge. Some Westerns suggest that in the absence of the well-established law and order supplied by fully developed political institutions, chaos will ensue and result in a Hobbesian war of all against all. Other Westerns express a more optimistic vision of human nature and the possibility of spontaneous order. In the archetypal image of a town spontaneously coming together to rebuild a burned-down barn, some Westerns embody the spirit of Tocqueville rather than Hobbes.[3]

In his classic book *Democracy in America*, Alexis de Tocqueville found a new spirit of cooperation in the United States, and he characterized Americans by their democratic propensity to form local associations on their own so that they can deal with their problems by themselves and without government intervention. America's great political debates have been played out again and again in its Westerns. Must order be imposed from above on otherwise unruly and ungovernable people by an all-powerful sovereign (Hobbes's position)? Or can order spring up from below, as people organize themselves into various forms of local associations (Tocqueville's position)? These are not easy questions to answer, and it is a tribute to the richness of the Western genre that its greatest practitioners, from John Ford to David Milch, have used the Western to contribute to our understanding of the issue of political order in the United States.[4]

As I worked on *The Invisible Hand in Popular Culture*, I began to see the way that the Western migrates to other genres and colonizes them. Science fiction also allows us to make thought experiments about political order, to imagine alien worlds in which the inhabitants are governed differently, or perhaps not governed at all. I realized that one of the most successful examples of science fiction, *Star Trek,* is actually a Western in disguise. Indeed its creator, Gene Roddenberry, famously pitched the series to NBC executives with the formula "*Wagon Train* to the stars." What after all is the "final frontier" of *Star Trek* but the Old West frontier projected into outer space? I explored this thesis by examining the way that Roddenberry's ideas for *Star Trek* evolved out of his work as the writer of twenty-four episodes of the classic TV Western *Have Gun—Will Travel*.[5] In particular, I showed that Roddenberry's experience writing episodes about Western towns dominated by corrupt local bosses or evil cattle barons translated into *Star Trek* episodes about Captain Kirk coming upon planets similarly exploited by despotic rulers.

I went on in the book to trace the migration of the Western to a major subgenre of science fiction, the alien invasion narrative (in movies such as Tim Burton's *Mars Attacks!* or television shows such as *Falling Skies*).[6] Once again, alien invasion makes possible a thought experiment. By toppling governments around the world, the aliens restore human beings to what is known in political philosophy as the state of nature, thus reopening the question of law and order. Some alien invasion narratives portray human beings as helpless in the face of superior alien technology, and the earthlings must accept some form of totalitarian rule from their interplanetary overlords. More optimistic versions of this kind of story portray resilient and resourceful human beings banding together to resist the alien tyranny and regain control of the planet. It is the same issue we will encounter in *The Walking Dead*—how human beings respond to a crisis threatening civilization, and whether they have the resources and the internal fortitude to take back control of their lives.

The Western is thus the prototype of a kind of narrative that recurs in American popular culture, one that allows Americans to imagine alternatives to the settled middle-class existence that prevails in their country, a way of life that they ordinarily take for granted and generally leave unexamined. One danger with the American dream is that at times it threatens to devolve into a narrowly middle-class conception of the good life, one that values security above all else. In the 1950s, middle-class suburban existence became the most common image of the American dream, as witness countless domestic sitcoms on television. This thorough domestication of the American dream provoked a reaction. Just as the middle class came to dominate the United States, culturally as well as politically, it was charged with complacency and conformity. Its vision of the American dream—comfortable life in the suburbs—was accused of narrowing the range of human possibility and leaving out many traditional forms of human excellence—for example, the whole realm of heroic virtue, which is in some ways antithetical to middle-class virtue. The middle class, with its emphasis on prudence and not rocking the boat, has always been suspicious of heroes, at least the traditional kind who keep risking their lives out of pride and a compulsion to excel.

As we will see in chapter 5, the reign of the domestic sitcom on television was oddly paired with the heyday of the Western, epitomized by such shows as *Gunsmoke, Have Gun—Will Travel, Wagon Train,* and *Maverick.* American viewers craved a break from the tepid world of the sitcom, in which typically the most serious domestic crisis involved nothing more troubling than an irksome neighbor, a missed birthday, or an obnoxious relative making an unwanted visit. Life on the old frontier was a lot more elemental than this, and, as Westerners, the characters got a chance to show their true mettle. Far from being just a face in the crowd, the Western hero often is a loner, willing to resist community pressures and take a stance on his own. What existentialism was in philosophy in the 1950s, the Western was in popular culture—a call for genuine commitment to real causes.

The vogue of TV Westerns in the 1950s and 1960s grew out of the public's desire to be served up something other than the placid world of the domestic sitcom and the suburban middle-class version of the American dream it reflected. When they grew tired of Ward Cleaver's affability and unflappability, Americans could turn to Matt Dillon's grim determination to stand up, alone if need be, for justice. The Western reminded people that there is more to human life than two cars in the garage, air-conditioning, and a color TV. There is, for example, the courage to face down an opponent in a life-or-death situation. That kind of courage may be needed in times of crisis to protect ordinary civic life, even though this masculine aggressiveness may be at odds with the middle-class desire for peace at any price. John Ford's Westerns—particularly *The Searchers* and *The Man Who Shot Liberty Valance*—keep coming back to the tragic story of a hero who is able to protect a community only with a kind of disposition to violence that makes it difficult for him to fit peacefully into the community he saves.

As I worked on this book, I came to realize that the gangster story, or the crime narrative in general, performs the same function of offering an alternative to settled middle-class existence. Gangster stories take us imaginatively into a world beyond the control of political institutions, evidently governed by rules very different from those that prevail in ordinary middle-class existence (although sometimes the rules turn out to be surprisingly similar). In works like the *Godfather* films or *Breaking Bad,* we see the way that outlaws operate outside a conventional legal framework and without government regulation. The results can be frightening and remind us of why we value our moral and political order in the first place—it protects us from crime and violence. But there can also be something intriguing and liberating about viewing the unconventional life of the criminal, who breaks all the rules and at least temporarily gets away with it. The criminal has a freedom we ordinarily lack, to pursue his dreams and desires without the fetters of ordinary morality, and, although we condemn him, we may also secretly envy him. Let's face it—middle-class existence can get very boring, and we take vicarious pleasure in watching the gangster break the taboos we normally have to respect. And it can be fun to see the gangster outwit the legally constituted authorities that we must dutifully obey in our daily lives. If we are honest with ourselves, we will acknowledge that we do not turn to popular culture only for edifying moral lessons. Sometimes we want to be thrilled by the daring of people who break the law or otherwise go beyond the normal limits of civic life.

Outlaw Heroes

That is why Americans have been fascinated by real-life criminals like Al Capone, Legs Diamond, Dutch Schultz, John Dillinger, Machine Gun Kelly, Pretty Boy Floyd, Lucky Luciano, and Bonnie and Clyde (sometimes colorful nicknames seem to help). America has made celebrities out of such criminals; they have passed into American popular culture—almost as folk heroes—and become the subjects of an endless sequence of films and television shows. These figures lead an existence that we can only fantasize about, and they take on larger-than-life stature. In a 2014 PBS documentary, *Al Capone: Icon,* Vince Gilligan showed that he understands this phenomenon, even though he finds it puzzling: "I think America is interested in antiheroes and criminals, gangsters. It's an interesting cultural phenomenon that we celebrate outlaws like Jesse James and Billy the Kid. Criminals that live a bigger than life kind of existence seem to live on in legend. . . . We all get this visceral thrill from stories about gangsters, be they fictional gangsters or real-life ones. . . . It's a strange thing how we celebrate our outsize criminals."

We know that for the sake of law and order—for our own safety—these criminals must be punished, and for that reason we can applaud the police who track such criminals down and take them out of circulation. But still, for a moment these lawbreakers give us a glimpse of a freer world, quite different from the ordinary middle-class existence in which we docilely abide by the rules and repress whatever antisocial impulses we may harbor. Fictional figures like the Corleones and Walter White exert a fascination on us. The criminals and gangsters in popular culture serve a cathartic function in our society. A gangster story allows us to play at being a criminal and to blow off steam, to release in a safe situation antisocial impulses that we may not want to acknowledge even to ourselves. There must be some reason why audiences are so attracted to gangster stories. They do not want to commit real crimes, but they would like to learn what it feels like to commit a crime. Vince Gilligan remarked: "I don't want to be a criminal, but I am fascinated by people who have the ability to do things I think are impossible."[7] To satisfy this kind of intellectual curiosity, fictional stories come to our aid. They allow us to experience safely in imaginary situations what would be too dangerous for us in real life.

Many commentators, including Vince Gilligan, were surprised—and some were appalled—by how many fans kept rooting for Walter White to the bitter end of *Breaking Bad*. As one of those fans, I can testify that, as powerfully realistic as the show was, I never thought for a moment that Walter White was a real human being who had actually killed people. I knew all along that he was a fictional character. Thus I never was rooting for an actual criminal to get away with his nefarious deeds. I was responding purely as a fan of a fictional television show. I rooted for Walter White because that was the only way to root for his story to continue (this is the subliminal trick by which crime narratives tempt us into sympathizing with and rooting for the criminals). After all, as soon as White got his "just deserts," *Breaking Bad* would be over. Like many fans, I had become fascinated by the Walter White character. Week after week, he kept surprising me and revealing aspects of human nature I had never quite seen before, as all great fictional characters do. Some of what he revealed was deeply disturbing, but some of it suggested qualities in him that raised him above (as well as lowering him below) the ordinary level of humanity.

To read many commentators on *Breaking Bad,* one would think that the only way to respond to films and television—to works of art in general—is with moral judgment. Moral judgment is important, but it does not constitute the full range of response to human experience. There is also, for example, aesthetic judgment, and, however immoral Walter White became, there is a kind of aesthetic beauty to the clever schemes he came up with to keep one step ahead of his enemies and the law.[8] I cannot believe that Gilligan and his team did not take a secret pleasure in dreaming up Walter White's unpredictable and shocking criminal moves. I rooted for him because I knew he was going to continue to surprise me, and I wanted to see what he would come up with next. Just as with literature, we do not turn to film and television solely to learn morality (which is, after all, already inculcated in us by many other forces in our world). Like literature, film and television are sometimes at their best when they offer us alternatives to the ordinary world we live in, and thereby deepen and broaden our knowledge and understanding of human nature. Shakespeare's tragedies do not provide us with simple lessons in morality, but instead give us glimpses into extraordinary human beings who go well beyond anything that most of us will ever encounter in our daily existence. I for one do not always turn to literature or film or television just to see mirrors of the ordinary reality with which I have to live every day. Sometimes I would like to see something different. And whatever else Walter White was, he was certainly different from any other fictional character I had ever seen. What most engages and energizes me in any form of art is a vision of something I cannot see in daily life. I already know the rules of middle-class existence; I have observed them all my life. What intrigues me is to see the extreme situations in which those rules are put on hold or pushed to their limits. Only then can we learn something new about their validity and applicability.

That is what attracts me to genre films and genre television shows. The Western, the alien invasion story, the gangster tale, the zombie narrative—what they all have in common is what I have been calling their potential to create thought experiments. In a variety of ways, each posits a kind of alternate or alien universe, in which the rules of ordinary middle-class existence are suspended, and we can observe what might result. The conclusion from these thought experiments might well be to return to our ordinary world with our original assumptions reinforced. It is a case of "beware of what you wish for."[9] We see that for all the drama and excitement we might gain, we really would not want to live on the dangerous Western frontier, or during an alien invasion or a zombie plague, or with a mob of freewheeling, gun-toting gangsters. Maybe one of the important functions of popular culture is to get our longing for an exciting but dangerous life out of our systems. Most of us are not born for the heroic life. But we also might learn something in the process of observing the alternative worlds of genre film and genre television. Perhaps the middle-class vision of happiness cannot fully satisfy all the longings of the human soul. Popular culture offers many stories of characters who feel trapped in the ordinary world of middle-class domesticity and yearn for something that transcends its narrow boundaries. The obsession with security and law and order may frustrate the desire for freedom and independence, a longing that is at the foundation of the frontier vision of American life. Some versions of the American dream involve fitting in perfectly to society and leading a peaceful and contented life. Other versions celebrate a more heroic path of standing out from the crowd and not letting social conventions dictate one's every action. In portraying the Westerner, the gangster, or the apocalypse survivor, popular culture reminds us that peaceful suburban life does not exhaust the whole range of human possibilities.

Here is perhaps the deepest fault line in the American dream. American literature has almost from the beginning been torn between visions of tranquil domestic life and visions of the Wild West in all its incarnations—home on the range rather than home in the suburbs. The common, middle-class version of the American dream puts a premium on security and contentment and thus ends up calling for conformism. In this version of the American dream, everyone ends up looking alike, but in the alternatives, everyone wants to look different. Those who feel alienated by the conformist vision, and who long for more freedom and independence, seek for ways to set off on their own as trailblazers and pioneers. They are not content with ordinary and moderate success; they want to do something extraordinary, maybe something that has never been done before. These are, for example, the heroic entrepreneurs who make the great breakthroughs in industry, commerce, and technology. But sometimes this kind of person goes too far and turns to what is known in the *Star Wars* universe as the dark side of the Force. As we will see again and again in this book, there is a thin line between exceeding normal limits and breaking with them entirely; that is how the entrepreneur shades over into the criminal, and therefore how the bright side of the American dream is linked with the dark side.

The freedom Americans prize can be misused and lead people to do not only what has never been done before but also what breaks the rules, even the law. *Huckleberry Finn* lays bare this problematic aspect of the American dream with relentless clarity. By doing so, Twain's novel exemplifies American popular culture at its best. With its ability to see both the bright side and the dark side of the American dream—and that they are in effect two sides of the same coin—popular culture shows that it can be genuinely thoughtful and perhaps even philosophic. And thus we come to the ultimate paradox of this book— by exploring the dark side of the American dream, we come upon something bright—the richness, vitality, and complexity of American popular culture. In reply to its many critics, we can say that films and television shows at times achieve the level of sophistication we associate with great literature. Despite initial appearances, American popular culture does not simply offer an unending sequence of Horatio Alger stories, bland tales of middling success that cater to the public's facile optimism. Rather, in works like the *Godfather* films and *Breaking Bad,* American popular culture recurs to some of the great tragic themes of classic literature and thereby serves up genuine food for thought.

1

ARISTOCRACY IN AMERICA

HUCKLEBERRY FINN *AND THE* DEMOCRATIC ART OF IMPOSTURE

> It is a saddening thought but we cannot change our nature—we are all alike, we human beings; and in our blood and bone, and ineradicably, we carry the seeds out of which monarchies and aristocracies are grown: worship of gauds, titles, distinctions, power.
>
> Mark Twain

Land of the Free, Home of the Fake

Mark Twain's *Adventures of Huckleberry Finn* is an American classic. It is at once a comic masterpiece and a serious exploration of what distinguishes the American character, above all, its love of freedom and independence. With its focus on children, it seems to celebrate the innocence of America, the land of perpetual youth and renewal. Although still widely read in its original book form, *Huckleberry Finn* has passed into the broader realm of American popular culture. It has been endlessly recycled in film and television adaptations, often in Disneyfied versions that turn it into musical comedy. It has become the sort of book that is commonly described as "beloved." Even though its racist language often keeps it from being taught to young people in schools, it is often classified as a children's book.

Yet *Huckleberry Finn* is a dark and deeply unnerving work. It is filled with a seemingly endless parade of con artists, impostors, vigilantes, lynch mobs, and other practitioners of fraud and deception or cruelty and inhumanity. Wherever one turns in the book, one finds murder or the threat of murder. At its most disturbing, *Huckleberry Finn* confronts the darkest blot on America as the land of the free—the crime of slavery in the South. The book seems misanthropic, anticipating Twain's cynical vision in his later work, especially the *Mysterious Stranger* fragments. To varying degrees, Twain seems to be questioning conventional morality and religious faith in *Huckleberry Finn*. Indeed, he must call these pieties into question because in Huck's world, they support slavery. In its corrosive skepticism, *Huckleberry Finn* seems to be the very opposite of a children's book as commonly understood.

All this leaves us with a paradox. In popular culture, *Huckleberry Finn* conjures up images of the fresh-faced All-American boy, to be played by cute child stars like Mickey Rooney, Ron Howard, or Elijah Wood. Yet in terms of the events and characters it portrays, the book has all the warmth and sweetness of a film noir. It seems like a cross between *Johnny Appleseed* and *Dial M for Murder*. For years I was puzzled by *Huckleberry Finn*—how could such a classic story of America be so dark and misanthropic?

I began to put the two, seemingly contradictory sides of the book together when I came across this passage from the critic V. S. Pritchett:

> As Huck Finn and old Jim drift down the Mississippi from one horrifying little town to the next and hear the voices of men quietly swearing at each other across the waters; as they pass the time of day with scroungers, rogues, murderers, the lonely women, the frothing revivalists, the maundering boatmen and fantastic drunks of the river towns, we see the human wastage that is left in the wake of a great effort of the human will, the hopes frustrated, the idealism which has been whittled down to eccentricity and craft. These people are the price paid for building a new country.[1]

Pritchett grasps how the bright and dark sides of *Huckleberry Finn* fit together. If you are going to give people freedom, you are going to have to live with the ways they may misuse and abuse it. If a nation is to be dedicated to giving people a fresh start, a lot of them will make false starts. A country based on political idealism will end up with a lot of people cynically taking advantage of gullible idealists. *Huckleberry Finn* portrays both the American dream and its nightmarish dark side. Even as it offers an enduring tribute to the American longing for freedom, it reveals, as Pritchett suggests, that we may pay a great price for liberating the desires and ambitions of ordinary human beings.

Huckleberry Finn is thus a Tocquevillian meditation on the advantages and disadvantages of aristocracy and democracy as alternative ways of life. To oversimplify the differences: As opposed to democracy, aristocracy offers a fixed social hierarchy in which people are largely born into their stations in life. The different social ranks are readily identifiable by clear and fixed markers, such as clothing, speech patterns, and manners. The price the majority of people pay for living in an aristocracy is that they lack freedom and social mobility. But the very rigidity of an aristocratic society brings with it a kind of psychological comfort: a lack of anxiety about social status. "Once a serf, always a serf" is the basic principle of aristocracy. Since individuals cannot do anything about their place in an aristocracy, they need not torment themselves over their lack of status. Your social rank is not your fault, and you know your place; what is more, everybody else does, too.

Democracy, by contrast, tears down aristocratic hierarchies, introducing freedom and social mobility and thereby liberating human energies. The American dream is that anyone can become president of the United States; people do not have to be born into positions of power. Americans are taught as their birthright that they are free to rise in the world by their own efforts. That is a wonderful prospect, but it also means that it is now your own fault if you remain in a low station in life. Democracy's motto is, "You can always do better; you can always make a fresh start." Compared to aristocracy, then, democracy gives the vast majority of people reason to be dissatisfied with their current lot in life because they now have genuine hopes of improving on it. Democratic individuals always tend to crave more—more money, more status, more power. That is what is good about democracy—it energizes human efforts. Freedom, especially in the marketplace, can be a powerful force for human betterment.

But there is a dark side to the liberation of human desire and ambition that democracy brings about. Set free from aristocratic restraints, people in a democracy are beset by new fears, uncertainties, and anxieties. They can no longer be sure of their status in life. The prospect of rising in status is inevitably accompanied by the possibility of falling. Moreover, the clear aristocratic markers of social status dissolve, leaving people to sort out where they stand in relation to each other. It becomes difficult to distinguish the genuinely self-made man from the con man. The respected entrepreneur you meet at a party may be Bill Gates, but he may just as well be Bernie Madoff (Twain portrays a primitive Ponzi scheme at the end of chapter 8 of *Huckleberry Finn*). The freedom and openness of democratic society paradoxically make social identity less transparent, and a lot of confusion and deception results. The democratic world Twain portrays in *Huckleberry Finn* is filled with impostors.

Confusion of identity is the keynote of *Huckleberry Finn*. Huck is always carrying on one masquerade or another. At one point he even tries to pass as a girl, but he cannot quite bring off that deception. He adopts so many false names in the course of his travels that he has a hard time remembering who he is claiming to be at any given moment. Amid the Grangerford family, he suddenly finds himself at a loss for the alias he has been using: "I went to bed with Buck, and when I waked up in the morning, drat it all, I had forgot what my name was."[2] When he comes to the Phelps farm, he realizes that he has been mistaken for a family relative, but he does not know which one. His problem becomes to "find out who I was" (200). This is democratic America for Twain—you are not told who you are; you have to discover it.

Soon Huck learns that in the eyes of the Phelps family, he is none other than his old friend Tom Sawyer. Huck describes this discovery as "like being born again" (201), and indeed "born again," with all its religious connotations, is a phrase we associate with America and its fresh-start spirit. *Huckleberry Finn* is all about "born again" Americans, a democratic people who are constantly inventing and reinventing themselves. A Mississippi riverboat pilot named Samuel Clemens reconfigured himself as a writer named Mark Twain, and the rest is literary history. Samuel Clemens was in fact one of the first to understand that in a democratic society a man can use the modern media to invent himself as a celebrity. In Twain's presentation, America is a land of disguises. As a runaway slave, Jim in particular must continually be kept under wraps. In a bizarre development—of whose irony Twain must have been aware—in chapter 24 Jim ends up dressed in the theatrical costume of King Lear. One of the central motifs of *Huckleberry Finn* is the theatricality of democratic America. People are constantly playing roles in public, and changing their identities seems no more difficult than changing their costumes.

A Sucker Born Again Every Minute

How is all this deception possible? In the case of Aunt Sally's mistaking Huck's identity, the answer is simple: although Tom is her nephew, because she lives apart from him, she does not know what he looks like. The America of *Huckleberry Finn* is a land of widely dispersed families, often families that have been forcibly broken up. This issue is central to Jim's story—he is worried about his family being divided up among several different owners, as happened with depressing regularity to slaves in the antebellum South. Huck's family is broken up, and so is Tom's. The social mobility of democratic America goes along with geographic and sheer physical mobility. As Pritchett writes, "Movement, a sense of continual migration, is the history of America."[3] Epitomized by Horace Greeley's famous injunction, "Go West, young man," America has set its population in perpetual motion. *Huckleberry Finn* is accordingly a picaresque tale, with its characters always on the go in their journey down the Mississippi. It is not just Jim who must keep moving to preserve his freedom. Many of the characters are seeking some kind of a fresh start, and that requires framing a new identity on the fly. Twain understood the role that a wide-open frontier played in shaping the American character. With its con men, hucksters, gamblers, thieves, and murderers, the world of *Huckleberry Finn* is an early example of what came to be known as the Wild West. Throughout American history, the frontier—the line between civilization and barbarism—kept shifting (generally westward). At the end of Twain's novel, Huck, feeling engulfed by civilization, is ready to "light out for the Territory ahead of the rest" (262). That is another way of saying that Huck, like the infamous criminals of the Old West, wants to stay one step ahead of the law, and, like those desperados, he is always willing to disguise himself to do so.

That is why nobody knows for sure anymore who anybody is in *Huckleberry Finn*. In the aristocratic world of the old regime in Europe, most people were immobile, tied to the land. That is what it meant to be a serf. When people live in small villages, everybody knows who everybody else is, and imposture becomes impossible. The simple answer to the village impostor is, "You're not a duke; I know you—you're John the blacksmith." But Twain's America is a land of wide-open spaces, and that makes it much easier to become an impostor, a stranger in a strange land. This is perhaps the best example of how all the criminality in *Huckleberry Finn* is linked to the new democratic freedom and mobility. This explains why the con man has been such a central theme in American culture. Before Twain, Herman Melville had chosen to name a novel about America *The Confidence-Man*. And con men have been a mainstay of American popular culture, especially its comedies, as the films of W. C. Fields and the Marx Brothers attest. Fields's taglines—"Never give a sucker an even break" and "You can't cheat an honest man"—have a distinctively American ring to them. The country of George Washington—who could not tell a lie—is also the country of P. T. Barnum, who made a fortune doing just the opposite.

The most irrepressible impostors in *Huckleberry Finn* are the king and the duke. They succeed in their fraudulent behavior by always staying one step ahead of the lynch mob. As long as they keep moving from town to town, they can use the same old con game by finding new—and therefore still gullible—victims. In their shameless impostures, they represent the dark side of all that is best in America, its spirit of enterprise. When they first team up to defraud the public, they assess their range as impostors:

"What's your line—mainly?"

"Jour printer, by trade; do a little in the patent medicines; theatre-actor—tragedy, you know; take a turn at mesmerism and phrenology when there's a chance; teach singing-geography school for a change; sling a lecture, sometimes—oh, I do lots of things—most anything that comes handy, so it ain't work. What's your lay?"

"I've done considerable in the doctoring way in my time. Laying on o' hands is my best holt—for cancer, and paralysis, and sich things; an I k'n tell a future pretty good, when I've got somebody along to find out the facts for me. Preachin's my line, too; and workin' camp-meetin's, and missionaryin around." (111–12)

The range of this false expertise is remarkable; the king and the duke can "master" science, technology, and medicine. We are struck by their commitment to pseudosciences, such as mesmerism and phrenology, but their careers are a good reminder that it has always been difficult to separate real science from pseudoscience in freewheeling, democratic America. Americans are perennial optimists, believing firmly that with freedom comes opportunity, and with opportunity comes progress and improvement. With enough effort, any problem can be solved, and, in particular, any disease can be cured. That is why Americans are so susceptible to the siren song of the medicine man. Democratic America has led the world in the development of modern medicine, but for that very reason it has also produced more than its share of medical quacks. Free markets allow for a wide range of experiments in technology and medicine, but for every true cure discovered, many false cures may be tried out. The hope of course is that the market will, over time, sort out the true products from the false. The comeuppance eventually suffered by the king and the duke is proof that you cannot fool all of the people all of the time. But still, their initial success as con men is a troubling consequence of the freedom America allows its citizens.

An element of theatricality runs through all these impostures; indeed the theater itself is one of their con games. The king and the duke know how to put on a show. They have been printers, actors, and public lecturers. Like their creator, Mark Twain, they know how to exploit the modern media to gain an audience and milk it for all it is worth. Twain hints that authors may be con men, too, putting on an act for their readers. Most audaciously, Twain allows his con artists' deceptive performances to culminate in preaching, thus presenting a sermon as no better than a medicine show. Another area in which the king and the duke can exploit the gullibility of the American public is religion. They have a temperance scam in which they play upon the moral fervor of their spellbound audience in order to extract donations for the noble cause of teetotalism.[4] Americans, as part of their democratic character, like to think the best of people. This is no doubt an admirable trait, but again, it makes Americans especially susceptible to con games. They love to hear stories of religious conversion, of criminals who discover the evil of their ways, confess their sins, and claim to have reformed their conduct. That is why the king and the duke include preaching among their con games. Their ability to exploit religion for financial gain is the dark side of the genuine power of evangelical movements in the United States.

Religious con games epitomize the paradox of democracy that Twain explores in *Huckleberry Finn*. With no established church in America, anybody can set himself up as a preacher. In the absence of any official form of validation, preaching must become self-validating and therefore rely on the charisma of the preacher. Unable to count on a captive audience, American preachers must create their own congregations. This makes for powerful preaching. It is no accident that democratic America has produced such peculiar religious phenomena as televangelism and the megachurch. What amounts to a free market in religion in the United States has energized American churches.[5] Europeans, with their state churches, have long marveled at the vitality of religion in America, above all, the periodic mass religious awakenings and the emergence of whole new sects, such as the Mormons. America has produced a remarkable number of religious leaders in its history, but according to the logic of democracy that works throughout *Huckleberry Finn,* the United States has turned out many false prophets as well (and of course one person's religious leader is another's false prophet). The very religious vitality on which Americans pride themselves is inextricably linked to their vulnerability to fraudulent piety.

King for a Day

Twain's central insight is that the con man is the evil twin of the American hero—the entrepreneur, the self-made man, the rags-to-riches genius.[6] Yet there is something peculiar about Twain's principal con men. These products of democracy nevertheless choose to impersonate aristocrats. One of them claims to be descended from the "eldest son of the Duke of Bridgewater" from England (112), and the other claims to be the French Dauphin, the son of Louis XVI and Marie Antoinette, and thus the rightful king, Louis XVII. A further paradox of democracy in America is the widespread allure of faux aristocracy. Among the false starts, false cures, and false prophets in America are the false aristocrats. The United States has broken with European aristocracy, but it remains fascinated by it.[7] Perhaps Americans are fascinated by aristocracy precisely because they have broken with it. Once the United States set itself up as a democracy, Americans began perversely yearning to recapture something of the old aristocratic aura. Virtually from the moment Americans chose to split off from England, they fell into the grip of Anglophilia, deriving much of their culture—their literature, their music, their painting, their architecture—from English sources. The patriotic hymn to US liberty, "My County 'Tis of Thee," is paradoxically sung to the tune of England's "God Save the King." American Anglophilia has particularly focused on English aristocratic trappings, with images of Buckingham Palace, Westminster Abbey, and Tower Bridge at the center of the cult of all things English. The obsession with Princess Di in the United States reflected the aristocratic bent of American Anglophilia. One got the impression that Americans feel deprived because they have never had a royal princess of their own.

In *Huckleberry Finn*, Twain dwells on this strange aspect of American gullibility—the way democratic Americans become suckers for anyone or anything that smacks of English aristocracy. The goal of American democracy was for all its citizens to be equal. Evidently, faced with that prospect, Americans balked and longed for ways to distinguish themselves from their fellow citizens, to stand out in the crowd in some new form of aristocracy. Americans still crave the trappings of aristocracy, various forms of dress, speech patterns, and manners that give an aura of "class." Some Americans have even cultivated phony English accents to make themselves seem elegant. The fox-and-hounds set among American upper-class society is a good example of this aristocratic Anglophilia. Americans are always trying to recapture something of the hierarchical character of aristocratic society. Aware of this potential problem, the Founders had the wisdom to forbid titles of nobility in the US Constitution (Article I, Section 9, Clause 8). But Americans keep seeking ways to get around the fact that genuine aristocracy is outlawed in the United States. They strive to re-create aristocracy on a democratic basis. That tendency is evident in the phenomenon of gentlemen's or ladies' clubs (often created on English models) and other social organizations with well-defined ranks. "Democratic aristocracies" have emerged in such fields as sports and entertainment, with titles like the Sultan of Swat and the King of Rock & Roll (not to mention the Duke of Earl). Above all, democratic politicians have often tried to position themselves as a new elite, with many of the traditional trappings of aristocracy, including political dynasties. The Kennedys even got themselves identified with Camelot.

In *Huckleberry Finn* Twain explores the ways in which a democratic America continues to live in the shadow of European and especially English aristocracy. The king and the duke learn of a substantial inheritance from England, and in a classic con game pretend to be the two designated heirs in order to claim the money. Twain presents average Americans at their most gullible in this sequence. The imposture should be transparent to all; even Huck is able to see right through it. But the simple townsfolk grasp at any signs that they are dealing with a superior class of people from England, and the king and the duke prey upon their ignorance. Even when they betray their own ignorance by using the term *orgies* instead of *obsequies* to refer to the funeral ceremony, the would-be Englishmen are able to give off an aura of aristocratic superiority. They trade on snob appeal: "I say orgies, not because it's the common term, because it ain't—obsequies bein' the common term—but because orgies is the right term. Obsequies ain't used in England no more, now—it's gone out. We say orgies now, in England. Orgies is better, because it means the thing you're after, more exact. It's a word that's made up out'n the Greek *orgo,* outside, open, abroad; and the Hebrew *jeesum,* to plant, cover up; hence *inter.* So, you see, funeral orgies is an open or public funeral" (153–54). The fraudulent inheritance plot generates some of the funniest moments in the novel, but it has a serious significance. Twain suggests that America's whole inheritance from England is basically one gigantic fraud, especially when it takes the form of superficial pretensions to aristocratic superiority.

Southern Comfort

The theme of sham aristocracy is at the heart of *Huckleberry Finn.* In Twain's view, the antebellum South was characterized precisely by its false pretentions to aristocracy.[8] Rich landowners in the South tried to create a new species of aristocracy in the midst of democratic America. In the form of the southern plantation, they sought to transpose the way of life of landed aristocrats in England to an American setting. Twain subjects the southern aristocratic ideal to scrutiny in his portrait of the Grangerfords. This aristocratic family is at first presented as in many respects admirable. Huck initially looks up to Colonel Grangerford as a true "gentleman": "He was well-born, as the saying is, and that's worth as much in a man as it is in a horse, as the Widow Douglas said, and nobody ever denied that she was of the first aristocracy in our town" (97). Huck is impressed when he looks at his aristocratic better in the form of Colonel Grangerford:

> His hands was long and thin, and every day of his life he put on a clean shirt and a full suit from head to foot made out of linen so white it hurt your eyes to look at. . . . He carried a mahogany cane with a silver head to it. There warn't no frivolousness about him, not a bit, and he warn't ever loud. He was as kind as he could be—you could feel that, you know, and so you had confidence. . . . He didn't ever have to tell anybody to mind their manners—everybody was always good mannered where he was. (97)

This is the aristocratic ideal of southern gentility, and I believe that Twain genuinely admired it (he certainly dressed in public like the Colonel). Even Huck admires aristocratic poise when he sees it. Colonel Grangerford is the opposite of Huck in every respect, partly because he has everything that Huck lacks. As a wealthy landowner, Grangerford can afford to live a life of noblesse oblige and set an example of elegant manners for his community.

But the emphasis in this passage is on Grangerford's appearance and the clothing he wears. Is the suggestion that his aristocratic character is something merely external, something just for show? Is his nobility just an aristocratic veneer? As we learn elsewhere in the book, democratic Huck likes to go naked along with Jim: "We was always naked, day and night, whenever the mosquitoes would let us—the new clothes Buck's folks made for me was too good to be comfortable, and besides I didn't go much on clothes, nohow" (109). For Huck, clothing is a matter of utility, not nobility; when he does not need clothing, he does not wear it. The way people are dressed is symbolic in *Huckleberry Finn*, and Twain raises the issue of whether clothes make the man in Huck's vision of the king's new raiment:

> We had all bought store clothes where we stopped last; and now the king put his'n on. . . . The king's duds was all black, and he did look real swell and starchy. I never knowed how clothes could change a body before. Why, before, he looked like the orneriest old rip that ever was; but now, when he'd take off his new white beaver and make a bow and do a smile, he looked that grand and good and pious that you'd say he had walked right out of the ark, and maybe was old Leviticus himself. (144)

Huck may be momentarily taken in by the king's appearance, but Twain seems to question whether new clothing has genuinely transformed the con man.

We thus need to take another look at the Grangerfords: "Bob was the oldest, and Tom next. Tall, beautiful men with very broad shoulders and brown faces, and long black hair and black eyes. They dressed in white linen from head to foot, like the old gentleman, and wore broad Panama hats" (98). Here the emphasis is almost exclusively on the external appearance of this aristocratic clan. And then we see what all this southern gentility is based on: "Each person had their own nigger to wait on them. . . . My nigger had a monstrous easy time, because I warn't used to having anybody do anything for me. . . . [T]he old gentleman owned a lot of farms, and over a hundred niggers" (98). This aristocracy—this leisured class—is made possible only by slavery. Southern efforts at re-creating aristocracy were inextricably linked to the institution of slavery. Twain traces the darkest blot on America—the continuation of slavery in a democratic land—to the lingering allure of aristocracy. The southern aristocracy's belief in their elevated status was derived from their ruling as masters over slaves. They derived a false sense of superiority by treating fellow human beings as if they were inferior by nature. In Twain's view, it was all a masquerade, but tragically, in the Civil War southerners proved willing to die for it.

Twain explores the link between aristocracy and violence in *Huckleberry Finn*. The Grangerfords are not only well dressed; they are also well armed: "The men brought their guns with them. It was a handsome lot of quality" (98). These are clannish men who are perpetually looking for a fight. They meet their match in another family: "There was another clan of aristocracy around there—five or six families—mostly of the name of Shepherdson. They were as high-toned, and well born, and rich and grand, as the tribe of Grangerfords" (98). The Grangerfords and the Shepherdsons hark back to the Old World of Scotland and its Highland clans.[9] In a world archaically divided into tribes, the stage is set for the classic manifestation of southern aristocratic pretensions: the feud. At the heart of the aristocratic sense of honor is the code of vengeance, and it typically leads to endless cycles of violence, since the nobles can prove their nobility only by risking their lives in deadly quarrels. The destructiveness of the nobles' sense of honor has been chronicled in centuries of aristocratic literature, from Homer's epics to the Icelandic sagas to Shakespeare's histories and tragedies.

Life Imitating Art

Twain regarded aristocratic literature as part of America's baleful heritage from Europe. He focused his ire particularly on the Waverley novels of Sir Walter Scott, which in the nineteenth century were extraordinarily popular in America, especially in the South. Twain believed that Scott's romantic evocation of the spirit of medieval chivalry in novels such as *Ivanhoe* had taught the wrong lesson to the American South. Would-be cavaliers in the South modeled themselves on Scott's nobles, especially in their disposition to fight on behalf of lost causes (as happens most famously in *Waverley*, with its Scottish Highlanders nobly but vainly championing Bonnie Prince Charlie). Only half-jokingly, Twain blamed the most famous of American lost causes—the Civil War—on Scott's novels.[10] He felt that too many southerners rode to their destruction in battle thinking of themselves as Scott's knights in shining armor. It is no accident that the wrecked ship Huck and Jim encounter is named the *Walter Scott* (68). In Twain's eyes, Scott had wrecked the South. He wrote *A Connecticut Yankee in King Arthur's Court* to debunk the kind of romantic chivalry Scott sought to revive. For Twain, reading European novels that glorify aristocracy only reinforced the unfortunate American tendency to imitate models inimical to a democracy.

In *Huckleberry Finn*, Tom Sawyer's head is so filled with the novels of Alexandre Dumas that he needlessly and endlessly prolongs Jim's slavery in an effort to weave him into the romantic fantasy of an aristocratic escape narrative. Tom is bored with ordinary democratic life in America; he wants something more heroic and hence something out of Europe's aristocratic past.[11] Complaining that Jim does not understand "the custom in Europe" (216), Tom wants him to imitate the legendary Man in the Iron Mask in all his sufferings (219), when in fact at this point Jim could walk free anytime he likes.

Twain even uses *Huckleberry Finn* to ridicule the popularity of Shakespeare's plays in nineteenth-century America. When the king and the duke stage their Shakespeare performances, they butcher the plays so badly that one can only suppose that the audience is drawn by a kind of snob appeal. The impostors, as always, stress their European aristocratic pedigree; their playbill announces that they have performed at the Royal Haymarket Theatre in London and also at Royal Continental Theatres. They can appear for "one night only" "on account of imperative European engagements" (126–27). They are trading on the cachet of their connections with Europe. Twain evidently worried that, with ignorant and naïve provincial audiences, Shakespeare's plays appealed to the lingering taste for aristocratic culture in the United States. As an American author, Twain dreamed of the country's developing its own native culture and not always turning to Europe for its art, which threatened to infect America with the aristocratic bias of the old regime's literature. The king and the duke choose Shakespeare's *Richard III* and his *Romeo and Juliet* for their repertoire. The history play concludes Shakespeare's panoramic account of the Wars of the Roses and thus centers on feuding aristocrats. The tragedy also dwells on an aristocratic feud—between the Montagues and the Capulets—and it dramatizes the failure of the young lovers to bridge the gap between their aristocratic houses. In the story of Sophia Grangerford and Harney Shepherdson in chapter 18, Twain had just told a kind of "Romeo and Juliet in the South" tale of feuding families and rebellious lovers. We cannot say for sure that the young lovers in *Huckleberry Finn* were inspired by *Romeo and Juliet,* but Twain evidently was concerned that, more generally, in the southern feud, America was recapitulating a tradition of aristocratic violence it had inherited from Europe.

Feuds and Frauds

Twain suggests that the aristocratic feud is not native to America by showing that the innocent Huck is ignorant of even what a feud is. His friend Buck Grangerford must explain the concept to him: "A feud is this way. A man has a quarrel with another man, and kills him; then that other man's brother kills *him;* then the other brothers, on both sides, goes for one another; then the *cousins* chip in—and by-and-by everybody's killed off, and there ain't no more feud" (99). In chapter 3, we will see the same logic play out in Corleone in *The Godfather I* and depopulate the town—until the young men emigrate to America, once again bringing Old World clan violence to the New. Huck finds this kind of violence un-American; he simply cannot understand it. Buck cannot even explain how the Grangerford-Shepherdson feud got started. The cause of the original quarrel has evidently been forgotten: "They don't know, now, what the row was about in the first place" (100). It is characteristic of aristocratic feuds that their origins are shrouded in the mists of time. Aristocratic societies remain trapped in the past and cannot find a way to move on. They are the opposite of fresh-start America. In the Grangerfords and the Shepherdsons, we see an aristocratic form of violence, feuding for feuding's sake. The many murders they commit shock Huck and leave him wishing that he had never met these southern aristocrats. Their aristocratic pretensions and their exaggerated sense of honor make it impossible for them to live together peacefully in civil society. As in the case of Colonel Sherburn later in the novel, Twain shows that men who take the law into their own hands because they think that they are above the law are a threat to democracy. The tension between aristocracy and democracy runs throughout *Huckleberry Finn*. In particular, the lingering allure of aristocracy in democratic America continually threatens to undermine the peace of society and lead to outbreaks of violence.

Thus for all Twain's awareness of the dark side of democratic life, he clearly is no partisan of aristocracy, a system he condemns as rooted in slavery (he makes the same point at length in *A Connecticut Yankee in King Arthur's Court*).[12] In fact, Twain seems to suggest that democracy goes wrong precisely when it clings to aristocratic ideals and tries to re-create them, even at the cost of perpetuating slavery. Twain includes a conversation between Huck and Jim in which Huck criticizes a whole series of European monarchs for their bad behavior, including Charles II, Louis XIV, Louis XV, James II, Edward II, and Richard III. Henry VIII comes in for special criticism for the tyrannical way he treated the women in his life: "He used to marry a new wife every day, and chop off her head next morning" (140). Huck is trying to explain to Jim that the real kings of Europe were far more evil than the false kings they have encountered in America: "That's the kind of a bug Henry was; and if we'd a had him along 'stead of our kings, he'd a fooled that town a heap more than ourn done. I don't say that ourn is lambs, because they ain't, when you come right down to the cold facts; but they ain't nothing to *that* old man, anyway. All I say is, kings is kings, and you got to make allowances. Take them all around, they're a might ornery lot. It's the way they're raised" (141).

Twain shows that democracy encourages fraudulent ways of life, but as the case of the king and the duke demonstrates, at least there is a chance of unmasking the imposture. The king and the duke are not really convincing in their aristocratic roles, largely because they were not born to them. As Huck explains to Jim, men born as kings make the most successful impostors. In Twain's view, aristocracy simply *is* fraud; it is all an illusion, based on mere externals, based on show, as again Huck explains to Jim: "I read considerable to Jim about kings, and dukes, and earls, and such, and how gaudy they dressed, and how much style they put on, and called each other your majesty, and your grace, and your lordship, and so on, 'stead of mister" (71). For Twain, aristocracy is by its very nature imposture, some people claiming falsely that they are by birth entitled to rule over others. But people born to rule seem to do a better job of convincing others to accept their slavery. That is why, in the debate between aristocracy and democracy, Twain ultimately comes down on the side of democracy. Democratic life makes certain forms of imposture possible, but they are still an aberration and can be exposed.

Exposing the falsity of aristocracy was Twain's mission in life. He constantly worried about the way that democracy's supporters are nevertheless prone to fall prey to the illusions of aristocracy. In Twain's late work *The Chronicle of Young Satan*, the devil complains about the tendency among democrats to pay tribute to aristocrats: "While they scoff with their mouths, they reverence them in their hearts. That democrat will never live who will marry a democrat into his family when he can get a duke."[13] To counter aristocratic illusions, Twain pinned all his hopes on humanity's sense of humor. Like his devil, he looked forward to the day when people could laugh aristocratic pretensions away: "Will a day come when the race will detect the funniness of those juvenilities and laugh at them—and by laughing at them destroy them? For your race in its poverty, has unquestionably one really effective weapon—laughter. Power, Money, Persuasion, Supplication, Persecution—these can lift at a colossal humbug,—push a little—crowd it a little—weaken it a little, century by century: but only Laughter can blow it to rags and atoms at a blast. Against the assault of Laughter nothing can stand."[14]

Here is Twain's self-conception as an author—he will subject the idols of aristocracy to the corrosive critique of humor and dissolve them. The best-selling status of his writings encouraged him to pursue his goal in democratic America. As we see in the case of the king and the duke in *Huckleberry Finn,* in a democracy the inferiority of those with aristocratic pretensions is more obvious. For Twain, in a true aristocracy, as practiced in Europe, imposture is a way of life; it provides the foundation of the regime. We have seen that *Huckleberry Finn* does have a dark side and refuses to paint a rosy picture of democracy in America. But Twain persists in championing the freedom of democracy over the slavery of aristocracy. America pays a price for building a new nation, but for Twain that price is worth paying for the sake of leaving the old regime of slavery in Europe behind.

2

THE TALENTED MR. DUKENFIELD

W. C. FIELDS AND THE AMERICAN DREAM

The most important thing in show business is sincerity. Once you can fake that, you've got it made.

Anonymous

Postmodern Hollywood

As the twenty-first century approached, 1999 was a banner year for postmodernism in American cinema. Three excellent films were released that all flirt with paradoxes of identity, specifically with the notion of identity as something constructed rather than natural: *Being John Malkovich, Boys Don't Cry,* and *The Talented Mr. Ripley.* As different as these three films are, they have one thing in common: each deals with the desire to be something one is not. *The Talented Mr. Ripley* tells the story of an impoverished young man who is sucked into the world of what Robin Leach used to call the lifestyles of the rich and famous. He is so dazzled by the luxurious existence of an expatriate American in Italy that he eventually murders him and uses his talent for mimicry and forgery to take his victim's place in Rome. Based on a true story, *Boys Don't Cry* portrays the brief and sad life of Teena Brandon, a girl who rejects her sexual identity and re-creates herself as Brandon Teena, a teenage boy who succeeds in having a love affair with a woman. Although the film focuses on the Brandon Teena character, it gives a poignant portrait of the depressing lives of a representative group of lower-class Americans, all of whom wish that they could be something other than what they are. The most brilliant and innovative of the films, *Being John Malkovich,* takes this principle to the level of absurdity. Through a marvelously comic premise—the discovery of a portal into the mind of John Malkovich (played with consummate subtlety and understatement by John Malkovich himself)—the film shows that ordinary Americans would pay good money for the chance to get into the head of a famous actor, if only for fifteen minutes while he orders towels from a catalogue over the phone.

All three films deal with gender issues and specifically pose paradoxes of identity to call into question traditional sexual roles. This is most obviously true of *Boys Don't Cry*, which in postmodern fashion asks us to entertain the possibility that sexual identity is not a biological given but rather a matter of conscious choice. Since *Being John Malkovich* allows women as well as men to enter the actor's mind, it, too, produces moments of sexual ambiguity and in particular explores a variety of lesbian possibilities, including the idea of two women as parents. *The Talented Mr. Ripley* has strong homoerotic undercurrents, and the emptiness of the protagonist's life is reflected in the fact that he desperately craves love from both men and women. But the issue of class is as important as that of gender in these films. This is clearest in *The Talented Mr. Ripley*, which focuses on the efforts of a lower-class character to take his place in the world of the upper class. But many of the problems of the characters in *Boys Don't Cry* are also generated by their lower-class status. A good deal of the frustration of Brandon Teena/Teena Brandon stems from his/her poverty and the limited options he/she has in life. And *Being John Malkovich* turns on the fact that celebrities constitute the only aristocracy Americans have and thus form the horizon of their social aspirations. In all three films, the desire to be someone else is at least partly a desire to rise in social class.

As the most postmodern of the three films, *Being John Malkovich* explicitly connects the desire to be someone else with the logic of the motion picture as an art form. The film basically claims that we all go to a movie in order to be John Malkovich. To see a movie is to want to be someone else, to identify completely with an actor up there on the big screen, to live vicariously the lives of celebrities. The ultimate protagonist of *Being John Malkovich* is the movie camera itself, which is the real portal into the actor's brain, the magic device that allows the audience to share the experiences of many of the characters in the film and to see the world as Malkovich sees it. The American dream is to be someone else and thereby rise in social status, and cinema is the medium that most powerfully allows Americans to indulge in this fantasy. The dream of being someone else is quintessentially American because it is quintessentially democratic. In an aristocratic society, one is born into a certain role in society and must accept it. But in a democracy, social roles are not fixed by birth, and at least in theory anyone may aspire to any position in society.[1] America is, after all, the land where every youngster can dream of being president someday. *The Talented Mr. Ripley*, *Boys Don't Cry*, and *Being John Malkovich* deal with what it is to live in this kind of democratic world, in which all boundaries—economic, social, sexual—begin to look fluid and no longer set limits to human desire. As sympathetic as the three films are to this urge to escape fixed identities, each sees something dark and troubling in this desire to be someone else—they suggest that it may be a formula for perpetual frustration and even disaster. For one thing, this desire inevitably leads to some form of fraud or imposture or acting a part, thereby linking it to Hollywood and its escapist fantasies.

At the time, these three films seemed to be cutting-edge works of art, but they were anticipated by movies made way back in the 1930s—by the great comedian W. C. Fields. If it seems at first implausible to compare Fields's work with these complex and unnerving contemporary films, recall that Fields's comedy always had an edge, and several of his films had a distinctly dark side. In fact Fields was constructing his identity—and making comedy out of it— long before postmodernism and poststructuralist French philosophy were ever heard of. The construction of identity is the principle that unites Fields the man and Fields the artist. In both his life and his art he thrived on creating illusions, sometimes in vertiginously complex ways that in retrospect seem to point ahead to postmodern art. Fields himself once reportedly described his situation: "We are sitting at the crossroads between art and nature, trying to figure out where delirium tremens leaves off and Hollywood begins."[2]

From Vaudeville to Broadway to Hollywood

Born William Claude Dukenfield, he reinvented himself as W. C. Fields and conquered first the world of vaudeville, then the world of Broadway, and eventually the world of the mass media as well, including movies and radio. The comic persona he crafted over the years is basically the all-American con man, part carnival barker, part patent medicine salesman, part circus showman, part cardsharp, and part stockbroker. The main characters of *The Talented Mr. Ripley, Boys Don't Cry,* and *Being John Malkovich* are all in one way or another contemporary versions of the con artist. Fields reminds us that this archetype has deep roots in American culture. In the nineteenth century, it produced such literary embodiments as Herman Melville's *The Confidence Man* and several of Mark Twain's most memorable figures, including Tom Sawyer and Huckleberry Finn. In Fields's vision, America is ultimately one gigantic con game, and he was determined to come out on the winning side, both in his life and in his art. His greatest discovery was that show business itself may be the biggest con game of them all. At their best, his films turn inward on Hollywood and expose the fraudulence of the magic world of cinema. Before the Frankfurt school and its Marxist theories of American popular culture, Fields understood that Hollywood is a dream factory.[3] And long before *Being John Malkovich,* Fields grasped the connection in America between movies and the desire to be somebody else.

W. C. Fields both lived the American dream and tried to expose it as an illusion. In his own life, he acted out a classic rags-to-riches story, rising from obscurity to become one of the biggest stars of Hollywood. In addition to his contradictory personal mottoes—"You can't cheat an honest man" and "Never give a sucker an even break"—he might well have adopted Tom Ripley's credo: "I always felt it would be better to be a false somebody than a real nobody." And yet precisely because Fields was so good at creating illusions, he was haunted by the thought of the illusoriness of his own celebrity, living in fear that it might at any moment evaporate, and fighting, sometimes desperately, to maintain it. That may explain why so much of his comedy is devoted to satirizing get-rich-quick schemes, social-climbing ambitions, and in general people's efforts to construct their identities and become something other than what they are. Fields knew both how to construct illusions and how to deconstruct them.

The son of James Dukenfield and Kate Felton-Dukenfield, Fields was born in Darby, Pennsylvania, on January 29, 1880. Even this fact is disputed; his first biographer, Robert Lewis Taylor, gives his birth date as April 9, 1879.[4] Since the Dukenfields were married on May 18, 1879, we sense what may be at stake here. This is typical of the situation with regard to Fields's biography. Over the years, he told so many stories, tall tales, and outright lies about himself that it is difficult for his would-be biographers to sort out fact from fiction. Fields reveled in the curious institution of the Hollywood publicity department, allowing and even encouraging studio publicists to invent the most outrageous stories about him. As a result, W. C. Fields has become a mythic figure. As happened with Samuel Clemens/Mark Twain, the public has confused the persona Fields created with the real man in a way that is not the case with the other great comedians of his era (Charlie Chaplin, Buster Keaton, Harold Lloyd, Laurel and Hardy, and the Marx Brothers). No one has ever believed that Charlie Chaplin was really a tramp, and most people understand that Groucho was not just a grouch, but almost everybody believes that W. C. Fields was really a drunk. He did in fact drink heavily, especially toward the end of his life, but a man whose comedy relied on precise timing and adroitly executed physical business could not have been habitually drunk in the ordinary sense of the term, particularly given the fact that for much of his career he was performing live before audiences with no chance for retakes. Another widely believed legend about Fields is that he squandered his money or squirreled it away in banks all over the country under false (and improbable) names, thus making it irretrievable after his death. Louvish shows that throughout his life, Fields was careful about financial matters, and left an estate valued at $771,428, a very substantial sum in 1946, the year of Fields's death. As one myth dies, however, another gains new life: Fields's remaining stock of liquor was valued at $1,553.[5]

Simon Louvish takes great pains to debunk the myth of Fields's bleak childhood, and he even shows that W. C. may not have hated his hometown of Philadelphia quite as much as legend has it (alas, his gravestone does *not* say: "All things considered, I'd rather be in Philadelphia").[6] Nevertheless, Fields's childhood was tough enough, and he did drop out of school at an early age, perhaps by the fourth grade. The young William Claude Dukenfield was determined to make something of himself, and that something turned out to be "W. C. Fields, juggler extraordinaire." Today we know Fields mainly for his movies, and thus we tend to forget that he came to Hollywood relatively late in life (not until his fifties). For him, film was basically the third stage in an already highly successful entertainment career. It is a tribute to Fields's ability to invent and reinvent himself that he was twice able to make the difficult transition from one phase of show business to another, first from a juggler in vaudeville to a musical comedy star on Broadway, and then from the stage to the screen—a career move that has proved over the years to be a stumbling block for many famous stars of the theater.

Fields may not have been the greatest juggler of his era, but he was the most popular and successful. Up until World War I, he played all over the world and was a huge star, especially in England and Germany. That Fields was a marvelous juggler with a variety of objects, particularly cigar boxes, we can see for ourselves because he incorporated juggling routines into a number of his movies. Still, no matter how proficient a juggler may be, he is bound to make mistakes in live performances, and Fields quickly learned to incorporate his errors into his act, making them seem intentional and making light of them. He realized that a little comedy could help him out of tight spots, and it was as a comic juggler that Fields scored his greatest successes, usually dressed as a tramp in a way that eerily foreshadows Charlie Chaplin's screen persona (both were working from precursors in the English music hall tradition). Fields had a favorite trick with five cigar boxes tied together by hidden strings. He first performed it to his audience's amazement and then revealed the secret to them. As Fields wrote about "the great cigar-box trick" in a 1904 magician's handbook: "The experiment possesses an advantage over many others, inasmuch as the performer nearly always brings the house down with appreciation for his almost miraculous dexterity, and afterwards secures a laugh so hearty as to nearly shake the foundations of the theatre when the audience see how they have been sold."[7] Illusion—disillusion: here in his early days as a juggler, we already see in miniature the characteristic rhythm of Fields's comedy. He loved to cast a spell over an audience, but he took equal delight in exposing his own magic as a fraud.

The outbreak of World War I made it impossible for Fields to continue his world tours as a juggler, and he seized the opportunity to make the transition from the variety circuit to the Broadway stage. He accepted an offer from the greatest theatrical impresario of the day, Flo Ziegfeld, and first appeared in the famous *Ziegfeld Follies* in 1915. Fields gradually became one of the biggest names on Broadway, appearing with such legendary performers as Eddie Cantor, Will Rogers, and Fanny Brice. With Ziegfeld he was featured in the sort of brief comic sketches that served as interludes between the main attractions of the show—the song-and-dance numbers for beautiful women that were Ziegfeld's specialty. Fields eventually got to star in full-length Broadway plays in the 1920s, several of them worked up specifically as vehicles for him and his particular talents. It was in the course of these performances that he developed and perfected the comic persona that he was later to display in his films, and indeed some of his films, such as *Poppy* (1936), were remakes of plays he had done on Broadway.

Perhaps the most famous of all Fields's comic routines was first performed as "The Stolen Bonds" on Broadway in 1928 and then immortalized in 1933 as *The Fatal Glass of Beer*, a short film Fields made for Mack Sennett, the king of Hollywood comedy in the silent era. *The Fatal Glass of Beer* is a condensed parody of a kind of melodrama that was popular in the nineteenth century (epitomized by a play called *The Drunkard*, which Fields incorporated into his 1934 full-length film *The Old-Fashioned Way*). Such stories of moral reformation—of a man who succumbs to the temptation of vice and learns to overcome it—clearly rubbed Fields the wrong way, especially when the vice in question was insobriety.[8] The ridiculously stylized and stilted acting in the short film makes fun of the moralism these melodramas purveyed. Having been firmly opposed to Prohibition, Fields loved to ridicule the demonizing of rum, beer, and other alcoholic beverages. But as comedy, *The Fatal Glass of Beer* transcends its immediate satiric target. The action shows Fields at his absurdist best, from his impossibly bad zither playing and singing to his going off "to milk the elk." Above all, Fields makes fun of movies themselves throughout the short. As Louvish writes, "The staginess of the film, which made it, at the time, a box-office disaster, seems to show a wonderful contempt for the motion-picture conventions, which fits our 'post-modern' conceits."[9]

The way Fields's stage sketches overlap with moments in his films shows that there was no sharp break between his career in theater and his career in motion pictures. Like any good gambler, Fields hedged his bets. While he was making his debut on Broadway, he was still appearing in vaudeville shows. Similarly, Fields did not make the move from Broadway to Hollywood in one abrupt step but tested the California waters several times before committing himself. In fact, he was quite prescient and saw very early that the motion picture was the wave of the future in entertainment. He appeared in a silent film as early as 1915, and by the 1920s he was starring in full-length versions of his Broadway hits.

Just as World War I effectively brought Fields's vaudeville career to an end, the Depression and its devastating impact on Broadway business finally convinced Fields to give up the stage and devote himself fully to a movie career. In 1930 he left New York and moved to the Los Angeles area for good, following the path westward that is forever linked with the American dream, even in Fields's own film, *It's a Gift*.

Fields in the Movies

The motion picture industry never knew quite what to do with Fields. Given the quirkiness of his comic imagination, he needed more freedom to develop his ideas in film than the studio system of his day was willing to grant him. He was often teamed with writers and directors who did not share his vision, with the result that his films suffer from inconsistency. Some of Fields's problems in Hollywood no doubt resulted from his own limitations. He was, after all, roughly fifty years old when he finally decided to commit himself wholeheartedly to motion pictures, and as adaptable as he was, he had spent almost his whole life on stage in one form or another and brought many theatrical habits with him to Hollywood. Louvish quotes Fields: "The hardest thing for a former stage player to get used to in movie work is to do your stuff minus applause or encouragement before a handful of cameramen and technical directors. You wonder if you're getting across, and there's no way of finding out."[10] Unlike comedians such as Charlie Chaplin and Buster Keaton, Fields never developed a truly cinematic imagination and contributed very little to the art of the motion picture. His movies often feel as if they are merely filmed versions of stage plays. The fact that he often appeared in films based on his Broadway successes did not help him learn what is distinctive about cinema as a medium. For that matter, the plays that Fields had appeared in were not exactly models of dramatic construction to begin with and often consisted of a series of comic sketches loosely strung together like his famous cigar boxes.

One could argue that Fields was fundamentally a sketch comedian. As brilliant as his comic mind was, he tended to think in terms of individual routines, perfectly molded within blocks of time, but for that very reason they were self-contained and difficult to integrate into a larger drama as a whole. Thus the plots of Fields's movies often seem designed merely to provide an excuse for him to go into one of his favorite routines—the golf sketch, the pool sketch, the Pullman car sketch, or the back-porch sketch.[11] Before pronouncing too negative a judgment on Fields's film career, we should, however, recall that he never had creative control over his movies in the way that Charlie Chaplin did over his. To see the distinctive nature of Fields's comic vision, it might be best to look at *The Bank Dick* (1940). In that case, Fields got to write the film largely by himself (under one of his marvelous pseudonyms—Mahatma Kane Jeeves), and the director, Edward Cline, gave him more freedom than he usually had to shape one of his movies. The result is Fields's motion picture masterpiece. With generally faster cutting than in his other films, *The Bank Dick* is well paced, less stagey, and more cinematic.[12] The multiple plots and subplots are well integrated, with all of them coming together in the pure cinema of the chase sequence at the end. Fields drew on many of his favorite routines for the movie, but, as Louvish writes: "For the first time one does not get a sense of comic episodes strung together for the sake of convenience, but a coherent whole, knit together and flowing from point to point with inexorable logic."[13] And in its satiric targets, the film serves up a compendium of Fields's comic preoccupations.

In *The Bank Dick*, Fields plays the aptly named Egbert Sousé (he pointedly puts the accent on the second syllable of his last name with everyone he meets). The film begins with one of the dysfunctional family scenes that are Fields's trademark—the breakfast table from hell. Fields always portrayed family life as a nightmarish labyrinth of tensions—between husbands and wives and parents and children, with in-laws, suitors, and assorted hangers-on thrown in to make life even more complicated and unpleasant for the characters. The many dysfunctional families in Fields's films no doubt reflect his own unsuccessful and troubled domestic life. He broke up with his wife after having one child and spent the rest of his days maintaining an uneasy relationship with the estranged Hattie Fields, largely in the hope of staying in touch with his son, Claude Jr.

Sousé is the typical family man in Fields—henpecked by his wife and mother-in-law, mooched off by his children, and harassed by all sorts of outside forces, including snooping neighbors. Fields is particularly negative about the way women try to domesticate men. Sousé must fight a constant battle just to have the opportunity to smoke and drink. All the forces arrayed against him are summed up when his daughter priggishly complains at breakfast: "My Sunday school teacher Mr. Stackhouse told me that he saw my father coming out of a saloon the other day and that dad was smoking a pipe!"[14] Like many of Fields's heroes, Sousé seeks refuge from the stifling world of women in a masculine retreat—in this case the Black Pussy Café, presided over by the friendly bartender Joe (played by Shemp Howard, of *Three Stooges* fame). From a historical perspective, Fields's comedies represent a male backlash against what today would be called female empowerment in the first quarter of the twentieth century. No doubt Fields saw women as the chief political force behind Prohibition, and he never forgave them for that. Like many of Fields's heroes, Sousé is threatened with emasculation. Belittled by the women in his life, dismissed as uncouth and unproductive, he is not the master of his own household. In particular, his mother-in-law accuses him of being a worthless dreamer, whose idea for supporting his family is to enter puzzle contests or to suggest advertising slogans and hope for the best.

The American Scheme

Here is where the American dream enters Fields's comic universe. For Fields, the get-rich-quick scheme is a way for a man to recapture his dignity and reassert his authority in his family. The Fields hero has usually been emasculated in the first place because of some form of economic irresponsibility. Unable to bring home the bacon, he no longer gets to sit at the head of the table. Sometimes the Fields hero is a misunderstood genius, like the inventor Sam Bisbee in *You're Telling Me* (1934), with his revolutionary puncture-proof tire, or the memory expert Ambrose Wolfinger in *Man on the Flying Trapeze* (1934), with his eccentric but unfailingly accurate filing system. Fields's *It's a Gift* (1934) opens to the upbeat strains of "California, Here I Come," signaling that it will explore a classic incarnation of the American dream. The film's hero, Harold Bissonette, will follow Horace Greeley's injunction to Americans—"Go West, young man"—in his effort to make something of himself. Bissonette had initially failed, according to his shrewish wife, in his "scheme to revive the celluloid collar." She says that it "was going to make us a fortune," but she pointedly asks, "Where is it?" But Bissonette does not give up—he cannot stand his life as a harried grocery store proprietor, at the mercy of his demanding customers, including a man who insists on purchasing no less than ten pounds of kumquats and a blind man who turns out to be the original bull in a china shop. Living in New Jersey, Bissonette finds the West Coast beckoning, and he dreams of making his fortune by purchasing his own orange grove.[15] In the face of warnings against his venture, Bissonette sticks to his guns the way an American entrepreneur should: "I got my heart set on a thing; I'm going through with it." After a long trek to California with his grumbling family in tow, Bissonette finds that his dream grove is in reality a nightmare of totally unproductive land. But at the last minute, Bissonette's story has a happy ending. A neighboring race track desperately needs his land to build its grandstand and buys him out for many times what he originally paid—and throws in a functioning orange grove to boot. Bissonette's move from the East Coast to California to realize the American dream turns out to be almost as rewarding financially as Fields's own move to Hollywood.

Sometimes the Fields hero is an outright con man; a good example is the 1939 movie *You Can't Cheat an Honest Man*, in which Fields plays Larson E. Whipsnade, a circus owner who is always just one step ahead of the law. Short one act, Whipsnade steps into the center ring himself as Buffalo Bella—"the only bearded-lady sharpshooter in the world"—and later he substitutes for the absent Edgar Bergen in what must be the worst ventriloquist performance in the history of show business. But even when Fields plays a legitimate business-man like Sam Bisbee, there is an element of larceny in his soul. Bisbee meets a real aristocrat, Princess Lescaboura, on a train, and she devotes herself to reha-bilitating his fallen reputation with the social elite in his hometown. But Bisbee thinks that she must be an impostor when he hears the Fieldsian moniker Les-caboura: "That's a funny name; how did you think that up? I hope we can put it over on my wife." Even when the whole town turns out to welcome the famous princess, Bisbee thinks that she is playing a part: "This princess stuff is work-ing like a million dollars—keep it up." We might as well be back in the world of the king and the duke in *Huckleberry Finn,* and the idea that in America all aristocracy is phony.[16] Bisbee cannot believe that a real princess would come to his aid, but he is happy to accept help from a fraud. Like all Fields heroes, he will do anything to restore his place in the community—except hold down a regular job. Instead of bringing home a weekly paycheck, the Fields hero usually plays for higher stakes and looks to make one big killing.[17] His family despises him for not pursuing the ordinary middle-class route to financial solvency, but his great hope is that if just one of his schemes pays off, he will be back on top again and secure in his masculinity. Winning a lottery has often been viewed as the epitome of the American dream, and Fields grasped the deep connection between the entrepreneur and the gambler in America (a subject that we will see come up in both the *Godfather* films and *Breaking Bad*).

In *The Bank Dick,* Fields weaves together several configurations of the American dream. In the main plot, Sousé becomes a local hero by accidentally thwarting a bank robbery. In gratitude the bank president gives him a "hearty handclasp" and a job as a guard. In Sousé's improbable success story, Fields sought to expose the arbitrariness of fame and the hollowness of heroism. The way he has the coward Sousé revel in his newfound reputation as a hero reminds us that Shakespeare's Falstaff—perhaps the greatest drunkard in all literature— was one of the ultimate sources of Fields's comic persona. Just as the number of highwaymen who attack Falstaff in *Henry IV, Part One* famously multiplies as he recounts the incident, the knife a bank robber supposedly pulls on Sousé grows and grows in his retelling of the tale, until "the sword that Lee surrendered to Grant was a potato peeler by comparison."

Another version of the American dream in *The Bank Dick* is financial. The boyfriend of Sousé's daughter, Og Oggilby (played by Fields's favorite screen dunce, Grady Sutton) ends up buying five thousand shares of stock in Beefsteak Mines at Egbert's insistence: "You don't want to work all your life—take a chance!" (the motto of gamblers and lottery participants everywhere). The stock is being peddled by J. Frothingham Waterbury, a slick and fast-talking con man—the part Fields usually played himself in his movies. Waterbury first tantalizes Sousé with his own version of the American dream: "Sixteen cylinder cars—big home in the city—balconies upstairs and down—home in the country—big trees, private golf course—streams running through the rear of the estate." It is hilarious to hear first Sousé and then Oggilby try to repeat this materialist mantra and get it all jumbled up in the process. Fields shows how elusive the American dream can be, even when one is just trying to formulate it. Although Oggilby at first appears to be in deep trouble—right after he "borrows" funds from the bank to buy the worthless stock, an auditor shows up—the Beefsteak proves to be a bonanza and Og can look forward to rolling in money (which he generously agrees to share with Sousé, whom he dubs "a financial wizard"). Og has done nothing to deserve his financial windfall; Fields thereby makes fun of the arbitrariness and even absurdity of another archetypal American road to success—the stock market. A victim of the 1929 crash, Fields liked to satirize the world of Wall Street—with its high-pressure sales tactics, mad speculation, and wild ups and downs, it struck Fields as just another con game.

The Bank Dick embodies Fields's insight into the fantasy element of motion pictures. He exposes the way movies pander to the masculine dream of becoming a hero and/or striking it rich—in a Depression world in which obscurity and poverty had become the fate of many people. With his genius for parody, Fields piles up the Hollywood clichés in *The Bank Dick* and reveals how male frustration generates the stock plot twists of cinematic melodrama, especially the abrupt reversals of fortune. Fields makes explicit the connection between the American dream and the motion picture industry itself. In one of the subplots, a film company arrives in Sousé's hometown and gets in trouble when its director goes off on a ten-day bender. Ironically, the usually inebriated Sousé gets to save Hollywood from the effects of the director's insobriety. Meeting the film's producer in a bar, Sousé starts reminiscing: "In the old Sennett days, I used to direct Fatty Arbuckle, Charlie Chaplin, Buster Keaton, and the rest of them. I can't get the celluloid out of my blood." Drawing upon his self-proclaimed expertise as a director and screenwriter, Sousé takes over the film and is soon remaking it into a typical Fields vehicle: "I've changed everything—instead of an English drawing room drama, I've made it a circus picture" (although the only scene we see Sousé rehearsing is a football story).

Delighted with his own work, Egbert is soon proclaiming in tried-and-true Hollywood rhetoric, "We're making motion picture history here." Fields is merciless in ridiculing all the Hollywood stupidities he had lived with for years, including the miscasting he often suffered from himself. The film pairs a very tall leading man with a very short leading lady. But above all Fields shows how perfectly congruent the shabby dreamworld of a cheap Hollywood production is with the shabby dreamworld of small-town America. Indeed the producer links the two forever when he complains: "We've got a thirty-six-hour schedule and a stinko script . . . and it opens in this very town the day after tomorrow."

In the best concluding chase scene in all his movies,[18] Fields mixes together small-town heroism, Wall Street, and Hollywood in a grand cocktail of the American dream. Sousé once again becomes an inadvertent hero and gets a five-thousand-dollar reward for accidentally apprehending one of the original bank robbers a second time. In the process he saves Og's stolen Beefsteak stock, and the movie producer shows up to offer him ten thousand dollars for a script idea he let drop on the set of the film he was directing. Sousé thus ends up a rich man, and in the last scene he presides over a mansion, living in the lap of luxury and finally commanding the respect of his family. Of course, the women in the family claim the credit for Sousé's transformation. His mother-in-law observes to his wife: "What a changed man! You deserve a lot of credit, Agatha." She piously intones, "It hasn't been easy." But Fields leaves us laughing at the idea that money has actually changed Egbert Sousé. He concludes the film with an image of Sousé following the siren call of Joe the Bartender. You can take the Fields hero out of the saloon, but you can't take the saloon out of the Fields hero. In Fields's cynical dissection of the American Dream, family life and middle-class domesticity turn out to be incompatible with a man's yearning for the freedom of the open road.

In Fields's next—and in effect his final—film, *Never Give a Sucker an Even Break* (1941), he chose to drop his mask and for once play himself, a character named W. C. Fields. In postmodern fashion, the film opens with Fields in front of a billboard for *The Bank Dick,* forced to listen to some street urchins badmouthing his recent film. Since "W. C. Fields" was already one of Fields's creations, the character he plays in *Never Give a Sucker an Even Break* turns out to be not very different from the persona he had been portraying for years. Although the movie is uneven in quality, it brilliantly continues Fields's satiric attack on Hollywood. Most of the film consists of Fields trying to peddle an inept script to a producer at Esoteric Pictures. Fields makes fun of the crazy logic or rather lack of logic in Hollywood movies. The producer constantly interrupts Fields to point out holes in the plot he is spinning, such as having a woman supposedly raised in seclusion on a remote mountain top in Russia go into a song-and-dance routine that evidences familiarity with the latest American trends in "jumpin' jive." With its artistic self-consciousness—it is after all a film about making a film—*Never Give a Sucker an Even Break* ends up being Field's most postmodern production. In one scene, he pans from sound stage to sound stage, exposing the artificiality of the world of Hollywood as he reveals the cameras, boom microphones, and other studio paraphernalia that go to make the movie. The moment when some goose-stepping Nazi soldiers march right through a musical production number by costar Gloria Jean could have been the inspiration for Mel Brooks's "Springtime for Hitler" sketch in *The Producers*.

Never Give a Sucker an Even Break was not quite Fields's farewell to the screen—he appeared in several cameo roles in later films before his death in 1946—but it provided his final word on the Hollywood he both loved and hated. Fields keeps interrupting the story with reminders of the phoniness and tawdriness of the cinema, but at the same time he is still able to work the old magic and keep us laughing at the absurd lameness of his own ways of telling the story. It is the old cigar box trick writ large.

Fields for President

In his long career, Fields had one more trick up his sleeve. His interest in the American dream and especially the con man's version of it inevitably led him to politics, the realm in which the American talent for deception and fraud has reached its greatest heights—and depths. As the quintessential con man, Fields sensed that he might belong in politics. Accordingly, in 1940, Fields lived the dream that all Americans by birth are entitled to pursue—he ran for president of the United States.[19] Records of such minor details as his officially registering as a candidate or getting his name on ballots across the country are sadly unavailable, but like so many politicians in our day Fields definitely got a book deal out of his campaign. *Fields for President* was originally published in 1940 by Dodd, Mead and Company. With show business in his blood, Fields intuited something about democratic politics in America—that it has many links to the world of entertainment and the mass media. Looking back on Fields's presidential run in 1940 from the vantage point of what we know today, we cannot help noticing that he anticipated many of the dubious trends in American politics in the decades since his death. In an age when politics seemed at its most serious—right after the Depression and during World War II—Fields saw the comic, ignoble, and indeed the seamy side of American democracy and grasped the way that political reputation and celebrity might come to fuse in a democratic arena. Above all, Fields sensed the link between the politician and the con man, in a passage that anticipates Coppola's *Godfather* films in the way it runs together business, government, and crime: "If he knows nothing else, a President should at least understand the secret of success in the business world. For, after all, what is the Presidency but a glorified business—or, at least, a fine racket?"[20]

Although Fields did not develop a coherent political philosophy, his reflections on government and its function (or dysfunction) have a certain consistency and in general lean in a libertarian direction. Fields planned his campaign around a variant of a familiar slogan—"A chickadee in every pot"[21]—and he was unusually candid in addressing the American people: "When, on next November 5th, I am elected chief executive of this fair land, amidst thunderous cheering and shouting and throwing of babies out the window, I shall, my fellow citizens, offer no such empty panaceas as a New Deal, or an Old Deal, or even a Re-Deal. No, my friends, the reliable old False Shuffle was good enough for my father and it's good enough for me."[22] Fields cut through the usual campaign rhetoric and got right to the heart of what is on the minds of voters: "The major responsibility of a President is to squeeze the last possible cent out of the taxpayer."[23]

Fields's obsession with the federal income tax threatened to turn him into a one-issue candidate. He kept harping on the dreaded moment when payments to the IRS come due: "That is the day when all the citizens of our fair land may practice their inalienable rights of sending a fat slice of their yearly increments to Washington; in return, our Congressmen will forward packages of radish seed or intimate camera shots of themselves weeding their farms or kissing their grandchildren."[24] Fields's antipathy to the tax authorities dated all the way back to the days when he toured the world as a juggler. In 1913, he complained about being stopped by a policeman in Prague: "I was informed that I would have to pay a tax of five cents for coming home at that hour. (It appears they tax everyone who remains out after nine o'clock.) I asked the policeman what would happen if I didn't come home at all. He said I wouldn't have to pay in that case. And, ashamed as I am to tell it, I must admit that I strolled away and didn't come back to my rooms for two weeks—and then I left without paying half the taxes I owed the city."[25] Over the years, Fields was to become more adept at evading taxes, and with good reason. He was especially incensed when President Roosevelt proposed capping Hollywood actors' annual incomes at twenty-five thousand dollars.[26] Fields became famous for his ongoing battles with the IRS over his aggressive deduction strategy on his tax returns. He is rumored to have claimed as a business expense twenty-five thousand dollars spent on milk for entertaining the press.[27] One year he supposedly tried to deduct his liquor bill as a legitimate business expense.[28] After all, he did have a public image as a drunk to maintain.

Beyond Fields's rants about taxes, he spoke out in the name of freedom in several areas of American life. In a Hollywood that generally favored Roosevelt's New Deal policies, and sometimes celebrated them on-screen, Fields refused to jump on the Democratic Party bandwagon and proved to be the great contrarian. He had the audacity to make fun of one of the central planks of the New Deal— FDR's new labor policy, specifically the new power granted to labor unions by the 1935 National Labor Relations Act, popularly known as the Wagner Act. In Fields's *You Can't Cheat an Honest Man,* Larson Whipsnade's struggles as a small-town circus manager are made even more complicated by a labor thug who barges into his office with the ominous words, "You don't want no trouble with the unions, do you?"—a line that had more resonance for the Hollywood of Fields's day than most filmmakers would have dared to admit in public. When the union goon says, "Now you take the Wagner Act," Fields's character replies, "*You* take them. We had them last summer—the worst acrobats I ever saw." In a Hollywood whose New Deal sympathies were soon to culminate in John Ford's film of John Steinbeck's *Grapes of Wrath,* a joke at the expense of the Wagner Act was a rare exception.[29]

For Fields, the central symbol of what was wrong with federal government policy was of course the Noble Experiment, Prohibition. A lifetime devotee of potent potables, Fields had no sympathy for the US government's attempt to impose a temperance policy on its citizens. Throughout Prohibition, he reveled in making fun of the stupidity of the antialcohol policy. We have already discussed his hilarious short *The Fatal Glass of Beer,* which skewers temperance melodramas. As with Fields's animus against the IRS, his hatred of Prohibition had a personal basis, but a more general attitude toward liberty emerges in his comedy as a whole. The great target of satire in Fields's works is the busybody, the person who in the time-honored American puritan tradition tries to tell you how to live your life. It may be your boss, your wife, your mother-in-law, a snoopy neighbor, a temperance preacher, a policeman, or an agent of the federal government. But in each case, someone tells you what is good for you, and it never turns out to be what you yourself want to do—whether it is drinking, smoking, or simply going to the wrestling matches in the afternoon. Fields evidently was struck by how much time and effort some people devote to interfering in other people's lives for no reason beyond the pleasure of exercising power over them.

Fields's vision of how overregulated our lives have become is caught perfectly in his short film *The Golf Specialist* (1930). According to a wanted poster, the film's protagonist, Effingham Bellwether, stands accused of a multitude of transgressions:

BIGAMY.

PASSING AS THE PRINCE OF WALES.

EATING SPAGHETTI IN PUBLIC.

USING HARD WORDS IN A SPEAKEASY.

TRUMPING PARTNER'S ACE.

SPITTING IN THE GULF STREAM.

JUMPING BOARD BILL IN 17 LUNATIC ASYLUMS.

FAILING TO PAY INSTALLMENTS ON A STRAITJACKET.

POSSESSING A SKUNK.

REVEALING THE FACTS OF LIFE TO AN INDIAN.[30]

With his genius for the absurd, Fields exaggerated the bizarre lengths to which society will go to regulate human conduct, but if he were alive today, he might find that life has outrun art. With contemporary concerns over the environment, animal rights, and cultural sensitivity, it would not be surprising to find that all of Bellwether's activities are by now illegal in one jurisdiction or another.

Fields himself sometimes ran afoul of the authorities in ways that made him an early martyr to political correctness. In 1928, he was hauled into a New York court on charges of cruelty to a canary. The local Humane Society had accused him of mistreating the bird in one of his dentist sketches on Broadway and being responsible for its death. Fields was acquitted on the grounds that the canary had actually been killed when the Humane Society officers tried to have it photographed as evidence and the smoke from the flashbulbs asphyxiated it. This story may be apocryphal—Louvish suggests that the affair may have originated as a publicity stunt—but in any case it offers an apt parable of how do-gooding can backfire.[31]

Mistreating canaries was undoubtedly not the cornerstone of Fields's achievement as a comedian, but in one respect his conflict with an overintrusive society went straight to the heart of his art. He found himself constantly at odds with the Hollywood censors. Fields's humor was often off-color, with sexual innuendo or double entendre in the dialogue, as well as sight gags that bordered on the obscene (notably in the 1932 short film *The Dentist*). What strikes us now is the incredible pettiness of the censors Fields had to deal with. In 1939 he got into trouble over a line in the script for his film with Mae West, *My Little Chickadee*: "I know what I'll do. I'll go to India and become a missionary. I know there's good money in it, too." As Louvish documents, these lines were challenged by Joseph Breen, censor-in-chief with the motion picture censorship board. The now infamous Hays Production Code ruled out anything "suggestive of an unfavorable, or derogatory, or comedy, reflection on the gentlemen of the cloth." Hoping to salvage his script in foreign markets, Fields wrote directly to Breen in a desperate attempt to keep the line: "Will this also have to be deleted from the European version or does that not come under your jurisdiction? I've got to get a laugh out of this picture somewhere even if it's down in India."[32] Fields's humor was evidently lost on Breen, who became even pickier when dealing with *Never Give a Sucker an Even Break*. Breen was determined not to let Fields get away with anything this time, and his memo to the studio is quite explicit and peremptory: "Any and all dialogue and showing of bananas and pineapples is unacceptable by reason of the fact that all this business and dialogue is a play upon an obscene story."[33]

In a heroic gesture on behalf of denture-wearers everywhere, Breen put his censorious foot down: "The business of the man taking out his false teeth

strikes me as a piece of business which will give offense to mixed audiences"[34]—
a sentence so preposterous it sounds like something Fields might have written
himself. Faced with the ultimate busybody in Breen, he could only respond by
making censorship itself the butt of his comedy in *Never Give a Sucker an Even
Break,* with the famous line, "This scene was supposed to be in a saloon, but
the censor cut it out."

The Libertarian Comedian

Fields's vision might best be described as absurdist anarchism or anarchic
absurdism. He ridiculed all figures of authority mercilessly, revealing them as
petty, pompous, and silly, while exposing their efforts to govern our lives as
meddlesome, misguided, and inept. He celebrated the spirit of individualism
and enterprise, even when the entrepreneurship took eccentric or even morally
questionable forms, like the gadget inventor, the carnival barker, or the patent
medicine salesman. As a champion of free speech and an opponent of the federal income tax, Big Labor, puritanical experiments such as Prohibition, and
intrusive regulation in general, Fields was an early champion of what is today
known as libertarianism.

With his successful careers in vaudeville, Broadway, Hollywood, and radio,
Fields could lay claim to being *the* representative figure of American show business
in the first half of the twentieth century. As we have seen, Fields quite consciously
and deliberately made himself into a star. He understood what today would be
called the constructed nature of celebrity and knew how to exploit all the media
institutions of the modern age to fashion the public image he desired. And he
made the frustrating and endless struggle to become someone else the theme
of his films, as he debunked a variety of incarnations of the American dream.
Beginning with his juggling act, his own ability to create illusions, which he found
mirrored everywhere in Hollywood, made him obsessive about the hollowness
and evanescence of celebrity, especially his own. In the end, though, the joke was
on Fields. For all his frustrations and unhappiness in life, his achievement as a
comedian has turned out to be lasting, and ironically the very medium whose
reality he questioned—the motion picture—is what allowed him to create images
of himself that have fixed him in the public eye forever. However cynical he may
have been, Fields himself offers proof in his life story that there really is something
to the American dream after all. Where else but in America could the humbly
born William Claude Dukenfield have had the chance to become W. C. Fields—
a major star, wealthy and famous beyond the wildest dreams of his childhood?

3

"I BELIEVE IN AMERICA"

THE GODFATHER FILMS AND THE IMMIGRANT'S TRAGEDY

Prohibition was the dumbest law in American history. . . . It was never gonna work, not ever. But what it did create was the Mob. Those dummies with their books and their investigations, they think the Mob was invented by a bunch of Sicilians in some smoky room someplace. Probably in Palermo. Bullshit. The Mob was invented by all those self-righteous bastards who gave us Prohibition. It was invented by ministers, by southern politicians, by all the usual goddamned idiots who think they can tell us how to live.

Frank Sinatra

Gemeinschaft versus *Gesellschaft*

"I believe in America"—those are the first words we hear at the very beginning of Francis Ford Coppola's *The Godfather I*. The film thus signals that it is going to examine the faith in the American dream. By linking that dream to the immigrant experience, *The Godfather I* and *The Godfather II* tell a foundational American story, perhaps *the* foundational American story. Together they chronicle life in America in roughly the first half of the twentieth century (1901–59). America is a land of immigrants, and they are drawn to its shores by the American dream. The *Godfather* films explore two components of that dream: family and business. One aspect of the American dream—a role traditionally assigned to men—is to build a solid foundation for one's family, to provide a good home and to promote one's children's growth and education. Another component is the classic American rags-to-riches success story. One should build a business empire and become rich beyond one's wildest dreams. At a minimum, one should have a business of one's own because the American dream is a declaration of independence. An American should not have to work for someone else; an American should not have to take orders from anybody.

The dream of being self-employed developed in conscious opposition to the centuries-old European nightmare of servitude. As we have seen in *Huckleberry Finn*, in the American imagination, Europe is the land of feudalism and autocracy, where the many are forever enslaved to the few. Historically, many Europeans left a variety of forms of oppression in the old country to come to America as the land of freedom and opportunity, with the Statue of Liberty as its welcoming beacon. The dream of founding a family and the dream of founding a business go together in America. Ideally the business should provide the financial foundation for the family, and it may even develop into a family business. A man dreams of his son going into his business (perhaps his daughter too). Like the family farm, the family business is at the heart of the American dream. In America, the land of optimism, all good things should be compatible. One should be able to combine family and business to the benefit of both.

In interrogating the American dream, the *Godfather* films turn on these two polarities: family versus business and Europe versus America (or more broadly: the Old World versus the New). But the *Godfather* films do not accept the American dream of moving easily between these poles. Instead, the films show them in tension. Devotion to one's family often comes into conflict with commitment to one's business. The demands of his business may draw a man away from his family, just as family loyalties may get in the way of business responsibilities. The *Godfather* films also question whether it is possible to make a smooth transition from the Old World to the New. Their epic scale gives a wide geographic and historical scope to the films. Coppola portrays what it is to move from Europe to America and from the nineteenth century to the twentieth, and neither journey goes well for the immigrant. Carrying over Old World habits to the New may interfere with pursuing the American dream, while adapting to the fast pace of change in America can be disorienting to the Old World immigrant. The New World way of life may undermine the immigrant's Old World customs and traditions, leaving him without a moral compass. The *Godfather* films present America as the land of modernization, but they also raise questions about modernity as a way of life.

The *Godfather* films are tragic in the way they present the immigrant experience, with characters caught between family and business, Europe and America, the Old World and the New. In Coppola's view of the immigrant experience, the American dream is elusive and perhaps delusive, and turns all too easily into a new nightmare. He chronicles the way in which fresh-start America threatens to become false-start America. The immigrant, precisely because he is not fully accepted into mainstream America, is forced to survive on its margins and thus is tempted by and drawn into a life of crime. Many of the core virtues that make a good American paradoxically turn out to make a good criminal as well—the drive to make something of oneself, the compulsion to succeed, the willing-ness to stand up for oneself, a commitment to hard work and self-discipline, a sense of self-reliance and refusal to become dependent on anyone, the courage to respond to challenges. The *Godfather* films tell a tragic story of how a life of crime, sometimes motivated by understandable reasons, becomes self-defeating. The central theme is that, if a man turns to crime to make his fortune and pro-vide for his family, he may in the process lose that family. Thus the films raise profound doubts about the American dream. They question whether the pursuit of the dream really is open to all who come to the United States, and they raise doubts about whether it is possible to separate legitimate activities in pursuit of the American dream from illegitimate.

The opening of *The Godfather I* brilliantly encapsulates the fundamental dilemma of the immigrant experience. The first words are spoken by an Italian American undertaker named Amerigo Bonasera, who epitomizes the immi-grant pursuing the American dream: "I believe in America. America has made my fortune."[1] Successful in his chosen profession, he has tried to assimilate into the American way of life and to bring up his children as Americans: "And I raised my daughter in the American fashion." Bonasera hoped that he could achieve a happy medium between the Old World and the New, not imposing the strict discipline of the traditional Italian Catholic family on his daughter while still preserving an old-style conception of family honor: "I gave her freedom, but I taught her never to dishonor her family." Unfortunately, Bonasera's hope that he could combine Old World Italy with New World America proved to be unfounded in the case of his daughter: "She found a boyfriend—not an Italian." The looser morality of young American males led to a disaster for Bonasera's daughter. When she refused to yield to the boy's advances, he and a friend beat her savagely and disfigured her face. Still, Bonasera tried to remain a solid citizen of his adopted land: "I went to the police, like a good American." Continuing to believe in the American dream, he assumed that, even as an immigrant, he could get justice from the American legal system. But to his dismay, the judge in the case suspended the sentences for the boys' crimes, and "they went free that very day." Bonasera's belief that America had accepted him into the ranks of its citizens was shattered by his failure to obtain justice from its courts.

At that point, Bonasera decided to turn to Don Vito Corleone to grant him Old World justice for his daughter. As the local Mafia chieftain, Don Corleone stands for the Sicilian code of vengeance, the primitive notion of an eye for an eye, and Bonasera begs him to murder the young men who beat up his daughter. The Don understands what Bonasera is going through, and, from long experi-ence, he knows how seductive the American dream can be: "You found para-dise in America. You had a good trade, and you made a good living, the police protected you, and there were courts of law, and you didn't need a friend like me." As a Sicilian, Vito insists on pure reciprocity—the young men will be beaten up, not murdered—all as part of his demand that the transaction be "Old World" in character. Vito is insulted when Bonasera offers to pay him money for the act of vengeance. That would turn it into a commercial transaction, something that smacks too much of modern America for the Godfather. For him, it must be a traditional act of friendship: "Accept this justice as a gift on my daughter's wedding day." Don Corleone turns his interaction with Bonasera into a case of Old World patronage.[2] His encounter with the undertaker ends with an Old World ritual moment, as Bonasera bows to him and kisses Don Corleone's hand, finally swearing allegiance to him as his Godfather. Bonasera might as well be back in Europe, submitting to the rule of an aristocrat and committing himself to do his patron's bidding when the time comes. To obtain Old World justice, Bonasera must submit to Old World servitude. Both the *Godfather* films grow out of the logic of this opening moment of part 1, during which we see the virtues and the defects of both the Old World way of life and the New.

The opening of *The Godfather I* introduces us to the conflict between two forms of community that will play out in the rest of both films. In German sociology, this conflict is famously known as *Gemeinschaft* versus *Gesellschaft*—a small, tight-knit, organic, traditional community (represented by the village) versus an extended, cosmopolitan, artificial, modern community (represented by the nation-state).[3] On the one hand, *Gemeinschaft* is a form of community characterized by concrete personal bonds and relations, in which people generally know each other and form a kind of extended family. These communities are generally ethnically homogeneous and governed by custom and tradition. Social status trumps other considerations in most transactions. Gift exchange is a prominent mode of interaction and creates a web of obligations that binds people to each other. Relations between people tend to be personal, and "who you are" and "who you know" are crucial in determining your success or failure in the community. On the other hand, *Gesellschaft* is a form of community built on abstract and impersonal bonds and relations, which thus does not require ethnic homogeneity. In order to extend the number of people who can be included in the community, relations must be depersonalized, since there are just so many people that any one individual can know personally. In the extended community, economic exchange generally replaces gift exchange, as people enter into markets whose function is precisely to allow them to deal with strangers. Markets are impersonal—people give money for the commodities and services they want rather than exchanging personal gifts. The principle of contract replaces the principle of status, as people freely enter into relations with each other as equals, rather than being woven into webs of domination and subordination (patronage).[4] Extended communities are characterized by the rule of law, not of men. People seek the impersonal justice of a legal system rather than the personal justice of a vendetta.

Bonasera is caught between these two conceptions of community. As a newly minted American, he turns to the law and its reputation for justice, and, even when disillusioned with that system, he expects to pay with money for any services he receives from Don Corleone. The Godfather has to remind Bonasera about the Old World he came from, where justice was done as a personal favor and everything hinged on whom he knew and whose personal authority he accepted. Don Corleone wants Bonasera to believe, not in America (which is indifferent to him), but in his Godfather, who, as his patron, will take care of him as a friend.

The geography of the *Godfather* films reflects this fundamental tension between small, traditional communities and extended, modern communities. The village of Corleone is the epitome of the small community, and its traditional way of life is both a curse and a blessing, something people flee from but also long to return to. The United States is the epitome of the modern nation, with its claim to impersonal justice and the rule of law, and its tendency—for good or ill—to turn every human interaction into an economic transaction. Las Vegas—an essentially artificial community springing up out of the Nevada desert—represents the hypertrophy of America as an extended, impersonal community. The New York of the *Godfather* films is in effect halfway between Corleone and Las Vegas, and indeed the halfway point in the Corleone's family's journey from the Old World to the New. As Vito's son Michael Corleone understands, the family cannot become fully American until it follows the classic American injunction ("Go West, young man") and moves to Nevada. Don Vito's neighborhood in New York—Little Italy—is only half American; it is still half Italian. It is appropriately the place where the Corleones begin their transition from the Old World ways of the village to the New World ways of the modern nation, but they cannot complete their journey in New York. As the place where the Old World meets the New, where the traditional way of life intersects with the modern, Vito Corleone's New York is at the center of his family's tragedy.

In the *Godfather* films, the American dream, precisely insofar as it liberates people from the shackles of the Old World, subjects them to the new constraints of the modern world. Dealing with the immigrant experience, the *Godfather* films explore the tragedy of modernization, portraying what happens when people uproot themselves from their traditional communities to pursue the American dream of freedom and autonomy. In Coppola's dark vision, the American dream of independence transforms into a new nightmare of servitude, as Michael Corleone becomes trapped in a life of crime. Struggling to liberate and legitimate his family, he ends up subjecting it to the impersonal forces of a modern corporate America, which drain the life out of it.[5]

It Takes a Village

As presented in the *Godfather* films, Corleone is the poster town for emigration to America. Corleone appears in the Sicilian interlude in *The Godfather I,* when Michael hides out there to escape the New York police and his mob enemies. We see the village again in *The Godfather II* in the flashback sequences that portray the childhood of the man originally named Vito Andolini, as well as his return later, after he, as Don Corleone, has become a successful mob boss. One can easily see why the American dream would seem attractive to the inhabitants of Corleone. In scenes in *The Godfather I,* set in Corleone just after World War II, young Italian men beg US soldiers still stationed there: "Take me to the America, GI." Corleone is characterized by crushing poverty and offers few outlets for ambitious young men, whose aggressive impulses are directed into murderous feuds. When Michael Corleone asks about the lack of young men in Corleone, he learns that vendettas have claimed many of their lives.

Corleone is small enough so that everybody seems to know everybody else, but if the town is one big family, it is not a happy one. Corleone is a patriarchal society, dominated by a Mafia overlord, Don Ciccio, who treats the town as his private domain. Apparently the citizens of Corleone have no legal authorities to appeal to if Don Ciccio treats them unjustly.[6] When Vito's father insults Ciccio, the Don has him killed, and then he has Vito's brother Paolo shot as well, to prevent him from seeking vengeance for his murdered father. The young Vito is next in line to be killed; only by sacrificing her own life is his mother able to save him. With young men having little to look forward to in Corleone and facing a limited life expectancy as well, no wonder they long to leave for America. From what they learn from their relatives who have gone to the United States, and from watching American movies, the people of Corleone, especially the young men, think of America as the Promised Land, a place where they will be free to pursue a fulfilling life for themselves and their families. One of Michael's Sicilian bodyguards, Fabrizio, asks him point-blank, "Is America as rich as they say?" His companion, Calo, is so sick of the American dream that he tells Fabrizio, "Stop bothering me with this rich America stuff."

Although Corleone is stifling and suffocating as a community, especially for young men, the town does have its good side. Michael's stay in Corleone brings him back to life after his shattering experience in New York, where he had to murder the police captain McCluskey and the rival mobster Sollozzo. In Corleone, Michael is thunderstruck by the beauty of a young Sicilian woman named Apollonia; he falls in love with her, and he gets to marry her. But in his pursuit of Apollonia, he gains more than just a beautiful bride; the process integrates Michael into the Corleone community. He gets back in touch with his family roots in Sicily.[7] He discovers what a small town like Corleone has to offer—a sense of belonging. To court Apollonia, Michael must participate in a series of age-old customs and rituals. On his first official "date" with Apollonia, a crowd of local women shows up as chaperones.[8] Gift giving is a prominent part of the courtship ritual in Corleone and creates personal bonds between Michael and Apollonia and her family. The courting process culminates in the ultimate village ceremony, marriage, presided over by the unifying cultural force in Corleone, the Catholic Church.[9] Michael marries into a whole family in Corleone and momentarily finds a home. This Sicilian idyll is shattered when an attempt to assassinate him goes awry and Apollonia is blown up instead. Although devastated by this outcome, Michael has at least gotten a taste of the warmth and fellowship of village life in Corleone.

The good side of the small town shows up again in *The Godfather II* when Vito returns to the place he had to flee as a young boy. Don Ciccio had wanted to exterminate every male in the Andolini family, and the small size of Corleone seemed to make that outcome inevitable. How could young Vito survive if the Mafia boss's henchmen could scour every corner of Corleone and proclaim that anyone who hid the boy would be killed? Yet here the tight personal ties of the small town come to Vito's aid, as townspeople risk their lives to smuggle the young boy out of the clutches of Don Ciccio and on his way to America. There, after a long struggle, he establishes himself as Don Corleone, a powerful man in the New York Italian American community. Among other things, he founds an olive oil company, which imports its product from Sicily. Vito is thus able to return triumphantly to Corleone, with his wife and three boys. For the townspeople, he is the living embodiment of the American dream, a wealthy and respected man in the New World, maintaining business ties with the Old.

Back in Corleone, Vito is reunited with his relatives at ceremonial occasions, which center around the obligatory gift giving, including a miniature Statue of Liberty (evidently a popular item in Sicily). Some happy memories must have brought Don Vito back to his hometown, and, as Michael does years later, he momentarily gets back in touch with his Sicilian roots. But before we sentimentalize this other Sicilian idyll, we need to remember that Vito has another reason—more pressing than nostalgia—for returning to Corleone. He finally gets his revenge for the murder of his father by personally killing an aged, nearly senile Don Ciccio (in deleted scenes, Vito murders two other men who were complicit in his father's death).

Coppola gives a complex portrait of Corleone in the two *Godfather* films. The village is visibly rooted in the distant past, but that is another way of saying that it is virtually in ruins. We see the virtues of the village community—its ties are personal and run deep, family bonds are strong, people help each other, their lives are anchored in religious faith, and they are guided and supported by a whole array of customs, traditions, rituals, and ceremonies. In Corleone, you need never be alone, and you will never be left to your own devices. But that strong sense of community also creates a stifling environment in the town. You will never be left alone. Corleone is too small—it lacks the resources to help young people flourish and it makes it all too easy for a local boss like Don Ciccio to dominate its affairs. The worst aspect of the town's traditionalism is that it is caught up in cycles of vengeance that appear to be unending. For both Vito and Michael, Corleone turns out to be the proverbial nice place to visit, but they are lucky that they did not have to grow up there. Only America, with its much broader horizons, gave them a chance to rise above the level of an ignorant peasant. If they had been raised in Corleone and remained there, no one would ever have heard of them.[10] Instead, by coming to America, they achieve a kind of national prominence, if only as crime bosses. They get their names in the newspapers; indeed, they draw the attention of the federal government and become national news. Only in America can a Corleone become somebody important, a serious man.

Living the Dream in Little Italy

Vito's transformation from a frightened boy into the powerful Don Corleone does not occur immediately when he comes to America, largely because the America he finds is initially not all that different from the Italy he left. In one of the many ironies in *Godfather II*, Vito Andolini's first taste of the Land of the Free is imprisonment. Immediately upon arrival, he is quarantined on suspicion of smallpox in a medical ward on Ellis Island. In one of the film's most poignant moments, the sad and lonely boy sings to himself with the Statue of Liberty visible through what look like the bars of his "cell" window. This is Vito's first sign that America may not be the welcoming land of opportunity it claims to be. He grows up and reaches manhood in a neighborhood in Lower Manhattan that is still known today as Little Italy. Although technically Vito is now in a nation called the United States, effectively his life is confined to a few city blocks in either direction, giving Little Italy the feel of an Old World small town.[11] Vito still speaks Italian (in a Sicilian dialect) among his family and friends, and he still follows Old World customs. As an immigrant, he finds that his economic opportunities remain limited. To support his growing family, he is forced to take a menial job in a local grocery store.

Worst of all, Vito finds that even in democratic America, he is still subject to the whims of an Old World big shot. Just as Don Ciccio dominated Corleone, Don Fanucci rules the neighborhood in Little Italy. Well-dressed and affecting a kind of Old World charm, Fanucci struts around the neighborhood running a protection racket that extorts money from local merchants who fear his power. Throwing his weight around, Fanucci gets Vito fired from his grocery store job in order to replace him with his own nephew. Just as in Corleone, there is no civic authority to whom Vito and the other denizens of Little Italy can turn to protect them from Don Fanucci and his Mafia connections. Vito is puzzled by this situation and asks his friend Genco about Fanucci, "If he's Italian, why does he bother other Italians?" Genco replies, "He knows they have nobody to protect them." As we have already seen in the case of Bonasera, the much-touted American rule of law does not extend to Italian American immigrants. New York's Little Italy maintains much of the warmth and community feeling of an Italian village, but it is also plagued by the same kind of lawlessness that allowed the Mafia to flourish back in the old country.

It is this lack of any kind of legal protection that impels Vito Corleone into a life of crime. With his livelihood and his family's future at risk, Vito gets involved in petty theft with some fellow Italian Americans named Clemenza and Tessio. Their close proximity in their small neighborhood brings them together, and they are drawn into their partnership in crime by doing a series of favors for each other, not by signing a formal contract. Unfortunately the close quarters in Little Italy also mean that Fanucci, as the local boss, knows all the details of what they are stealing and how much they are selling it for. Fanucci is actually surprised that a man of Vito's mettle has escaped his scrutiny; he asks him, "How come I never heard of you before?"

When Fanucci tries to muscle in on the trio's meager action, Vito decides to take the law into his own hands and murder Fanucci. Given the fact that we have seen Fanucci to be a glorified thug and we have also seen Vito's need to take care of his wife and children, it is easy to sympathize with his violent act. Fanucci acts like a patron of the community, ostentatiously giving money to the Catholic Church, but he is in fact bad for the neighborhood. Vito becomes a hero for liberating Little Italy from Fanucci's tyranny. He gains a reputation for being a man of consequence in the community. Vito's increased stature in Little Italy is clear in a deleted scene when he goes to buy some fruit from a street vendor and the man will not let him pay for it: "I don't want your money. Take it as a gift." We are squarely within the Old World gift economy, especially when we hear Vito's reply: "If there's something I can do for you, you come, you talk." The Godfather is born.

Coppola made an interesting choice in the way he shows Vito's emergence as the local godfather in Little Italy. We have already seen him assert his dominance over Clemenza and Tessio, his initial partners in crime, who will go on to become his captains, the caporegimes, in his crime organization. At this point, we might expect the film to move on to show Vito establishing the rackets that will soon form the core of his crime empire. How did the Corleone family become involved in bootlegging? How did they gain a foothold in gambling? How did they establish their control over powerful labor unions?[12] Instead of answering these obvious questions, Coppola made an odd choice to show Vito's newfound stature in Little Italy. We see him settling a minor dispute between a landlord and a tenant. An old woman, Signora Colombo—who happens to be a friend of Vito's wife—comes to beg him to get her reinstated in her apartment. Her noisy dog has given her landlord an excuse to evict her and rent out the apartment for more money. This is not exactly the stuff of the St. Valentine's Day Massacre.

Playing the younger Vito, Robert de Niro does a great job of subtly conveying the new godfather's bewilderment and annoyance at being drawn into such a trivial dispute and having to waste his time settling it. Nevertheless, Vito does meet with the landlord and tries to reason with him to take the woman back, calmly and politely appealing to Don Roberto's sense of decency.[13] He evokes the communal spirit of the small town, speaking of the plight of the poor widow: "She has nobody to take care of her. . . . All she has is this neighborhood." When the landlord refuses to comply with Vito's request, he simply suggests that Don Roberto inquire about Don Corleone in the neighborhood. The landlord returns in the next scene, obviously scared to death, and quickly makes one concession after another on the merest hint from Vito, bidding against himself to lower the widow's monthly rent. Vito gets the greedy landlord to become an Old World gentleman and admit that "money isn't everything." When he leaves the offices of Genco Olive Oil, the rattled landlord is clearly relieved to have escaped with his life.

This sequence is brilliantly contrived to show that Vito has indeed become the criminal equivalent of the new sheriff in town. We do not have to see a scene in which the landlord asks around and learns to his dismay that Vito is the man who killed Don Fanucci. Don Roberto's nervous fumbling with the door lock as he tries to get in and out of Vito's office tells us all we need to know. The word is out in Little Italy that Don Corleone is a man to reckon with—and to be feared. This scene does a better job of conveying a sense of Vito's newfound status and power in the community than the more obvious tactic of showing him coming into his own in an organized crime situation.

The landlord-tenant sequence is part of a larger strategy that is vital to the overall effect of the *Godfather* films. The triviality of the dispute is precisely the point. It reveals how much New York's Little Italy is like the town of Corleone.

Everything is focused on the immediate neighborhood. The old woman needs the neighborhood to take care of her, and all Vito needs to do to bring Don Roberto into line is to refer him to what the neighborhood now thinks of Don Corleone. Little Italy is still a kind of village, and whoever wants to dominate it must get involved in its day-to-day activities. That is integral to the all-important system of personal relations that characterizes both Corleone and Little Italy. Vito must be a hands-on godfather; he must intervene personally in the neighborhood's affairs if he wants to gain and maintain its respect. Even Don Fanucci, with all his gentlemanly pretentions, is willing to get his hands dirty as a criminal. He shakes down his victims in person. To use the language of the congressional hearing scenes in *The Godfather II*, the crime bosses in the early days of the Mafia do not yet have "buffers." They do not yet act only through intermediaries to insulate them from legal responsibility for the crimes they want done. When we see Vito emerge as the new godfather, it occurs in a kind of Old World context, a community in which he knows just about everyone in Little Italy and just about everyone in Little Italy knows him. And we do not see him entering into financial transactions; he does people favors, and he expects to be repaid with favors from them in turn. Of course, he wants money, but, as we saw with Bonasera, Don Corleone wants respect even more.

The way Coppola painstakingly creates on-screen the small-town environment in which Vito operates in the early stages of his crime career is key to the sympathy he generates for his protagonist. In their humanizing portrait of gangsters, the *Godfather* films represented something new in the history of cinema. In the classic period of Hollywood's gangster movies—the days of *Little Caesar* (1931), *Public Enemy* (1931), and *Scarface* (1932)—the mobster was generally presented as a psychopath or a sociopath.[14] He was portrayed as an outsider, a lone wolf, at war with society, a kind of monster in his inability to participate in normal human relationships. If he has a family, it is somehow pathological, as in Tony Camonte's quasi-incestuous relationship with his sister in *Scarface*. The main point about the gangster in the earlier films is that he cannot fit into society and thus is denied our sympathy; at best he can be an antihero.[15] Coppola's *Godfather* films are much subtler and more complex than their precursors because several of his gangsters are well-rounded characters, developed as full human beings, who have families and friends. They thereby earn our sympathy for the humanity they share with us. They are gangsters, but we see them first as human beings (in *The Godfather I*, we first meet the Corleones at a family wedding party).[16]

How can we not sympathize with the emergent godfather when the first thing that we see Vito do with his newfound power is to take the side of a poor widow against a money-grubbing landlord?[17] To be sure, we see Vito cold-bloodedly commit murders. But the men we see him kill personally—Don Fanucci and Don Ciccio—are themselves gangsters, who have the particularly nasty habit of threatening and sometimes killing helpless women. Whatever else may be said against Vito, he is not a psychopathic killer. His murders, although clearly against the law, at least have understandable motives (self-preservation or vengeance). Vito uses the power he gains to do good in his community, and from everything we see of him, we can only conclude that he is a decent family man, faithful to his wife and always trying to do what is best for his children. In making the *Godfather* films, Coppola's genius was to take the stereotypical figure of the Italian American gangster and make him sympathetic by emphasizing, not the gangster part, but the Italian American part.[18] He fleshes out his principal gangster figure, giving him a family and a community in the context of which he can display his fundamental humanity. As an Italian American himself, Coppola was able to draw upon the rich immigrant heritage of his own family to bring an Italian American community to life on-screen.[19]

Marriage Italian-Style

Nowhere is Coppola's genius more evident than in the wedding sequence at the beginning of *The Godfather I,* a tour de force in capturing Italian Americans at their most ethnic. The Corleones are no longer living in Little Italy, but they still bring Italy with them to the suburbs (Long Beach, Long Island). They seem to be re-creating Corleone on some higher level, now that they have the wealth to do so.[20] The wedding is Italian-style, but it is one that poor Sicilians could only dream of. There seems to be an endless supply of food and drink. The wedding guests speak Italian, they sing Italian songs, they dance Italian dances, and they follow Italian wedding customs. All the emphasis is on family. Vito is not satisfied until the last of his sons, Michael, shows up to participate in the festivities. Gift giving is the order of the day. To be sure, the bride's purse is filled with envelopes stuffed with cash, but on such occasions, it is the thought that counts. This is still a traditional gift-exchange economy. As we have seen with Bonasera, a Sicilian father cannot refuse any request on his daughter's wedding day, and Vito is dispensing favors left and right, confident that someday they will be returned.

We thus see how Old World customs are still operating in the suburbs of New York. On balance, it is the good side of Don Corleone that is in evidence, as we see him use his powers to aid his clients. He is the champion of the family. He will get justice for Bonasera's daughter, he will help the baker Nazorine get the Italian son-in-law he wants, and he will come to the aid of his own godson, Johnny Fontane, by rescuing his faltering entertainment career. To be sure, accomplishing these "good" deeds will require violence, intimidation, and the use of Vito's connections with corrupt judges and members of Congress. But at least Vito is trying to help people, and we see the people who will be benefited and we do not see the people who will be harmed. The wedding sequence holds out the hope that the Old World might be successfully synthesized with the New. The Corleone family abides by its Sicilian customs, but it can now finance them with its New World wealth. No Italian wedding would be complete without an Italian singer, but the Corleones get the most famous crooner in America, no less than Johnny Fontane (a stand-in for Frank Sinatra).

The wedding sequence shows the Corleone family at its best, and indeed at a kind of pinnacle, from which it is soon to descend into tragedy. Vito appears to have achieved the American dream. He has provided a good home for his wife and children, and he is looking ahead to their future. Sonny has gone into the family business; as for Michael, Vito has sent him to an Ivy League college (Dartmouth), and, as we later learn, he has plans for Michael to enter politics and become a senator or a governor. Vito has also fulfilled the entrepreneurial side of the American dream. He has founded a joint venture and become successful in the olive oil business. His less legitimate enterprises are even more profitable and have made him a very wealthy man, just as the American dream calls for. He is involved in criminal activities, but his marginalized status as an immigrant seems to have forced him into a life of crime. We get glimpses of the violence that underpins Vito's success, but in both films we mostly see Vito helping family and friends. He has become a pillar of the Italian American community and earned the honorific title of Don Corleone.

Vito seems to have learned how to deal with the inner tensions that threaten to make the American dream problematic. He has managed to combine success as a family man with success as a businessman, largely by compartmentalizing the two sides of his life. He insulates his wife and all the women in his family from any danger stemming from his criminal business activities. He does not allow family business to be discussed at the dinner table. At the beginning of *The Godfather I,* he thinks that he has successfully kept Michael's hands clean and that his youngest son is poised to pursue the kind of legitimate success that has eluded Vito. At this point, the mobsters seem to have a gentlemen's agreement to keep family and business separate. Michael does not need to go about with a bodyguard because the family's enemies know that he is a "civilian" and thus is off-limits for their vengeance.[21] According to the Mafia code, you do not attack a man's family, and his house remains a safe refuge. If a gang war breaks out, the mobsters "go to the mattresses," moving out of their homes and into rented quarters in order to avoid civilian collateral damage. As long as the Corleones and the other mafiosi can keep family separate from business, they can hope to combine the best of the Old World and the New. The mafiosi can maintain the personal family values and the sense of honor characteristic of the Old World village, while pursuing their business activities and piling up wealth on the model of the heroic American entrepreneur.

"Drugs Is a Dirty Business"

As we have seen, the *Godfather* films have a geographic and a historical dimension. They deal with the movement from the Old World to the New, which is correlated with the movement from a traditional way of life to a modern. In particular, the films deal with the Mafia in transition, moving from a backward-looking, quasi-feudal institution, rooted in Old World values and based on an almost chivalric code of honor, to a forward-looking, quasi-corporate model, more suited to liberal democratic America, in which commercial interests predominate, often at the expense of traditional considerations, including moral scruples. *The Godfather I* focuses on a development that brings these issues to a head, an important crossroad in the Mafia's history—the question of whether the mob should get involved in drug trafficking.[22] This issue is at the center of the plot of *The Godfather I* and drives the action, especially the repeated attempts to assassinate Don Corleone. An upstart gangster named Virgil Sollozzo has set up an operation to import heroin into the United States, and he wants to partner with the Godfather for the sake of financing and obtaining protection from the police as a result of Vito's political connections—the politicians and judges he infamously has in his pocket. It turns out that Vito has brought a good deal of the Old World with him to America. By corrupting government officials at all levels, the Godfather has undermined the much vaunted rule of law in the United States and restored the rule of men, under a Sicilian-style system of patrons and clients. Sollozzo wants to exploit Vito's political connections to forge a new link between the Old World and the New through drug trafficking—the Sicilian connection.

The move into narcotics would mark a major departure for Don Corleone, who has been hitherto somewhat old-fashioned in his criminal activities. His younger associates are in favor of entering the drug trade. His eldest son, Sonny, sees the financial advantages: "There's a lot of money in that white powder." Vito's adopted son, Tom Hagen, his consigliere (his official counselor), is also in favor of taking Sollozzo's offer. He argues that the Mafia is at a turning point:

> There's more money potential in narcotics than anything else we're looking at. Now if we don't get into it, somebody else will—maybe one of the Five Families, maybe all of them. Now, with the money they earn . . . they can buy more police and political power. Then they come after

us. Now we have the unions, we have the gambling—and they're the best things to have—but narcotics is the thing of the future. Now if we don't get a piece of that action, we risk everything we have. I mean, not *now,* but in ten years from now.

Hagen's considerations are economic. He does not view drugs as a moral issue and does not seem at all concerned that moving into narcotics would mark a break with a family tradition. Hagen sounds like an American business executive, staring at the bottom line and looking for the next big thing, "the thing of the future." He takes the long view of the matter (looking out ten years into the future), and he thinks about the larger context. Ultimately his economic concerns turn out to be political. The profits from narcotics can be "invested" in building up the family's political connections and thereby forestalling any other mobsters' attempts to displace the Corleones. At several points in the *Godfather* films, people say, "Times are changing," and the challenge for the Corleones is to keep up with those changes.[23]

Caught between his customary way of doing business, which still has an Old World feel to it, and the wave of the future in the New World, Don Corleone decides not to break with what amounts to a family tradition. He turns down Sollozzo's proposal, offering his reasons: "I have a lot of friends in politics, but they wouldn't be friendly very long if they knew my business was drugs instead of gambling, which they regard as a—a harmless vice, but drugs is a dirty business. . . . It makes—it doesn't make any difference to me what a man does for a living, understand. But your business is . . . a little dangerous."[24] Don Corleone does not exactly make a moral argument against the drug trade; in fact, he claims to be indifferent to any moral considerations.[25] He simply argues that getting involved in drugs would be bad for business. But his argument is indirectly moral because it rests on a moral distinction between narcotics and other rackets. The community regards gambling (and presumably prostitution and several other mob activities) as victimless crimes. These are crimes only because the law prohibits them, not because they are inherently evil. Like many good Americans, Don Corleone puts drugs in a different moral category; for him, selling drugs is *not* a victimless crime, and thus he refuses to participate in it.

Prohibition—instituted by the Eighteenth Amendment, which outlawed the sale of alcoholic beverages in the United States—is the classic example of the issue Vito raises. The folly of Prohibition was the attempt to deny people a product that the majority of Americans did not regard as evil. In retrospect, the stupidity of Prohibition as government policy is crystal clear. It is a perfect illustration of what goes wrong when government regulation overextends itself and produces unintended consequences. Prohibition only succeeded in increasing alcohol consumption in the United States, and it was the greatest boon to organized crime in American history. By criminalizing a widely accepted activity, Prohibition made sure that only criminals would become involved in it, thereby giving the mob a lucrative business to finance all its other operations. The argument over the drug trade in *The Godfather I* is brief, but it is at the center of the plot and has a larger resonance. In rejecting the drug trade, Don Corleone in effect offers a defense of the Mafia as it has been operating up until this moment. Many of its businesses—bootlegging, gambling, prostitution—were criminal only because the government had made them illegal. The fact that these activities have at other times and other places been perfectly legal confirms the arbitrariness of outlawing them. It may or may not be good public policy, but it is not a matter of the inherently immoral nature of these activities.

Don Corleone suggests that he and his criminal associates have simply been acting like businessmen, providing products and services that American consumers want and approve. As immigrants, he and his fellow Italian Americans have been the victims of prejudice and blocked from pursuing many legitimate business opportunities.[26] The more dubious aspects of their behavior follow from the fact that they cannot operate out in the open and do not enjoy the protection of the law. For example, their need to enforce their contracts themselves leads directly to their use of their own "enforcers," murderous thugs such as Luca Brasi. The *Godfather* films are constantly drawing parallels between gangsters and legitimate businessmen. This is usually taken to be a way of showing that so-called legitimate businessmen are really gangsters, and that was certainly Coppola's stated intention. He famously said that *The Godfather I* is "a metaphor for capitalism."[27]

But this principle cuts both ways. It can also suggest that the so-called gangsters are just businessmen.[28] They are giving the public what it wants, and if their actions are criminal, the only reason they is that the government has declared them illegal. When we see the Genco sign being raised above Don Corleone's olive oil company, it is a scene right out of the American dream, the moment when the entrepreneur proudly opens his own store for business. Genco says: "God bless America. We're gonna make a big business." From *Huckleberry Finn* on, we have seen how thin the line between legitimate and illegitimate activities has been in American life. The *Godfather* films help explain this development by showing how that line keeps shifting, depending on what the government, sometimes arbitrarily, decides is legal or illegal. One moment Italian Americans are making a major contribution to the developing American wine industry by bringing their Old World skill and experience to the New. The next moment these perfectly honest entrepreneurs are put out of business by Prohibition. No wonder some of them are tempted to become involved in the Mafia's clandestine alcohol-making operations during Prohibition. The Eighteenth Amendment passes, and suddenly hitherto honest citizens become criminals or lose their livelihood.

Here is another respect in which the *Godfather* films depart from the traditional Hollywood gangster movie: they do not draw as sharp a line between their criminals and their representatives of the law. The early gangster films tried to paint in whites and blacks, whereas the *Godfather* films use a palette of grays. Generally it is easy to separate the good guys from the bad guys in films such as *Scarface* or *Little Caesar*. The criminals are thugs, shattering the peace of society, and they are dishonest to the core. By contrast, the police who pursue the criminals are usually representatives of law and order, and embody a whole series of familiar virtues, from honesty to courage. The representatives of government are clearly presented as morally superior to the criminals. The way Eliot Ness figures as Al Capone's nemesis in a whole series of films and television programs is a classic example of this kind of Hollywood stereotyping. Capone is at best presented as a charming rogue and more frequently as a murderous thug, whereas Ness is a boy scout with a badge—the untouchable, the incorruptible. There is no Eliot Ness figure in the *Godfather* films—no morally uncompromised figure who sets out to bring the gangsters to justice out of public-spirited motives. The very premise of the Godfather's power is that he has corrupted a vast number of public figures. He can rely on a network of judges, congressmen, senators, police officers, and journalists to do his bidding.

In both *Godfather* films, there are few, if any, prominent public officials who are upright and honest.[29] The gangsters may be sinister, but they often seem to have higher ethical standards than the people pursuing them. Most of the public figures are hypocrites—they will not show up at Vito's daughter's wedding, for fear of the publicity, but to remain in the Don's good graces, they make sure to send their greetings and a gift of money. The one major policeman in *Godfather I* is Captain McCluskey, and he is in the pay of Sollozzo, agreeing to act as a bodyguard for a known criminal. McCluskey is a party to the second attempt to assassinate Vito, when he is in the hospital recovering from the first. Without any legal justification, the police captain breaks Michael Corleone's jaw, at a time when the young man has no criminal record and is in fact a decorated war hero. Don Corleone and his associates commit a lot of crimes, including murder, but the government forces arrayed against them cannot claim any moral high ground in the conflict between them.

This pattern continues in *The Godfather II*. If anything, government figures appear in an even more dubious light. In the person of Pat Geary, we finally get to know a US senator, and he may well be the most contemptible figure in both films. He puts on a good show in public, pretending to be a servant of the people and glad-handing with the best of them. But in private, Geary is as sinister as any of the gangsters, attempting to shakedown Michael over a casino deal in Geary's home state of Nevada. Michael is justified in telling Geary, "Senator, we're both part of the same hypocrisy." Moreover, Geary turns out to be a sexual predator, unfaithful to his wife with prostitutes in both Nevada and Cuba. One would be hard-pressed to find a more vicious portrayal of a member of Congress anywhere else in popular culture—not even the despicable Frank Underwood in the television series *House of Cards.*

In the closing sequence of *The Godfather II,* it seems that Michael Corleone is finally going to be brought to justice by a congressional committee investigating organized crime. Our first hint as to the morally compromised status of this committee is the fact that Pat Geary is a member of it. Subject to blackmail by the Corleone family—they have effectively framed him for killing a prostitute in a rough sex game—this man, who earlier in private castigated Michael and his associates for "trying to pass [themselves] off as decent Americans," gives a fulsome public speech in praise of Italian Americans as his main contribution to the committee hearings. In his panegyric, he pulls names like Enrico Fermi out of his hat, and he has the nerve to say, "Some of my best friends are Italian American." We later learn that the committee's lead lawyer is in the pay of the rival gangster Hyman Roth. What appears to be the pursuit of justice is actually just part of a clever mob attempt to destroy Michael Corleone.

In sum, far from being presented as the mob's antithesis in the *Godfather* films, the government is repeatedly presented as in league with it, deeply implicated in its worst crimes. The films are anticapitalist in conception, but they are by no means progovernment and do not suggest that government is the answer to the problems supposedly created by capitalism. In fact the films suggest a continuity between the quasi-feudal lords of Sicily, the crime bosses of New York, and the politicians in Washington, DC. Each one is, in the terms of the film, a *pezzonovante,* a "big shot" who uses his position of power to exploit common people. In that sense, the problem with capitalism is not that it is at odds with a genuinely public-spirited government trying to regulate it. The real problem is not the free market, but what is known as "crony capitalism," the way government officials are constantly in bed with businessmen and allow them to manipulate public policy to enrich themselves at the public's expense.[30] With all the judges and the politicians in his pocket, Don Corleone is the poster boy, not for the free market, but for crony capitalism. After all, his origins are in Old World feudalism, not New World capitalism.[31] In historical terms, the *Godfather* films repeatedly show that the oppression and injustice ordinary people endure result from the ways that Old World feudalism has carried over into the New World. For all the talk of democracy, common people in America are still under the thumbs of big shots. It was government interference in the operation of free markets that generated gangsters. It was Prohibition—the reductio ad absurdum of market regulation—that set in motion mob violence on an unprecedented scale.[32] Prohibition is the classic case of government regulating, not too little, but too much.

A National Crime Syndicate

The fact that the government forces arrayed against the criminal figures in the two *Godfather* films are not portrayed as superior, morally or otherwise, does not justify the crimes of the Corleones. But it does make it difficult to present them as moral monsters, a few uniquely evil men in a world of moral sanctity and government officials who unequivocally stand for justice. The *Godfather* films depict not good versus evil, but a thoroughly corrupt world, with bad guys on both sides. Again, this does not excuse the Corleones, but it forces us to qualify any condemnation we wish to make of them. They are the product of the morally compromised and fundamentally corrupt world in which they live. If anything, the criminals in the *Godfather* films at times appear to be more virtuous than the forces supposedly bringing them to justice. At least some of the gangsters are good family men. Unlike Senator Geary, Hyman Roth, for example, seems faithful to his wife.[33] They are in fact presented as almost a stereotype of an elderly middle-class couple, peacefully living out their twilight years in Florida.

The forces of law and order in the films, if not downright evil themselves, tend to be faceless bureaucrats, with no private lives to speak of and hence no private virtues. The FBI agents assigned to guard Frankie Pentangeli in *The Godfather II* seem perfectly content to spend the rest of their lives playing cards with the gangster-turned-government-witness. We are used to seeing the FBI in a more heroic role in gangster movies. In *The Godfather II*, it turns out that they cannot keep Frankie Pentangeli alive; despite all their elaborate precautions, the Mafia is still able to get to him. In *The Godfather I*, the FBI first appears in the diminished role of wedding crashers. As they intrude upon this private family occasion to take down the license plate numbers of the cars parked outside the compound, Sonny Corleone, with some justification, says, "Goddamn FBI doesn't respect nothin." Paradoxically, the gangsters are generally more decent and humane than the representatives of the law in the *Godfather* films.

This is another way in which these films depart from cinematic tradition and create sympathy for some of their gangster protagonists. It would not be unreasonable to argue that Vito Corleone, all things considered, is the most admirable main character in both films (admittedly, in a world of generally less than admirable human beings).[34] For all his faults and all the evil deeds he commits, he exhibits some of the traditional virtues, above all, as a family man. Accordingly, unlike the traditional Hollywood gangster, Vito does not die in the street in a hail of bullets, getting his just deserts for a life of crime. It tells us a great deal about Coppola's distinctive vision that, in a deeply moving scene, Vito gets to die of natural causes at the end of a long life and in the company of his grandson Anthony. In a brilliant bit of improvisation, Marlon Brando shows Vito only pretending to be a monster just to scare the little boy in play. In the end, Vito seems to deserve the lavish funeral he is given.

By comparison with traditional screen gangsters, Don Corleone is a decent human being (this may not be saying much, but it *is* saying something). He is not particularly aggressive or vindictive (certainly not by Sicilian standards), and he repeatedly shows that he is a man who can be reasoned with. Even his worst enemy, Don Barzini, pays tribute to him: "We all know him as a man of his word—a modest man, he'll always listen to reason." Vito claims to reject Sollozzo's drug deal out of purely prudential considerations, but it is hard to believe that some form of moral scruples on his part is not involved. He seems to be old-fashioned in his ways, and contrary to an American entrepreneur, he is out of touch with the latest business developments. As Vito moves further into the twentieth century in America, he starts to become an anachronism, a throwback to the Old World (just as earlier Fanucci—a throwback to the old-style Moustache Petes in Little Italy—had become an anachronism by the time Vito killed him). In some ways, Vito's tragedy is his failure to adapt more fully and more quickly to American ways. He does not remain wholly true to the village ethos of his native Sicily, but he does not completely abandon it either and go over to life in the fast lane in modern America, letting nothing stand in the way of making money. A fully Americanized gangster would have taken Sollozzo's drug deal.

Once Vito turns down Sollozzo's offer, his fate is sealed; he has earned the enmity of all the gangsters who want to take the Mafia into the drug business. In the aftermath of the attempt on Vito's life and Michael's retaliatory murder of Sollozzo, an all-out gang war erupts between the Corleones and the Five Families. We are reminded of the fact that gangsters are violent men and that they do kill people. But even in this sequence, Coppola is careful to maintain sympathy for the gangsters. We see very little of the actual violence of the gang war. It goes by quickly in a montage, and we mostly just get glimpses of it in newspaper headlines: "Police Hunt Cop Killer," "City Cracks Down: Pressure on Organized Crime," "Police Captain Linked with Drug Rackets," "Mobster Barzini Questioned in Underworld Feud." Coppola spends much more time on Clemenza's giving Michael an extended cooking lesson, and indeed there is something strangely domestic about the scenes of the gangsters going to the mattresses, sustained by Clemenza's Italian cooking and Chinese takeout. Assigned to kill the traitor Paulie on a trip to Manhattan, Clemenza remains the consummate family man as they leave: "Watch out for the kids when you're backin' out." Clemenza has combined the errand of rubbing out Paulie with a shopping trip on behalf of his wife. In perhaps the most memorable line in both the *Godfather* films, the actor who plays Clemenza, Richard Castellano, improvised what amounts to Paulie's epitaph in words that seem to epitomize the choice between crime and family: "Leave the gun. Take the cannolis."[35]

In this whole sequence, Coppola does his best to normalize the gang warfare by routinizing it, suggesting that it is periodic, inevitable, and predictable, as Clemenza explains to Michael: "These things gotta happen every five years or so—ten years—helps to get rid of the bad blood. Been ten years since the last one. You know you gotta stop 'em at the beginning, like they shoulda stopped Hitler at Munich. They shoulda never let him get away with that. They were just askin' for big trouble. You know, Mike, we was all proud o' you. Bein' a hero and all. Your father too." At first a gang war seems as far removed from normal and decent human behavior as possible, but Clemenza reminds us that war is a common and legitimate human activity and sometimes a necessary one. In the American imagination, World War II is the good war, and one of the heroes it produced was Michael Corleone.[36]

In *The Godfather II*, the last conversation between Tom Hagen and Frankie Pentangeli again associates the Mafia with the events leading up to World War II. Trying to persuade Pentangeli to commit suicide so that he can never again be used to testify against Michael Corleone, Hagen mentions that Frankie was "always interested in politics and history" and points out that he was worried about Hitler as early as 1933. Tom then extends the parallel between high-life politicians and low-life gangsters further back in time and indeed offers a classical precedent, reminding Frankie how the Mafia modeled itself on the Roman Empire: "They based it on the old Roman legions and called them regimes—the capos and soldiers." Waxing nostalgic, Frankie says proudly: "Those were the great old days, you know. And we was like the Roman Empire. The Corleone family was like the Roman Empire." Michael draws similar parallels between politics and crime when discussing his father with Kay: "My father's no different than any other powerful man. . . . Any man who's responsible for other people—like a senator or president." Kay tries to draw a distinction: "You know how naïve you sound? . . . Senators and presidents don't have men killed." Michael shoots back: "Oh, who's being naïve, Kay?" Both films seem to take Michael's side in this argument. Associating the mafia with grand political parallels casts gang warfare in a much better light. Perhaps this internecine strife will have positive results too and bring a lasting peace to gangland.

But more violence must occur before that peace becomes possible. Vito must endure the murder of Sonny in a particularly brutal fashion by the rival mobsters. In the depths of his grief, Don Corleone once again shows that he is not a common thug. He suppresses his violent impulses, foreswears all retaliation, and sets the course for peace. He tells Tom Hagen: "I want no enquiries made. I want no acts of vengeance. I want to arrange a meeting with the heads of the Five Families. . . . This war stops now." Ultimately, Don Corleone proves to be a peacemaker. With the meeting Hagen arranges, the Mafia takes a decisive step forward—out of the old world of the Sicilian small town and into the new world of the American nation-state. As we have seen, the mafiosi, rooted in Little Italy, had in effect re-created Corleone in New York—with predictable results. The principle of vendetta was on its way to destroying the Mafia just as it had done in Corleone, as one mobster after another was wiped out in retaliation for prior murders. Just to preserve themselves, the mafiosi must make the transition from *Gemeinschaft* to *Gesellschaft* and seek a more abstract and impersonal way of dealing with each other. The Mafia must start operating more like an institution united for business and less like a family divided against itself. Accordingly, under the leadership of Don Corleone and Don Barzini, the Mafia reorganizes itself on an American corporate model.[37]

To bring home this point, Coppola shows the mob bosses getting together as if they were business executives at a corporate board meeting. The script specifies that the scene take place at "the boardroom of a bank." To lend authenticity to the scene, Coppola shot the exteriors at the Federal Reserve Bank of New York and the interiors at "the boardroom of the Penn Central Railroad in Grand Central Terminal, 32nd floor."[38] The goal of the meeting is to organize the Mafia into a larger organization that will go beyond the parochial limits of the families that comprise it—in short, to create a national crime syndicate. The various families will reach beyond their local boundaries and learn to deal with each other at a distance. Don Corleone gives a sense of the expanded geographic scope of the meeting as he greets and thanks the participants: "And also the other heads of the Five Families, from New York, New Jersey, Carmine Cuneo from the Bronx, and from Brooklyn—Philip Tattaglia—and from Staten Island, we have with us Victor Stracci. And all the other associates that come as far as from California, Kansas City, all the other territories of the country." The Mafia will no longer be restricted to a single city; having expanded throughout the United States, the mob must become a truly national organization.

This development marks a major departure from tradition for the Mafia. Back in Sicily, it had long served as a bulwark against the encroachment of the emergent Italian nation-state, largely based in the north, on local affairs in the south.[39] The Mafia's hostility to the nation-state is the crux of the argument between Michael and his family that breaks out in the final scene of *The Godfather II*. News of the Japanese attack on Pearl Harbor is threatening to spoil Vito's surprise birthday party. When Tessio says, "I understand thirty thousand men enlisted this morning," Sonny calls them "a bunch of saps." Michael questions Sonny's judgment, provoking his brother to reveal his Sicilian clannishness: "They're saps because they risk their lives for strangers." Here is the old spirit of the Sicilian village—moral obligations do not extend beyond the immediate family, or at least not beyond people you know personally. Michael shows that he is the most modern of the Corleones when, thinking in terms of an extended, impersonal community, he speaks up for patriotism: "They risk their lives for their country." Sonny sticks to the Old World attitude when he insists: "Your country's not your blood." Placed where it is, this scene is completely out of chronological order, but it was a brilliant decision on Coppola's part to end the two *Godfather* films with a dialogue that crystallizes the conflict between the Old World and the New—"your blood" versus "your country." This ending harks back to the "I believe in America" scene at the beginning of *The Godfather I*, thus rounding out both films effectively. It turns out that Michael has already enlisted in the Marines that morning, a sign that he has broken with his family and embraced the ethos of the modern nation-state of America.[40]

Faced with the unending violence of mob warfare, the Mafia after World War II has to follow Michael's lead and Americanize itself. Leaving the small towns of Sicily behind, the Mafia must finally acknowledge that it is operating in a modern nation-state in America. The organization of the Mafia will mirror that of its host nation—a kind of federal system in which each of the regional powers will be represented.[41] Don Barzini speaks of the historical significance of this moment: "Times have changed. It's not like the old days when we could do anything we want." As we have seen ever since Sollozzo's initial proposal, the drug deal is necessary for the mafiosi to move out of the past and into the future.

The mobsters reach an agreement on expanding into the drug trade, based on compromise. They behave like decent businessmen, willing to make concessions to each other to get a deal settled. They will go into narcotics, but they will regulate it—no free market for them—and they start to act like a government themselves. A gangster named Zaluchi insists, "I want to control it as a business, to keep it respectable." As paradoxical as it sounds, by entering the drug business the Mafia will finally go legit. Zaluchi specifies how he would regulate the drug trade: "I don't want it near schools. I don't want it sold to children. That's an *infamia*. In my city we would keep the traffic in the dark people, the colored." Note the federalism of this proposal—within the overall framework of the agreement, local authorities may set up their own local regulations. Zaluchi anticipates future politicians (perhaps because he knows them so well): he is already calling for drug-free zones around schools. He and not the free market will determine who the customers are. Zaluchi shows that at least some of the mobsters still have moral reservations about drug trafficking. To sell drugs to children would be, as Zaluchi says, an *infamia*, a shameful deed that would cost someone his reputation (and, in ancient Roman law, all legal protection). He wants to remain loyal to his Old World morality, even as he consents to expanding into a New World business.

The overriding need to put an end to gang warfare dictates the successful outcome of the conference. As Don Corleone says: "I hoped we could come here and reason together. And as a reasonable man, I'm willing to do whatever's necessary to find a peaceful solution to these problems." Spoken like a good citizen of America. The mafiosi are moving from the rule of men to the rule of law. Having created a kind of legislature for themselves, they are finally setting up rules to govern their conduct. As Barzini concludes: "Then we are agreed. The traffic in drugs will be permitted, but controlled."[42] The mafiosi have come up with a system that will allow them to operate successfully on a much larger scale, indeed a national scale. They will no longer be a set of local families perpetually at war with each other, bogged down in territorial disputes. It will be far more lucrative to have a national organization and peaceful ways of settling conflicts before they erupt into gang warfare. The Sicilians have learned a lesson from America. In their own way, they have become patriotic Americans, with the Cold War mentality that gripped the country in the 1950s. When Don Barzini acknowledges that Don Corleone must profit from this deal, he reassuringly says, "After all, we are not Communists."[43]

But the old country habits run deep, and some of the mafiosi are skeptical about this new organization. Philip Tattaglia hesitates to accept the peace deal: "But I must have assurance from Don Corleone. As times goes by and his position becomes stronger will he attempt any individual vendetta?" It is understandably difficult for a longtime mafioso to believe that the mob can ever move beyond the Sicilian principle of vendetta. Don Barzini tries to make light of the matter: "Look, we are all reasonable men here; we don't have to give assurances as if we were lawyers." Barzini suggests that the mafiosi are actually more honorable than conventional businessmen; they can trust each other without legal guarantees. But Barzini is missing the point. What Tattaglia doubts is precisely whether they as gangsters can successfully make the transition to the rule of law. In fact what he wants is an Old World form of assurance—not a signed legal contract, but a good old Sicilian oath from Don Corleone. And that is what Tattaglia gets from Vito: "I swear—on the souls of my grandchildren—that I will not be the one to break the peace we've made here today." The mafiosi still have one foot in the Old World, even as they take a bold step into the New.

It is Don Corleone's fate never to make the full transition from Sicily to America. He lives to see the Mafia reorganized on an American, corporate pattern, and he goes along with and even promotes this development. But he does not get to enjoy the benefits of this new agreement. From the moment it is concluded, Don Corleone goes into semi-retirement and soon into complete retirement. He acknowledges that his day is over. As Michael explains to Kay: "My father's way of doing things is over; it's finished. Even he knows that."[44] In retirement, Vito retreats to his garden, and, in a profound irony, he goes back to being a Sicilian peasant, tending to his lettuce, tomatoes, and peppers, and playing with his grandchild.[45] Just when the Mafia expands to embrace the whole of America, Vito's horizons contract to a suburban backyard. He does at least achieve a peaceful death, a fate seldom granted to gangsters, at least in popular culture.[46] The last words he hears are "I love you" from his grandson. In external terms, he does seem to have achieved the American dream: a big house, a large family, a successful family business, and great wealth—remarkable achievements for an immigrant who arrived in the United States not speaking a word of English and with few possessions and not a penny to his name. Talk about rags to riches.

Vito's rise in the world is guided by an important lesson he learns from his paisan Clemenza. In a deleted scene, Clemenza tells him the story of his father, who worked twelve hours a day building the New York City subway but never even got to ride on it. That is why Clemenza turned to a life of crime: "Nobody orders me around. I'm my own boss." Vito never forgets those words. With his death approaching, he offers a moving reflection on his life: "I work my whole life, I don't apologize, to take care of my family, and I refused to be a fool, dancing on a string held by all those bigshots."[47] Vito speaks his own epitaph: "I refused to be a fool." It is the epitaph of a true American, a man who would never let himself be pushed around by pseudo-aristocratic elites.

But Vito's realization of the American dream is tainted with failure. He has lived to see the bullet-ridden corpse of his eldest son. His dreams of his youngest son's becoming a governor or a senator have been shattered. He had hoped to keep Michael free of the taint of the family business, but precisely in defense of his father, Michael has become deeply involved in Mafia business—and a cop-killer fugitive in the process. There is something heroic about Vito's rise to power in America, but if he is a hero, he is a *tragic* hero.[48]

"Go West, Young Man"

It is up to Michael Corleone to fulfill his father's hopes for him and his family, but he fails more fundamentally and ends up a tragic figure as well. Michael's challenge is to complete the Americanization of the Corleone family, to leave their Old World ways behind and fully embrace the modern United States. As Al Pacino described the character he so brilliantly brought to life on-screen, Michael is "caught between his Old World family and the postwar American dream."[49] To embrace that dream, Michael follows Horace Greeley's famous injunction to Americans: "Go West, young man"—a pattern we have already seen illustrated in the lives and works of both Mark Twain and W. C. Fields. The geographic logic of the *Godfather* films is relentless. The Corleone family must keep heading west.[50] Coming from Sicily to New York does not complete their journey, because for them New York means Little Italy, and at first their story proves to be a case of "You can take Italians out of Italy, but you can't take Italy out of Italians." As we have seen, the home the Corleones find in New York is not all that different from Sicily and confronts them with similar problems. As the site where immigrants to America first arrived, the East Coast remains tainted by its European heritage.

To free his family from the stigma of being immigrants, Michael must engineer a move to the American West. That is the site of the American frontier, where people can leave the European corruption of the East Coast behind and get a fresh start at becoming Americans. Everyone except Native Americans are immigrants to the West, and traditionally westerners care only about who you are, not where you came from. If America is the land of the fresh start, then the West is America in its purest form, because it lets people recover from any false starts they might have initially made. Accordingly, even before Vito dies, Michael is already planning to move the Corleone family west to Nevada.

Nevada is crucial to Michael's plans because it has legalized gambling. *The Godfather I* does not stress this point, but it is the reason for the Mafia's development of Las Vegas in the first place and also the premise of all Michael's scheming.[51] The fact that gambling is legal in Nevada is a good reminder of the arbitrariness of its being illegal in other states. There is nothing illegal about gambling that a state legislature cannot change at a moment's notice. Indeed, today many states run their own gambling operations—calling them "lotteries"—a particularly insidious form of gambling because it attracts poor people, especially given the heavy television advertising behind it. If the Mafia runs a lottery, it is called the "numbers racket"; if a state runs a lottery, it is called "funding for public education," even though many states have diverted lottery funds from their original designated purposes.[52]

The issue of gambling has perpetually divided Americans and goes to the heart of the ambiguity in their self-conception as a nation. On the one hand, many Americans have opposed gambling on ethical and religious grounds, viewing it as an activity that subverts the family and other middle-class values. On the other hand, from the very beginning America was itself a kind of gigantic gamble. Explorers had to risk everything just to find it, colonists had to gamble with their lives to settle it, and its entrepreneurs became heroes precisely by their willingness to take risks that ordinary people are unwilling to assume. The issue of gambling thus helps to reveal a contradiction at the heart of the American dream. One version of that dream is a vision of security—a family protected from all risks, with a breadwinner's steady income, a fixed-rate home mortgage, and a drawer full of insurance policies. But another version of the American dream involves winning the lottery, or striking it rich in a risky venture, or correctly calling a longshot winner at the Kentucky Derby. Americans do not seem to know whether to avoid risks or to embrace them. Perhaps it is the signal achievement of Las Vegas that it has been able to domesticate gambling and transform it into a middle-class pastime, fun for the whole family. Especially, as it turns out, the Corleones.

Michael is hoping to make the Corleone family legitimate; he promises to his wife, Kate, that he will accomplish that goal in five years. Muscling into the legal casino business in Las Vegas appears to be a quick route to legitimacy and allows Michael to draw upon the family's long years of experience running illegal gambling operations in other states. As explained in *The Godfather II*, mob money financed the development of Las Vegas under the leadership of Moe Greene (a stand-in for real-life gangster Bugsy Siegel). If Michael can get control of several large casinos in Nevada, he will be much closer to his goal. He can continue to pursue one of the family's core businesses—gambling—but now it will be perfectly legal (although the film only hints at this point, casino operations involve huge cash flows and thus are very attractive to gangsters, who can use the technique known as "skimming" for various criminal goals, including money laundering and tax evasion).[53]

To prepare the way for the move to Nevada, Michael feels that he must first settle the score with the other families in the New York area. He will eliminate his competition and get revenge for the murder of Sonny (Vito swore that he would never take vengeance for his son, but Michael was not party to the oath). Michael's ruthlessness in dealing with his mob enemies reveals that his attitude toward crime is different from his father's. Michael is much more cold-blooded and calculating than Vito was. He lets nothing stand in the way of accomplishing his goals, including any Old World heritage of respecting family and religion. Michael has Carlo Rizzi killed because he set up the assassination of Sonny; the fact that Carlo is married to Michael's sister Connie means nothing to him. To compound his treachery, Michael lulls Carlo into a false sense of security by agreeing to be godfather to his new baby. In a brilliantly orchestrated sequence, Coppola shows Michael participating in the baptism of Carlo and Connie's newborn child while his orders to murder the heads of the Five Families (together with Moe Greene) are carried out.

To be sure, in *The Godfather II*, Vito is shown using a Catholic street festival as cover for his pursuit of Don Fanucci, and the murder is counterpointed with the moment of communion in a Catholic Mass. Still, Vito would never do anything as sacrilegious as Michael's participating in a sacred ritual at the very moment he is having his enemies assassinated. With Vito gone and Michael running the whole show by the end of *The Godfather I*, the mob is operating on pure business principles, with no regard for personal considerations. As we might expect, it is the most forward-looking of the gangsters, Virgil Sollozzo, who begins the movement to make the Mafia a pure business. When he kidnaps Tom Hagen and tries to convince him to support his drug deal, he tells the consigliere, "It's good business, Tom." Trying to avoid a gang war, Sollozzo insists: "I don't like violence, Tom. I'm a businessman. Blood is a big expense." In short, Sollozzo wants to replace blood feuds with economic calculation.

Hagen learns Sollozzo's lesson and tries to convince Sonny Corleone to react calmly to the attempts on his father's life; Hagen stresses: "This is business, not personal. . . . Even the shooting of your father was business, not personal, Sonny." For the moment, Sonny still reacts in personal terms to the attack on his father: "Well, then, business will have to suffer." When the Corleone family later plans the murders of Sollozzo and McCluskey, they toss the terms "business" and "personal" back and forth. As soon as Michael offers to do the shooting, Sonny jokes with him: "You're takin' this very personal. Tom, this is business and this man is takin' it very personal." In reply, Michael for the first time reveals his true colors: "It's not personal, Sonny. It's strictly business." The man who will succeed Vito Corleone as godfather has set his course for the future. The process of replacing personal with business considerations culminates in the death of Vito's old friend, Sal Tessio. When he is revealed to be in the process of betraying Michael to Don Barzini, Tom Hagen has him seized. Tessio says to Hagen: "Tell Mike it was only business. I always liked 'im." Making a last-minute plea for his life, Tessio asks Hagen: "Tom, can you get me off the hook? For old time's sake?" But having just admitted to elevating business over personal loyalty himself, Tessio can hardly expect Michael to let him live for personal reasons.

As we have seen throughout *The Godfather I*, the times are indeed changing, and Michael has fully adapted to the new era, which allows no room for nostalgia or any other archaic Old World traditions.[54] Paradoxically, for Michael to Americanize and modernize the mob is to make it more unfeeling, ruthless, and brutal. In his drive to run the mob more efficiently, on the model of an American business, Michael centralizes command and never lets his personal feelings interfere with his business decisions. Michael's crime empire operates more like a corporation than a family business, and Michael is its CEO.[55] In Coppola's vision, the more modern the Mafia becomes, the more inhuman and monstrous its operations turn out to be.

We get only a glimpse of Las Vegas in *The Godfather I,* but it is enough to show how it differs from the world of the Corleones in New York. Las Vegas is a land of hotels, not of homes. It is a totally artificial community that has been conjured up in the Nevada desert.[56] In Hyman Roth's moving tribute to Moe Greene in *The Godfather II,* he says that the New York gangster "invented" Las Vegas.[57] There is nothing natural about Las Vegas; it had to be invented. It seems nobody lives there on a permanent basis. Nobody puts down roots. They are all visitors. That makes Las Vegas the quintessential American city, a tourist paradise for a people perpetually on the move. As Michael's car drives down the Las Vegas strip, we see one hotel after another, with their neon lights: the Desert Inn, El Rancho Vegas, the Sands. There is something unreal about the city—it is a world of billboards and marquees, advertising the casinos' entertainment. The Corleone family will exploit its connections with Hollywood via Johnny Fontane to bring big stars to its casinos and thus attract customers. Culturally, Las Vegas is about as far as one can travel from Corleone, where Vito's journey began. In Corleone, the people have no local entertainment; the young men can only dream of the big stars they have seen in American movies (they reel off names like Clark Gable and Rita Hayworth as American GIs ride by them). In Las Vegas, the Mafia succeeds in making big stars available in person for the masses. Corleone is the epitome of the small town; Las Vegas is a totally artificial city with no ethnic neighborhoods and a totally transient population. In Corleone everybody knows everybody else. Las Vegas is where you go to be anonymous and be free of all moral accountability. When the mob sets up Pat Geary for a false charge of murder, Tom Hagen is able to reassure the bewildered senator that the incident will be covered up: "The girl has no family—nobody knows that she worked here. It'll be as if she never existed." What happens in Carson City, stays in Carson City.

To portray the full contrast between Nevada and New York, and to show what it means for the Corleone family to Americanize, Coppola begins *The Godfather II* with a scene that is clearly meant to be juxtaposed with the opening of *The Godfather I.*[58] The family is now living in a compound on the shores of Lake Tahoe in Nevada. As the film opens, they are once again celebrating a joyous family occasion, this time the first communion of Michael and Kay's son, Anthony. As many observers have noted, the two parties are carefully counterpointed to reveal how things have changed for the Corleone family under Michael's leadership. In *The Godfather I,* the opening party is, as we have seen, saturated with Italian ethnicity. But in *The Godfather II,* the Corleone family has been thoroughly deracinated.[59] There is nothing much Italian about this second party; it reflects Michael's attempt to assimilate into America. In honor of his son's first communion, Michael is making a gift to charity, but, unlike a traditional mafioso like Don Fanucci, Michael is not giving to the Catholic Church but rather to a secular state university in Nevada. This time a prominent politician has shown up at the party—Michael has achieved at least that level of respectability for the Corleones[60]—but Senator Geary, in private, speaks to him with nothing but contempt for Italian Americans. The number of Italian Americans in attendance at this party is drastically reduced, if only because Michael has killed off so many of his father's mob associates. By this time, the three surviving children of Don Corleone (Michael, Fredo, and Connie) are each married or engaged to a non-Italian.[61] The warm family feeling that permeates the opening sequence of *The Godfather I* is absent at the corresponding point in *The Godfather II*. Summing up his party, Anthony Corleone says: "I got lots of presents; I didn't know the people who gave them to me." With strangers, not family, giving the gifts, this time it is the money, not the thought, that counts.[62]

Frankie Pentangeli, who has replaced the recently deceased Clemenza in running the Brooklyn branch of the family, is the representative of Old World ethnicity at the party, and he is bewildered by what he sees. He has wandered into the Land of the WASPs. Most of the guests, we learn, are from Kay's family—the Adams family of New England.[63] Frankie comments on the absence of traditional Italian fare at the party; he finds waiters offering him fancy canapés, which he pronounces "can of peas." He searches in vain for Italian peppers and sausages, and has to ask for red wine in place of the champagne cocktails being served. Frankie sees a band of musicians and is amazed that there is not a single Italian American among them. He tries to lead them in a tarantella, but all the band can come up with is "Pop Goes the Weasel"—much to Frankie's humiliation.[64] This party is serenaded, not by an Italian crooner, but by the Sierra Boys Choir, who look as if they might be auditioning for the not-too-distant Mormon Tabernacle. In *The Godfather I*, the Italian guests dance spontaneously among themselves; in *The Godfather II*, the guests are entertained by a professional dance team with their slick moves. In this opening sequence of *The Godfather II*, we see that Michael has succeeded in moving the Corleone family into the American mainstream, but we also see the price he has paid for that. His family has almost completely lost touch with its Italian roots, and he has cut them off from their past connections. The party that begins *The Godfather I* is a joyous occasion, one that celebrates family ties. The party that begins *The Godfather II* seems devoid of joy and drained of all emotion. As a family, the Corleones seem to be a shadow of their former selves.

Pentangeli has traveled all the way to Nevada to complain to Michael about the situation back in New York. The suggestion is that Michael has lost touch with his roots and is now too distant from his own crime family.[65] Frankie is upset that evidently he now needs a "letter of introduction" just to talk to the head of his family. Pentangeli says to Michael, "You're sitting high up in the Sierra Mountains" while the family's foot soldiers battle it out unaided in the Bronx trenches. To Frankie, Michael appears too businesslike; he seems to be betraying his personal loyalties and siding with another crime family, the Rosato brothers, against his own family. Still attached to the Mafia's old ways, Frankie complains that the Rosato brothers have lost all moral scruples: "They do violence in their grandmothers' neighborhood." Vindicating Vito's decision not to go into the narcotics business, Pentangeli blames the gangsters' moral decline on the fact that the Rosato brothers are now dealing in drugs. The Rosato brothers are allied with Hyman Roth, one of Vito's old associates. Pentangeli cannot understand why Michael is taking the side of Roth, a Jew, in his struggle with Michael's old Italian American comrades: "You'll give your loyalty to a Jew before your own blood." In what becomes one of the major plotlines in *The Godfather II*, it turns out that Michael has indeed allied himself with Roth. His willingness to make common cause with a Jew, even at the expense of a Catholic paisan, is another sign of how alienated Michael has become from his traditional family and ethnic loyalties.

Michael's alliance with Roth marks the culmination of organized crime's evolution from its small-town origins to something much larger in scope. We have already seen the mob go national; now it is going international. Under Roth's leadership, the mob is striving to gain a foothold for its operations in a foreign nation: Cuba. In Nevada, the Mafia found a state willing to legalize gambling. But Cuba promises to become a gangster's paradise—a whole nation willing to promote gambling and presumably also to allow the mob's other nefarious activities. "This kind of government knows how to help business," Roth proclaims, and the Mafia will finally realize the crony capitalist's dream: "a real partnership with a government." Roth recognizes the historical significance of the moment; he tells Michael that the mob is entering a new phase of its evolution: "What we'll do together in the next few months will make history. It's never been done before. Not even your father would dream that such a thing could be possible." Michael has indeed moved well beyond the world of Vito Corleone.

As negotiations with the Cubans proceed—in a scene that clearly echoes the boardroom meeting in *The Godfather I*—Michael sits down at a table in the presidential palace in Havana with a group that goes well beyond an assembly of all the Mafia chieftains in the United States. He is joined by the Cuban president himself and his military aides, together with the heads of a number of multinational corporations, clearly meant to represent the likes of United Fruit and IT&T.[66] The Corleone family has come a long way since Vito, Tessio, and Clemenza sat down around a humble dining room table to parcel out the money they made selling stolen goods. Michael is now like a head of state; at least he is meeting with a head of state and the great captains of American industry.

The meeting in Cuba marks the pinnacle of Michael Corleone's ascent in the world and his Americanization—he literally gets to sit at the table as an equal with the CEOs of some of America's largest corporations. Elsewhere, Hyman Roth speaks proudly of the mob's ascent into the upper echelons of corporate America: "We're bigger than U.S. Steel." Coppola's aim is not to elevate the mob in our esteem but to lower its partners—to show that the business executives are little better than gangsters themselves. When Roth has his birthday cake with a map of Cuba on it cut up for his guests, we see what big shots do—they carve up a country for their own benefit. Lee Strasberg does a brilliant job of playing Hyman Roth (a stand-in for real-life gangster Meyer Lansky). Strasberg deliberately underplays the part. His Roth is no maniacal, machine-gun-toting Scarface. Instead, Strasberg's Roth comes across as a mild-mannered old and ailing man, taken care of in his declining years by his attentive wife, and calm and sweetly amiable in all his dealings. He seems more like a real estate developer than a mobster, which in a way is what he is, as he plans on creating a hotel empire in Cuba.

Michael Corleone and the Tragedy of the American Dream

Having reached the peak of his power in Cuba, Michael quickly begins his descent into tragedy. At a Havana nightclub he discovers a shocking truth: it was his brother Fredo who was the traitor in his organization and set him up for assassination back in Nevada. Treachery within the immediate family— that is something new and deeply disturbing in the world of the Corleones. Meanwhile, the Cuba deal turns sour. Michael had noticed the fanaticism of Castro's rebels in Cuba, and his doubts about the viability of the Batista regime prove to be well founded. Just when the deal is about to be concluded, Batista, unable to quell the Castro rebellion, flees the country, leaving the gangsters in the lurch. Another kind of mob violence breaks out in the streets of Havana—the Cuban people vent their anger after years of frustration by sacking the casinos and smashing their slot machines. The Mafia will not get its friendly government after all. Their Cuban venture turns out to be the Mafia's biggest gamble, and ironically in the end the high rollers crap out. Michael, ever-cautious and resourceful, manages to escape Cuba and return safely to the United States, but immediately his family life starts to fall apart.

Michael always claims to be a good family man and views that as part of his American heritage. At the congressional hearing, he prides himself that his goal has always been "to give my children their fair share of the American way of life."[67] Michael inherits his concern for his children from his father, who always was a staunch supporter of the family. Vito's conception of his manliness is intimately bound up with his sense of himself as the patriarch of a family. When Johnny Fontane comes to beg his godfather to help his career, he breaks down sobbing, "I don't know what to do." In a rare outburst of emotion, Vito slaps Fontane and shouts, "You can act like a man!" For Vito true manliness is manifested in the role a father plays in his family. He asks Fontane: "You spend time with your family?" and when he gets an affirmative answer, Vito explains why that is important: "Because a man who doesn't spend time with his family can never be a real man." His determination to be a real man is at the heart of all Vito Corleone's struggles with the world. He turns to crime to protect his family. His masculinity is obviously at play in his dealings with his fellow criminals. Standing up to them is vital to his maintaining his status and power in the criminal world. But it is part of the richness of Coppola's portrait of Don Corleone that his manliness is not simply a form of thuggishness; it is also a positive trait that plays a role in his dealings with his wife and children and makes him a fuller human being.

Thus, in Vito's last conversation with Michael, when so many other grave matters are weighing heavily on his mind, he still brings up Michael's relation to his family: "Your wife and children, are you happy with them?" Vito is carefully going over with Michael how to deal with the threat from Don Barzini, but in this case he cannot separate business concerns from family concerns: "I spend my life tryin' not to be careless. Women and children can be careless, but not men." In one way this statement is patronizing, but at the same time it reflects Vito's admirable sense of responsibility as a man to take care of his family. Throughout this powerful scene, Vito's thoughts wander back and forth between business and family. He keeps asking Michael about his son, and the aging Don is pleased to hear that his three-year-old grandchild can already read the funny papers. To the end, Don Corleone's sense of himself as a man is linked to his role as a father.

This proves to be a difficult act for Michael to follow. In *The Godfather II,* he insists that everything he has done has been to protect his family just as his father had done, but he begins to wonder if, in trying to protect his family, he has in fact destroyed it. The cruelty he has summoned to deal effectively with his enemies has dehumanized him. In a moving scene with his widowed mother, who has become the last bastion of Sicilian family values in his world, Michael speaks of his father as always "strong for his family," but then he hesitatingly asks her, "But by being strong for his family, could he lose it?" Mama Corleone tries to reassure her son: "But you can never lose your family." Yet that is exactly what happens to Michael in *The Godfather II.*

Appalled by Michael's cold-bloodedness and his unceasing lies to her, Kay decides to leave him and take their children with her. With all his power, Michael is able to prevent Kay from getting custody of their children. Still, Kay is able to deliver a mortal blow to Michael's consciousness of himself as a family man. While he was away from home pursuing his plots with Roth, Kay lost the baby she was carrying. Michael acknowledges that his absence constituted dereliction of his duty as a father, and he tells Kay that he will make up for it. Michael was told that the loss of the baby was from a miscarriage, but at the height of her anger with Michael, Kay reveals that it was an abortion. She knows that an abortion is the one outcome Michael could not accept. In the strongest words in either film directed against the Old World heritage, Kay speaks to Michael with contempt for "this Sicilian thing that's been going on for two thousand years." Enraged, Michael strikes Kay, and with this act of violence against a member of his immediate family—a woman—he has crossed a line from which he can never pull back.[68]

It is a short step from this crime against the family to Michael's ultimate familial sin—he has his brother Fredo murdered. To be sure, Fredo almost became responsible for Michael's being murdered when he breached the security of the Corleone compound in Nevada by giving inside information to agents of Hyman Roth. Many commentators become sentimental about Fredo because he is such a pitiful figure, and he did not think that he was involved in actually getting his brother killed. Still, Fredo's motives in helping out Roth were base—a combination of petty ambition, selfishness, envy, and spite. Michael views having Fredo killed as an act of retributive justice, yet another example of settling the score with his enemies. Nevertheless, in having Fredo killed, Michael kills something in himself, and he realizes that he has gone too far by attacking a member of his own family.[69] Michael participates in what he himself regards as the moral degeneration of the Mafia. He complains bitterly to Frankie Pentangeli that the assassination attempt on him in Nevada endangered his family: "In my home! In our bedroom, where my wife sleeps! Where my children come and play with their toys. In my home." As we saw in *The Godfather I*, traditionally the Mafia had tried to keep family and business separate, designating noncombatants off-limits to mob violence. But in *The Godfather II*, Michael and his family are attacked in his own home. Yet Michael turns out to be no better. First in hitting Kay and then even more so in having his brother Fredo murdered, Michael is guilty of bringing violence into his own family.[70]

Like his father, Michael ends up a victim of the American dream, particularly as it presents itself to the immigrant. Although coming from an immigrant family, Michael tries to grow up as an all-American boy. He goes to a good college, he enlists in the armed forces the day after Pearl Harbor, and he becomes a decorated war hero. Early in *The Godfather I,* when he is describing to Kay some of his father's more nefarious activities, Michael reassures her: "That's my family, Kay; that's not me." Michael hoped to show that in the second generation, immigrant families can completely assimilate in America. He planned on staying clear of any involvement in mob operations, and on pursuing some form of lawful career on his own. His father actually concurred with this plan, as he explains in their last conversation together: "I knew Santino was goin' to have to go through all this. . . . But I never—I never wanted this for you. . . . I thought that—that when it was your time—that *you* would be the one to hold the strings. Senator Corleone, Governor Corleone, somethin.'"

Having failed at successfully combining his family life with his life in crime, Vito hoped that Michael could escape the cycle of violence in which the gangster inevitably gets caught. But unfortunately, Michael's determination to save his father's life gets him entangled in exactly the kind of criminal activities he had hoped to avoid. One moment he is Christmas shopping with his girlfriend; a little while later he is shooting a New York police captain in cold blood. Although Michael does many horrific things as godfather, we should never forget that he is drawn into Mafia life as the direct result of a decent aim—trying to protect his father. Once enmeshed in gang warfare, he is driven from one violent act to another by the sheer logic of the situation. In a way Michael's problem is that he becomes too good a mob chieftain—he adapts too well to the new American setting for crime, and by making his crime operation more efficient, he makes it more deadly and corrupts his own soul in the process.

In the end, what the *Godfather* films say about the American dream is disturbing. The American dream rests on an optimistic premise—that Americans can have it all. They can have successful family lives while also being successful in business. The two activities need not be in tension. Decades of sitcoms offered this vision of America, even though we rarely knew exactly what business the fathers in these shows were in. To get technical, one might say that Americans believe that they can happily combine *Gemeinschaft* with *Gesellschaft*. Americans can take the best of the Old World and synthesize it with the best of the New. They can enjoy the kind of tight-knit, tradition-bound community epitomized by the family and the village, but they can also enjoy the economic benefits generated by the extended community embodied in a nationwide market. One might call this a kind of ethical federalism, in which Americans hope to combine the virtues that work at the local level with those that work at the national level.

In different ways, both Vito Corleone and his son Michael try to be true to the Mafia and true to America at the same time. In some ways, their achievements are impressive—neither is an ordinary man. In striving to be somebody, to make a difference, each is being profoundly American, but their ambition also leads them into distinctly un-American activities—the kind that have to be investigated by Congress. Vito and Michael build, but they also destroy. Michael ends up destroying the family life he tries to build. Vito and Michael are mirror images of each other, together illustrating the dilemma of the American immigrant. Vito prospers in America, but to the extent that he clings to his Old World habits and principles, he cannot keep up with the changing nature of crime in America, a reflection of the fast pace of change in general in the United States, with its entrepreneurial spirit and dynamic marketplace. As a result, Vito is in effect squeezed out of organized crime and forced to retire, but at least he has his family to retreat to, and he enjoys a peaceful death. Michael is not so fortunate. As a second-generation immigrant, educated in America, Michael Corleone is more adaptable to the ways of America and rises to new heights in the criminal world. Unlike Vito, he is able to defeat all his enemies, but in the process, Michael loses his soul and the family he claimed to be working for. He ends up in total isolation, with all the vitality evidently drained out of him, as we see in the final shot of *The Godfather II*. Both Vito and Michael are exemplars of the American dream but also its victims, and thus they end up as tragic figures. In telling their stories, the *Godfather* films explore the more general tragedy of immigration in America, tracing the ways that the American dream may draw newcomers to its shores and lead them into a self-defeating and self-destroying struggle to combine family and business.

Appendix

Godfather Hermeneutics: "I'm Gonna Make Him an Interpretation He Can't Refute"

Interpreting the *Godfather* films raises all sorts of thorny hermeneutical issues that I can discuss only briefly. In this chapter, I have chosen to analyze *The Godfather I* and *The Godfather II* together as a unified work of art, and in a kind of shorthand, I refer to the shaping force behind the films as "Coppola." Both decisions need to be explained and justified.

Film is a collaborative medium; despite the claims of the so-called *auteur* theorists of cinema, no one person—not even a great director—is responsible for everything that ends up on the screen (or the soundtrack). Francis Ford Coppola deserves—and generally receives—credit for the *Godfather* films. But the question of authorship is unusually complicated in this case. *The Godfather I* and significant portions of *The Godfather II* are based on a novel written by Mario Puzo. This novel contributed the basic plotline and created almost all the major characters that appear in the films. Many people who have seen the films first are surprised to discover how much of the dialogue is taken directly from the novel. This should in fact not be so surprising since, in a rare case of a novelist being allowed to write the screenplay for a film based on his work, Puzo was chosen to collaborate with Coppola on writing the scripts for the *Godfather* films. As a result, these films are rooted in their precursor written text to a degree unusual for Hollywood productions. Mario Puzo had a major say in the form that *The Godfather I* and even *The Godfather II* took, and he deserves credit for this role.

Moreover, as in any film production, many other people played a significant role in creating the *Godfather* films. Those involved in the production, as well as those who have studied it, give a great deal of credit to the director of photography, Gordon Willis, and the production designer, Dean Tavoularis. And who can imagine the *Godfather* films without Nino Rota's music? The magnificent cast of actors did a great deal to make the *Godfather* films what they are. They often improvised material that we now think of as integral to the film's original conception (such as Marlon Brando's use of a cat in the opening sequence and an orange peel in his last scene). It comes as a shock to learn that one of the most memorable lines in the films—"Leave the gun. Take the cannoli"—was a last-minute improvisation by the actor Richard Castellano, and that one of the greatest scenes in either film—the final meeting of Vito and Michael Corleone—was written, not by Coppola or Puzo, but by the script doctor Robert Towne (he was brought in at the last possible moment; he did, however, draw heavily on material in Puzo's novel and on the dialogue in several deleted scenes).

The magic of cinema is more mysterious than most people realize. We tend to think of artistic production on the Romantic model of the solitary creator. A single consciousness is supposed to be responsible for a work of art coming into being, and the process is supposed to happen according to a comprehensive plan, fully worked out in advance, and perfectly executed without deviation from the original intentions. As applicable as this model may be in some cases, it does not work in studying film and television. In these fields, collaborative work is the norm rather than the exception. Studies have shown that the proverb "too many cooks spoil the broth" is not a good guide for understanding film and television production. On the contrary, frequently a group of artists working together can create films and television shows greater than any one of them could have come up with working in isolation. Because the production of films and television shows takes place over long periods of time, their creation requires midcourse corrections, and, as a result of improvisation and feedback, a film or a television show can be improved by departing from the original production plans. I discuss the distinctive demands of interpreting popular culture in "Popular Culture and Spontaneous Order, or, How I Learned to Stop Worrying and Love

the Tube," the introduction to my book *The Invisible Hand in Popular Culture:
Liberty vs. Authority in American Film and TV* (Lexington: University Press of
Kentucky, 2012), 1–22, 356–64. For a detailed case study of multiple authorship
in the case of a famous Hollywood screenplay, see my essay "'As Time Goes By':
Casablanca and the Evolution of a Pop-Culture Classic," in *Political Philosophy
Comes to Rick's: Casablanca and American Civic Culture,* ed. James F. Pontuso
(Lanham, MD: Lexington, 2005), esp. 16–22.

Thus when I refer to "Coppola" as the creator of the *Godfather* films, the term
is shorthand for "Coppola and all the other talented people who contributed to
the genesis of these masterpieces." This kind of question of interpretation comes
up throughout this book. For the record, only in my chapter on *Huckleberry
Finn* can I speak of a single author—Mark Twain. In the case of W. C. Fields in
chapter 2, we see the downside of an artist not being able to create his works
single-handedly. We know from Fields's correspondence that he often complained
bitterly about studio interference in the production of his films, and he lamented
the fact that he did not have creative control over them. In my chapter on *Breaking Bad,* I often use the phrase "Gilligan and his team" in recognition of the fact
that, as Vince Gilligan is the first to admit, he worked with a remarkable writing staff and others in crafting the series. With *The Walking Dead* in chapter 5,
we are back to a situation almost as complicated as in the case of the *Godfather*
films. The television series is based on a precursor written text in the form of
a comic book with the same name, and the creative force behind these comics,
Robert Kirkman, is also one of the principal creators of the television episodes.

I mention these matters here in order to reassure readers that I am aware
of the complexities of interpreting film and television when it comes to questions of authorship. I have written elsewhere on the subject. See, for example,
my discussion of the relation of Edgar Ulmer's film *Detour* to the Martin Gold-
smith novel on which it is based, in *Invisible Hand in Popular Culture* (262–68).
Although I am fully conscious of these difficult hermeneutical issues, I have not
let them paralyze me when it comes to interpreting the works I cover in this
book. It may be difficult to pin down exactly whose intentions are at work in
these films and television shows, but I think it is still possible to speak of inten-
tionality in the works themselves. They all *look* as if they have been carefully
planned, even if they may be the result of improvisation or last-minute revision.
However these works may have come into being, they have ended up having an
artistic shape, and they form more or less coherent aesthetic objects, which we
can analyze for their patterns of meaning. Of course no one can ever come up
with an interpretation that cannot be refuted, but one can make a sincere effort
to consider all the evidence and search for aesthetic patterns in the works one
is discussing, and that is what I have tried to do in this book.

Now to explain why I am analyzing *The Godfather I* and *The Godfather II* together, as if they formed one larger coherent work of art. The alternatives would be to include *The Godfather III*, or to discuss the first two parts separately. Many critics have chosen to analyze the *Godfather Trilogy* (see, for example, Freedman in *Hollywood Crime Cinema*) and to integrate their analysis of the third part into their analysis of the first two parts. These critics can point to the fact that the three films have been released on DVD as the *Godfather Trilogy,* and Coppola sanctioned this decision. I would agree that *The Godfather III* is unified thematically with *I* and *II*. But for me, the gap in quality between *III* on the one hand and *I* and *II* on the other is just too great. *III* has its moments—it is after all still by Coppola—but as even many of the proponents of analyzing it together with *I* and *II* would admit, *III* is clumsily edited by comparison with the earlier films, the performances of the cast (especially in one notorious case) do not measure up to the standard of the first two films, some of the scenes go over the top in a way that does not happen in *I* and *II,* and so on. Above all, *III* never develops the kind of dramatic momentum that energizes *I* and *II* and makes them two of the greatest movies of all time. I admire the work of my colleagues who have discussed the *Godfather Trilogy* as a unit, and at a few points I too draw on the third film in analyzing the first two. If anything, the third film confirms what I claim about the way the first two trace the movement from archaic village life to globalized modernity. I just cannot bring myself to dwell on a film that I believe tarnished Coppola's reputation and that I wish had never been made.

Moving in the opposite direction, some critics resist the idea of discussing *The Godfather I* and *The Godfather II* together as one larger work of art. Instead they view *The Godfather II* as a revisionist take on *The Godfather I*. As one of the most intelligent of these critics, Thomas Ferraro, says of *The Godfather II*: "The film offers a very different perspective on the Corleones than either the novel or the first *Godfather* film. . . . In the standard interpretation, the film strips the Mafia of its sentimental familial wrappings and reveals it for what it is and perhaps always has been: capitalistic enterprise in its most vicious form" (*Ethnic Passages: Literary Immigrants in Twentieth-Century America* [Chicago: University of Chicago Press, 1993], 39). This interpretation is solidly based in remarks Coppola has made about *The Godfather II*. He was upset that audiences had rooted for the Corleones in *The Godfather I* and said: "I wanted to put a stop to that" and "What I tried to do in *Part II* is at least turn it around to a very harsh ending. This time I really set out to punish Michael" (Peter Biskind, *The Godfather Companion* [New York: HarperPerennial, 1990], 82). I respect critics who take this view of the two films, and I am tempted to defer to Coppola's authority about his own work, but I would counter that, as I have shown in this chapter, together the two films offer a historical take on the Mafia. They do not present two different views of the Mafia in two different films but rather one consistent view of the Mafia at two different stages of its history. My point is that together *I* and *II* trace the development of the Mafia over time from a comparatively sympathetic family-based enterprise, rooted in Old World values, to an ugly corporatized form, more suited to the impersonal society of modern America.

Thus, while acknowledging alternate ways of talking about the *Godfather* films, I stand by my approach in this chapter. I believe that together *The Godfather I* and *The Godfather II* tell a consistent story about the Mafia, a kind of historical chronicle of its development in America. My own narrative in analyzing the films basically follows this historical arc, from Corleone in Sicily to Little Italy in New York to the sleek hotels of Las Vegas and Cuba—a movement from the local to the global and from the archaic to the hypermodern. I confess that I have often worked from *The Godfather Epic,* the seven-hour reconfiguration of the story that Coppola prepared for television broadcast, which follows the tale chronologically, from Vito Andolini's childhood to Michael Corleone's final round of executing his enemies. This version incorporates the multitude of deleted scenes that were rightly cut from the theatrical releases of the films for the sake of pacing but that do add to our understanding of the grand narrative as a whole. The existence of *The Godfather Epic* is evidence that Coppola acknowledges the validity of treating the story in pure chronological order—in a way that creates continuity between *The Godfather I* and *The Godfather II*.

Anyone who writes about the *Godfather* legend faces a bewildering embarrassment of riches: Puzo's original novel, the two "canonical" Coppola films, all the scenes deleted from those films that have since been resurrected on the DVD versions, as well as in *The Godfather Epic,* and finally *The Godfather III,* which may or may not be part of the "canon." I decided to concentrate on *The Godfather I* and *The Godfather II,* but I have not been dogmatic in my approach. When it seemed useful for interpreting the two films, I have drawn on the Puzo novel, on *The Godfather III,* and on some of the scenes deleted from *I* and *II*. My aim has been to illuminate the larger significance of the Godfather story from as many angles as possible, while still keeping my focus on the two theatrical releases that constitute the major incarnations of what has become one of the great myths of American popular culture.

4

THE MACBETH OF METH

BREAKING BAD AND THE TRAGEDY OF WALTER WHITE

I care not whether a man is Good or Evil; all that I care
Is whether he is a Wise Man or a Fool.

William Blake, *Jerusalem*

One would make a fit little boy stare if one asked him: "Would you like
to become virtuous?"—but he will open his eyes wide if asked: "Would
you like to become stronger than your friends?"

Friedrich Nietzsche, *The Will to Power*

Double Lives and Secret Identities

Vince Gilligan—the creator and showrunner of *Breaking Bad*—famously declared of the show's protagonist, Walter White: "We're going to take Mr. Chips and turn him into Scarface."[1] This was a clever formula for peddling the show to television networks, but it mischaracterizes the story Gilligan actually told. Walter White does not begin as Mr. Chips, and he does not end as Scarface (especially not the Al Pacino Scarface referred to in the series).[2] Mr. Chips is the model of a good teacher, and he would never say, "Don't bullshit a bullshitter" to a high school student, the way Walter White does in 2/7, or write "Ridiculous" on a course assignment. Meanwhile, Pacino's Scarface gets a lot more fun out of life than Walter White ever does (he takes more pleasure in killing people, for example). In one of the many ironies of his story, Walt finds that he cannot spend his ill-gotten gains without tipping off the authorities as to his criminal activities. Even buying an expensive bottle of champagne—Churchill's favorite—is too dangerous for the hypercautious Walter White (4/3). Imagine Scarface fretting over a detail like that. Walt never gets to be fully Mr. Chips or fully Scarface. He is always somewhere in between, a mixture of the two, and that is what makes him so interesting as a character. Even while trying to be a decent high school teacher, he takes his frustrations out on his students, and even while achieving legendary status as a drug lord, Walt clings to a curiously bourgeois way of life, desperately trying to live in the same house and stay married to the same woman. There are no cocaine-fueled orgies in Walter White's life. In the final season, he ends up driving a Volvo, not a Ferrari. Walt would strike Pacino's Tony Montana as hopelessly middle-class to the very end.

Gilligan has earned the right to describe his creation any way he wants, but in order to understand *Breaking Bad,* we must reject his categories as too simple. Mr. Chips is a pedagogical saint and Scarface a criminal sinner, the archetype of a gangster. But *Breaking Bad* is not a straightforward tale of good guys versus bad guys. From beginning to end, the show is suffused with moral ambiguity.[3] The name of the company Walt cofounds is Gray Matter Technology. We learn that this name results from combining Walt's last name with that of the other founder, Elliott Schwartz (*schwarz* means "black" in German). This is a clear sign that *Breaking Bad* does not deal in the whites and blacks of melodrama, but only in shades of gray. The greatness of the show is precisely its moral complexity, the way it constantly unnerves us with the difficult choices its characters are forced to make. That is why audience reaction to the show remained divided up through the last episode. As Walt committed more and more heinous crimes, he lost the sympathy of many viewers. But Gilligan himself was surprised by how many fans—vocal fans—continued to root for Walter White right up until the end (count me as one of them).[4] Perhaps if Gilligan had not been thinking in terms of the sharp polarity between Mr. Chips and Scarface, he would have understood why many viewers, even confronted with Walt's criminal acts, continued to feel for him and wished that he could find some way to salvage his soul.

Almost all the characters in *Breaking Bad*—certainly all the principal ones—are morally ambiguous. That means that most of the characters against whom Walt commits crimes are in one way or another morally compromised themselves, sometimes as flawed in character as he is. To be sure, sometimes Walt is directly or indirectly responsible for the deaths of innocent people (such as the boy killed in the course of the train robbery in 5/5). But this is far different from saying that Walt is the lone monster in a world of unequivocally good characters. *Breaking Bad* portrays a nasty world populated by deeply troubled people who, unhappy themselves, inflict unhappiness on others, sometimes violently. Each in his or her own way feels frustrated, unfulfilled, and envious, and thinks that he or she has been dealt a bad hand by fate and thus denied the American dream. As a result, in *Breaking Bad,* the desire to be someone other than oneself is all-pervasive. Trapped in various forms of boring middle-class existence, the characters fantasize about more glorious ways of life. Walt's wife, Skyler, aspires to be a successful fiction writer, and, although she fails in print, in her real life, she turns out to be capable of spinning amazing yarns about Walt (see particularly 3/9). Her sister, Marie, is a kleptomaniac, shoplifting expensive items so that she can pretend that she is richer than she really is. Later in the series, she goes on a spree of visiting houses up for sale, creating false personas for herself with the real estate agents; for example, she poses in the more glamorous role of an astronaut's wife.

Reacting to their frustration, many of the characters in *Breaking Bad* create new identities for themselves, sometimes merely for the sake of becoming someone different. In the spell of the American dream of the self-made man or woman, they feel a need to reinvent themselves.[5] For example, frustrated by his miserable family life, Walt's son, Walt Jr., insists on being called Flynn White. Walt's sidekick Jesse Pinkman goes by the name of "Captain Cook" in the drug business. The shady lawyer we know as Saul Goodman turns out to be really named Jimmy McGill, and he brags that he once convinced a woman that he was Kevin Costner (3/11). Like a good American, he wishes he were a movie star. A nerdy chemist named Gale, who becomes Walt's assistant in manufacturing crystal meth, makes karaoke videos to get into different personas (4/4) and reimagine himself as a celebrity entertainer. The mastermind behind crystal meth distribution in the Southwest, Gustavo Fring, appears in public as an upstanding citizen, the owner of a chain of fast-food restaurants and a well-respected philanthropist. Gus prides himself on his ability to "hide in plain sight" by keeping his criminal identity secret (3/8). In 5/12, Marie's therapist sums up the basic situation in *Breaking Bad*: "We all lead double lives to some extent. We all have secrets." With all the imposture going on in the series, we once again see the dark side of the American dream.

Of course the greatest example of a secret identity in *Breaking Bad* is Walter White himself. To most people, he is a mild-mannered high school chemistry teacher who evidently would not hurt a fly.[6] But in criminal circles, he goes by the alias "Heisenberg," the much-feared king of meth production in the Southwest and ultimately the world. One of the best ways of understanding *Breaking Bad* is in terms of a classic pop culture pattern—the archetype of the superhero with a secret identity—or, if you insist, the supervillain (with today's superhuman figures, it is in fact hard to tell the heroes from the villains). Why has the figure of Superman been so popular? Because the story of Superman appeals to a basic male fantasy, especially an adolescent male fantasy. You are a nobody. People do not give you a second thought; above all, women do not give you a second look. If only they knew the *real* you. They would acknowledge your superhuman potential and worship you. If only people realized that behind the mild-mannered exterior of Clark Kent lurks the potent figure of Superman. "I am not a nobody; I am somebody"—that is what the Superman myth allows the average male to fantasize. The same logic is at work in the secret identities of other superheroes, from Batman to Captain America, from Spider Man to the Incredible Hulk. The superhero myth is a variant of the American dream of reinventing one's identity. Evidently, inside every American is a hero just waiting to burst loose—all he needs is a phone booth and a cape, and the sky is the limit.

Breaking Bad offers a contemporary variant on the traditional pop culture theme of the superhero and his secret identity.[7] Walter White even changes costume to become Heisenberg—think of the importance of his signature porkpie hat. The choice of his alter ego is perfect for Walt. We learn in the first episode that he was "crystallography project leader for photon radiology" in an important scientific project, and he was given a plaque for contributing to research that eventually was awarded the Nobel Prize in 1985 (1/1). A mere high school chemistry teacher in an obscure New Mexico school district, Walt takes the name of a Nobel Prize–winning scientist, Werner Heisenberg. Viewers can empathize with that. We all have seen our ambitions frustrated and know what it is to dream of their being fulfilled. One of the keys to understanding the widespread appeal of *Breaking Bad* is that the series taps into the same psychology that fuels the popular taste for superheroes and their secret identities.[8] Many people harbor an inner Heisenberg, and it is cathartic to watch a character who acts out his secret fantasies. In *Breaking Bad,* we get to experience vicariously what it would be like to indulge our aggressive drives and our feelings of superiority—to break free for once from all the normal rules and laws that hold us in check in civil society—and let our egoistic impulses run loose. In the story of Walter White, we are fascinated even as we are appalled by the results. Sometimes we turn to popular culture, not for a realistic mirror of our ordinary existence, but for an alternative to it—something more exciting, something more dangerous, something that appeals to our hidden fantasies. Because we have entered a fictional world, we can safely explore extreme possibilities that are denied to us in our everyday lives.

The curious production history of *Breaking Bad* offers another way of grasping this point. When Gilligan proposed that Bryan Cranston play the role of Walter White, executives at the AMC network balked at the prospect.[9] For seven seasons, Cranston had played the hapless father Hal in the sitcom *Malcolm in the Middle* on the Fox television network. Cranston had proved himself to be a master of comedy in playing the part of a henpecked husband, overwhelmed by his domineering wife, Lois, and by his mischievous, rebellious, and resourceful sons. The AMC executives could not picture the actor who played the bumbling Hal stepping into the role of the sinister Walter White. What they did not realize is that in fact *Malcolm in the Middle* provided Cranston with the perfect training ground for playing the Walt we meet at the beginning of *Breaking Bad.* He too is threatened with emasculation at the hands of a domineering wife, and he too is placed in one embarrassing and humiliating situation after another in his daily life. Indeed, Hal and Walt share a strange habit of showing up in public in their underwear (their tighty-whities) that calls into question their masculinity and at times even their sanity.[10]

If the AMC executives had studied *Malcolm in the Middle* carefully, they would have found that in season 2, episode 14 ("Hal Quits"), Cranston's character gets fed up with his boring life and decides to fulfill himself by becoming an artist. In retrospect, it looks as if Bryan Cranston discovered his inner Walter White in this episode, or rather his inner Heisenberg. It deals with Hal undergoing a midlife crisis and quitting his job, which has become meaningless to him. In his artistic endeavors, he displays the kind of obsessive-compulsive behavior we associate with Walter White, and for once he stands up to Lois and becomes the domineering one in the relationship. Season 2, episode 25 ("Flashback") provides another example of Hal getting frustrated with his subordinate situation at home and unleashing his anger on Lois, provoking their youngest son, Dewey, to worry that they will get divorced.[11] *Malcolm in the Middle* and *Breaking Bad* turn out to be mirror images of each other.

Gilligan and his team evidently realized this connection between the two series. As a supplement to the last season of *Breaking Bad* DVDs, they created a hilarious alternate ending to the series. With a nod to famous dream sequences in *Dallas* and *The Newhart Show,* it turns out that the whole story of Walter White was just Hal having a bad dream. Cranston wakes up in bed with Jane Kaczmarek, the actress who played Lois in *Malcolm in the Middle.* Back in character as Hal, Cranston whines about all the horrible things he has done and all the horrible people he has had to deal with. Meek as ever, Hal says: "The only thing that made sense in the whole business is that I still walked around in my underwear." Forever belittling Hal, Lois tells him, "You grow a beard and suddenly you think that you're Osama bin Laden." Evoking Gilligan's formula for *Breaking Bad,* Lois dismisses Hal: "Go to sleep, Scarface." As the scene concludes, the camera pans to Heisenberg's trademark hat.

This vignette is a stroke of genius; it also embodies a genuine insight into what *Breaking Bad* is about. If the Hal of *Malcolm in the Middle* had a fantasy life, he would want to become someone like Walter White/Heisenberg.[12] Not wearing the pants in his own household (sometimes literally), ridiculed by his wife, and outsmarted by his own sons, Hal would long for a situation in which he could be the boss ("You're not the boss of me now" is the refrain of the theme song of *Malcolm in the Middle*). Tired of the middle-class version of the American dream in the suburbs, Hal would fantasize about breaking out of his rut and becoming somebody, somebody who matters. The *Breaking Bad* team got it exactly right: *Malcolm in the Middle* and *Breaking Bad* are two sides of the same coin. They both interrogate the traditional American dream of middle-class suburban life. They both portray what it is like to be trapped in a frustrating family situation; they both explore the frustrations of middle-class existence in contemporary America—especially for men. It is just that the one show treats this material comically and the other show treats it tragically.

From Albuquerque to Dunsinane

Tragedy and *tragic hero* are in fact the concepts we need to analyze *Breaking Bad* properly. As long as we think in terms of Gilligan's Mr. Chips and Scarface, we are looking simply for good guys versus bad guys. Gilligan implies that Walter White must be either a pure hero or a pure villain, and thus we must either root for him or against him. That is the way most of the dramas on television work—they are melodramas. But there is something between the good guy in the white hat and the bad guy in the black hat—and it is the *tragic* hero.[13] The fact that television drama rarely attains the level of genuine tragedy means that media critics do not have the concept of the tragic hero at their fingertips. But as many have noted, in *Breaking Bad* Gilligan and his team have attained an almost Shakespearean level of drama. Accordingly, we have to analyze the series in terms derived from high culture, terms seldom applied to popular culture but appropriate in this exceptional case.

The tragic hero lies somewhere between the ordinary hero and the ordinary villain, and combines elements of both.[14] That is what makes him tragic, and that is what produces the complexity of audience responses, so that some will root for him, some will root against him, and some will not know how to react. The tragic hero *is* a hero—he embodies some form of nobility or excellence; he does impressive things for which we can admire him; he is a somebody, not a nobody; he is the kind of person who stands up for something and makes a difference. In short, the tragic hero stands out from the ordinary run of human beings. But the reason this kind of hero is tragic is that, through an unfortunate set of circumstances, something goes wrong in his life, something gets out of kilter. He makes a mistake, he oversteps the normal bounds of human life, he pushes a principle too far, he overestimates himself, he dares to break a taboo. The results appall us. The tragic hero commits a crime; he violates a sacred bond, such as that of family or nation; he disregards ordinary moral considerations; he arrogates to himself the right to break the rules and laws that normally confine human beings and provide the foundation of peaceful social coexistence. With his transgressive actions, the tragic hero poses a threat to the very fabric of society. For that, he must be condemned and punished. And yet we do not react to the tragic hero the way that we do to the ordinary criminal. He has broken a taboo, but we sense that he has not done so out of ordinary villainous motives. Even in his crimes, the tragic hero seems out of the ordinary. Somehow the evil he does seems to be bound up with the qualities for which we originally admired him. What makes him a good man in our eyes in the first place somehow leads him to do something we cannot help regarding as evil. And yet we still sense something of the original goodness in him and sympathize with him in his tragic fate. Showing that on some level he really does understand the character he created, Gilligan said of Walter White, "I love the idea of a good character, a good man, doing arguably bad things for a good reason."[15]

That is the paradox that I believe Gilligan was groping for in his formulation of Mr. Chips turning into Scarface. But tragedy is not a matter of a good man simply turning into an evil man. Tragedy involves opposites somehow being joined in one and the same figure. What is so disturbing about tragedy is that it forces us to rethink the moral categories with which we conventionally view the world. This does not mean that tragedy produces moral relativism. The great tragedies like *Oedipus tyrannos* and *King Lear* do *not* teach us that there is no difference between good and evil. If anything, they reinforce our sense that good and evil do exist. But tragedy teaches us that it is not always as easy to separate good from evil as we would like to think and that someone who is in some sense genuinely good can nevertheless end up doing something evil, even as he is pursuing a course of action that—however mistakenly as it turns out—he had reason to think of as good.

Before analyzing Walter White as a tragic hero, let us turn to a more familiar example of tragedy, Shakespeare's *Macbeth*.[16] Many will justifiably balk at speaking of Walter White as any kind of hero, "tragic" or otherwise. After all, does he not do terrible things? He lets a young woman die before his eyes when he might have saved her life; he poisons a child; he participates in a robbery that results in the death of another child. The list of his crimes goes on and on, and indeed at the foundation of his new career, he is one of the worst kind of criminals—the manufacturer of a drug that ruins the lives of thousands of people and sometimes kills them. For many, these facts place Walter White beyond the pale—he is a monster, not a human being; people frequently refer to him as a sociopath. In the hope of getting people to suspend their moral judgment for a moment and to reconsider their evaluation of Walter White, I want to remind them that we all know a famous figure in literature who is as criminal as Walter White and yet is generally accepted as a tragic hero—Shakespeare's Macbeth. Shakespeare's tragic heroes often commit criminal acts. Othello murders his innocent wife; Coriolanus betrays his country; Brutus assassinates his friend Julius Caesar; and so on. And yet Shakespeare creates sympathy for all these tragic heroes, and we admire them even as we are deeply troubled by the results of their actions. But in *Macbeth,* Shakespeare really seems to be pushing the envelope and seeing how criminal he can make a character and still present him as a tragic hero.[17] If even the murderous Macbeth can be a tragic hero, we might consider whether Walter White can be regarded as one, too.

Macbeth's rap sheet rivals Walter White's. He murders Duncan, the legitimate king of Scotland, while he is staying at Macbeth's castle and should, under the law of hospitality, be protected, not assassinated. To divert guilt from himself, Macbeth frames two of Duncan's servants for the murder and then kills them too. Macbeth goes on to order the murder of his friend and war comrade Banquo, and only by luck does Banquo's son, Fleance, escape the ambush. Just like Walter White, Macbeth becomes inured to criminal acts as his story progresses. At first Macbeth carefully debates the issue of killing Duncan, just as Walt in 1/3 runs over the pros and cons of murdering the drug dealer Krazy-8. But murder comes more and more easily to Macbeth, just as it does to Walt, and eventually he goes on a killing spree. Macbeth has an innocent woman and her children killed when his forces assault Macduff's castle. The bloodbath Macbeth unleashes is of Walter White proportions: "I am in blood / Stepp'd in so far that, should I wade no more, / Returning were as tedious as go o'er" (3.4.135–37).[18] Ultimately Macbeth plunges the whole nation of Scotland into a brutal civil war, thus becoming a monster in the eyes of his people (5.8.25). They see him as a "butcher," married to a "fiend-like queen" (5.9.35). In the end, the Scottish people do not regard him as a hero—they cut off his head and display it as a warning to would-be usurpers.

And yet this play is called *Macbeth,* and the titular character is its hero. How can the murderous Macbeth be regarded as a hero? In fact, Macbeth is being celebrated as a hero at the beginning of the play for his triumphs on the battlefield. King Duncan calls him a "worthy gentleman" and "noble" (1.2.24, 67) and rewards him with a new title. Macbeth is glorified specifically for an act of the utmost brutality—cleaving a man in half and decapitating him (1.2.21–23). At the end of the play, he is condemned for his aggressive violence, but at the beginning he is praised for it.[19] The difference between the two situations is of course obvious. At the beginning, Macbeth is fighting on behalf of his legitimate king; it is an entirely different matter to kill that king and illegitimately usurp the throne in Scotland. The same act—killing someone—takes on a different meaning depending on whether it is done legally or illegally. Actions that in wartime may be laudable may be condemned in peacetime.

But is the resolution of this paradox that simple? Scotland breeds Macbeth to be a fierce warrior and encourages his ferocity on the battlefield. Can the community turn around and legitimately condemn as murder in peacetime what it celebrated as "valor" in wartime (1.2.19)? It is easy to formulate the ideal we expect from the powerful; Shakespeare does so eloquently in *Measure for Measure*: "O, it is excellent / To have a giant's strength, but it is tyrannous / To use it like a giant" (2.2.107–9). But it is not easy to live by this ideal in reality. In a number of his plays (*Othello, Coriolanus, Richard III*), Shakespeare dramatizes the problem of a soldier carrying over the aggressiveness he displays in wartime into peacetime, with disastrous results. Of course in any conventional legal or moral sense, Scotland is right to condemn the tyrant Macbeth. But does conventional morality always tell the whole story about human nature? Shakespeare seems to be going out of his way to reveal a double standard operating in Scotland. Warriors in battle are judged by a code different from the one that governs them in peacetime situations.

Macbeth is a tragedy because it exposes a deep fault line in our ethical standards, revealing a conflict between two different conceptions of the good (this is the prototypical tragic situation, according to Hegel). At times we celebrate aggressive impulses and admire a man for his sheer strength and power, his ability to triumph in combat over others. The greatest monument to this attitude in our culture is Homer's portrait of Achilles in *The Iliad*. At other times, we assert the need to tame aggressive impulses and we brand them as evil, as the most significant impediment to achieving social order. The greatest monument to this attitude in our culture is the portrait of Jesus in the New Testament, with his un-Achillean injunction to turn the other cheek. *Macbeth* turns on the opposition between these two ethics, one classical, the other Christian. This opposition is reflected in the very conception of what it is to be a man in the play.[20] Duncan's heir, Malcolm, urges Macduff to let his anger at Macbeth's murdering his wife and children motivate him to rise up against the tyrant, but Macduff hesitates to do so:

> *Malcolm.* Dispute it like a man.
> *Macduff.* I shall do so;
>   But I must also feel it as a man. (4.3.219–21)

Two very different conceptions of what it is to be a man clash in this exchange. One we associate with the pagan warriors of ancient Greece and Rome—the classical idea that a man must assert himself, fight for his reputation and his rights, take vengeance on those who wrong him, and prove his valor in the most direct means possible—overcoming his enemies in combat. All of this is summed up in Malcolm's injunction: "Dispute it like a man." But when Macduff says that he "must also feel it as a man," he is referring not to the aggressive side of human nature, but to the compassionate. Part of being a human being is to feel for others, and that kind of human warmth and sympathy works against wanting to crush opponents and see them grovel in the dust. Instead, we speak of turning the other cheek, an ethical position deeply rooted in the teachings of Christianity, above all, in Jesus's claim, "Blessed are the meek: for they shall inherit the earth" (Matthew 5:5).

To portray a tragic conflict between pagan and Christian ethics, Shakespeare sets *Macbeth* at a special historical moment, when a pagan warrior community has been Christianized. The geography of the play reflects the fact that Scotland is at a crossroad. To the south lies the Christian kingdom of England, ruled by the saintly Edward the Confessor. To the north lies Norway, traditional land of the Vikings, from which, at the beginning of the play, pagan hordes are invading Scotland. Macbeth is caught between civilization and barbarism, Christianity and paganism. He is aware of how Scotland has been transformed—the "humane statute" of Christianity has "purg'd the gentle weal" (3.4.75). A fierce land of pagan warriors has been tamed by the new religion of peace. Part of Macbeth accepts this transformation, but part of him rebels against it and has contempt for the way Christianity has weakened Scotland's warriors in its attempt to pacify his country. This contempt surfaces when he is trying to enlist two men to murder Banquo, who, he tells them, has thwarted their ambitions:

> Do you find
> Your patience so predominant in your nature
> That you can let this go? Are you so gospell'd,
> To pray for this good man and for his issue
> Whose heavy hand hath bow'd you to the grave,
> And beggar'd yours for ever? (3.1.85–90)

Macbeth taunts the two men: have you been made so meek by Christianity—"so gospell'd"—that you will not take your just revenge on Banquo? To Macbeth's challenge, the murderers reply simply, "We are men, my liege" (3.1.90), showing that they know that it is their manliness that has been called into question. In effect, they are saying, "We are men, not Christians." They will embrace the old pagan conception of manliness—a man proves himself to be a man by standing up for his rights and aggressively defending them. No Christian turning the other cheek for them.

Shakespeare keeps showing that two conflicting ethical systems are abroad in the Scotland of *Macbeth*. People have fundamentally different conceptions of what "good" means. Lady Macduff is troubled by the fact that her moral goodness provides no defense in a world of savage warriors:

I have done no harm. But I remember now
I am in this earthly world—where to do harm
Is often laudable, to do good sometime
Accounted dangerous folly. Why then, alas,
Do I put up that womanly defense,
To say I have done no harm? (4.2.74–79)

Lady Macduff articulates the Christian rejection of the warrior's ethic. For pagan warriors, to inflict injury on opponents is a sign of strength and thus their idea of what is good; to turn the other cheek is a sign of weakness, and thus foolish and contemptible in their eyes; "weakness" is their definition of "bad." For Christians, the opposite is true. Goodness is forbearance and meekness, whereas aggressive violence is the very definition of evil. Note that Lady Macduff thinks of her Christian morality as a form of womanliness, the opposite of the pagan conception of manliness as martial virtue.

Paradoxically, Lady Macbeth becomes the champion of this kind of manliness. She worries that her husband is too Christian to do what he has to do to become king; he "is too full o' th' milk of human kindness" (1.5.17). Thus, as Macbeth later does with the murderers, Lady Macbeth challenges her husband's manhood to his face, accusing him of being a "coward" if he does not seize the opportunity to kill Duncan: "Art thou afeard / To be the same in thine own act and valor / As thou art in desire?" (1.7.39–41). Used to being celebrated as a valiant warrior, Macbeth rejects her doubts about his manliness: "I dare do all that may become a man; / Who dares do more is none" (1.7.46–47). Lady Macbeth is relentless:

When you durst do it, then you were a man;
And to be more than what you were, you would
Be so much more the man. (1.7.49–51)

As in the dialogue between Malcolm and Macduff, we see that the question, "What is it to be a man?" is at the heart of *Macbeth,* and two different answers—the pagan and the Christian—run throughout the play and are in tragic tension. Macbeth is tormented by doubts about his manliness. When Lady Macbeth ridicules his fear of Banquo's ghost—"Are you a man?," "What? quite unmann'd in folly?" (3.4.57, 72), Macbeth insists upon his manly courage: "What man dare, I dare" (3.4.98).

Macbeth's tragic dilemma is that he is torn between two conflicting ethics and cannot be a pure pagan or a pure Christian. He is a great warrior and has been lionized for his implacable cruelty on the battlefield. His wife keeps insisting that he live up to the warrior's code and display the courage of a true man, fighting for his status in Scotland. At the same time, Macbeth is aware of the teachings of Christianity and the appeal of the virtue of meekness. That is why he hesitates at first to kill Duncan:

> Besides, this Duncan
> Hath borne his faculties so meek, hath been
> So clear in his great office, that his virtues
> Will plead like angels, trumpet-tongu'd against
> The deep damnation of his taking off;
> And pity, like a naked new-born babe,
> Striding the blast, or heaven's cherubim, hors'd
> Upon the sightless couriers of the air,
> Shall blow the horrid deed in every eye,
> That tears shall drown the wind. (1.7.16–25)

Macbeth may be a fierce pagan warrior, but notice how richly articulated his Christian imagination is in this passage. His poetry shows that he appreciates the Christian virtues of meekness and pity; he can feel them in his blood. Tragically for Macbeth, he has a Christian soul in his pagan warrior's body.

Macbeth is a tragic figure because of this complexity in his character. He is tragically torn between antithetical conceptions of the good. He feels the pull of the pagan past, and the warrior virtues are celebrated in his country and held up to him as an ideal, above all by his wife, who questions his manhood if he does not pursue his ambition aggressively. At the same time, he feels the pull of Christianity, and the virtue of meekness is also held in high regard in his country. That is why, when he commits his crimes, he can do so only with a bad conscience. He is horrified by his own deeds, haunted before and after them by frightening images he himself produces of their criminality. Macbeth is not the simple "butcher" Malcolm accuses him of being. He is something far more complex, and that complexity maintains our sympathy for him and complicates our response to him, leaving us not knowing how to judge him. He does commit brutal crimes. But at first the Christian in him resists these deeds, and even when he plunges into a life of crime, he is deeply troubled by what he has done. If Macbeth were not torn in opposite directions, his life would be much simpler. If he were fully a Christian, he would never commit the crimes he does. If he were fully a pagan, he would not be so tormented by his deeds and would proceed without hesitation. But the Macbeth Shakespeare creates is torn between two conceptions of what it is to be a man, and that makes him a truly tragic figure.

Tragedy versus Melodrama

In real life, we feel it necessary to condemn people who become tyrants like Macbeth, and to take sides against them. But in the fictional world of drama, we have the luxury of temporarily suspending moral judgment and trying to understand and appreciate the inner complexity of a tragic hero like Macbeth. Macbeth has many admirable qualities and is initially respected for them in Scotland. He is a brave warrior and at first serves as a much-needed bulwark against the threat of domestic rebels and foreign barbarians in his country. The life of a warrior has made cruelty come easily to him, but he is not simply cruel. His imagination keeps confronting him with powerful images of the horror of cruelty, and as the plot progresses, he comes to understand that his ambition has led him to ruin his life and destroy everything that he once valued. We never see him enjoy being a tyrant. Because he is in fact sensitive to moral considerations, he is punished for his crimes internally by his conscience long before he suffers external punishment. We may at first be tempted to think that he and his wife are the only villains in Scotland. Yet Shakespeare reveals, not a black-and-white polarity in Scotland, but a continuous spectrum from good to evil, embracing many shades of gray in between. Is Banquo simply a morally good man? In fact, Shakespeare shows that Banquo, much like Macbeth, is gripped by ambition, and he cannot help thinking about the predictions the witches made about his sons ending up as kings (3.1.3–10). Like Macbeth, Banquo has trouble sleeping (2.1.6–9). He becomes an accessory after the fact to the murder of Duncan. He fails to reveal what he knows about the witches' prophecies, despite the fact that he suspects that Macbeth had a role in Duncan's death (3.1.1–3). In a cat-and-mouse game with Macbeth, Banquo in effect makes a deal to keep quiet about what he knows in return for future aid from Macbeth for his own ambitions (2.1.20–29).

Macduff also does not provide a purely good antagonist to Macbeth, the purely evil tyrant. In his eagerness to fight Macbeth, Macduff abandons his wife and children, with fatal results for them. His own wife accuses him of cruelty—"He wants the natural touch" (4.2.9)—and reproaches him for not caring about his own family. Macduff's treatment of his wife and children arouses Malcolm's suspicions. He worries about allying with a man who would betray his own family:

> Why in that rawness left you wife and child,
> Those precious motives, those strong knots of love,
> Without leave-taking? (4.3.26–28)

Shakespeare does not portray a Scotland in which Macbeth is the only cruel and ambitious male. The country is filled with them. From the beginning, rebellious thanes pose a serious threat to the meek Duncan's rule. One gets the sense that if any other thane had received a prophecy that he would be king, he might have acted just as Macbeth did. At the end, Ross, one of the thanes who triumphs over Macbeth, enunciates the same conception of manliness that induced Macbeth to murder Duncan in the first place. Ross is telling Siward, one of the English generals, about the death of his son in battle:

> Your son, my lord, has paid a soldier's debt.
> He only liv'd but till he was a man,
> The which no sooner had his prowess confirm'd
> In the unshrinking station where he fought,
> But like a man he died. (5.9.5–9)

When Siward affirms the nobility of his son's death and even calls him "God's soldier" (5.9.13), we see that—contrary to being uniquely evil—Macbeth lives by the same manly ethic that prevails on both sides of the political conflict in Scotland.[21]

Macbeth is a great tragedy—and not a melodrama—precisely because of the moral complexities and ambiguities it portrays. True tragedy does not provide us with simple moral lessons, such as "pride goes before a fall." Unlike melodrama, which simply appeals to our conventional moral beliefs and reaffirms them, tragedy is unsettling; it disturbs us and unnerves us by revealing that our ordinary moral categories do not necessarily or adequately cover the full range of human possibilities. The fundamental tragic aspect of life that Shakespeare points to is the perplexing fact that not all forms of human excellence are compatible with each other. In particular, moral excellence may be in tension with other forms of excellence. Not all goods are moral goods.[22] Our moral categories are so important in our daily lives that we would like to think that they are universally and unequivocally applicable in all circumstances, that all judgments are moral judgments. But as reassuring as that belief may be, it is simply not true. When I seek out a plumber, I am not looking for a morally good plumber: I want someone who has the ability to fix my sink. I would not want him to cheat me (at least not too much), but fundamentally I am concerned about his skill as a plumber. Similarly, aesthetic judgment is not the same as moral judgment. In evaluating a work of art, we invoke something other than moral categories, especially with regard to its formal properties. And from cases like Caravaggio and Richard Wagner, we know that a morally dubious person can create great works of art. In extreme cases, our moral judgment may ultimately override our aesthetic judgment, but they are still separate forms of judgment, which is why they can come into conflict with each other.

Understandably, we do not like to think about the problematic character of the human condition that Shakespeare exposes in his tragedies. We keep making the same mistake over and over—we think that people we admire for entirely nonmoral reasons—for example, our athletes and our entertainers—will be admirable in moral terms as well. But why should someone who happens to have a great voice or a strong body be especially moral in his or her daily life? We say earnestly that our idols in sports and entertainment should provide good role models to our youth, and we should be thankful that they often live up to that responsibility. But sometimes people who become famous for nonmoral reasons are corrupted by that very fame and start behaving immorally. Sometimes, as in the case of athletes, people are admired for traits—such as aggressiveness—that work against their behaving morally in their daily lives. The desire to have our heroes perfect in every respect—including morally—is an untragic view of life. It is premised on the questionable belief that all our values are perfectly compatible and never need to come into conflict with each other. Those who offer conventional moral interpretations of Shakespeare's plays miss the point of tragedy, which is to show that our ordinary moral categories, as important as they may be, do not explain the whole of human life and may interfere with our understanding of other forms of human excellence.

I realize that many will reject my interpretation of *Macbeth,* and others will say that, if it is correct, then so much the worse for Shakespeare. They will insist that no matter what Shakespeare may have thought, Macbeth *is* an evil man and nothing else, and certainly no kind of hero.[23] Our moral judgments are so important in our daily lives that it is difficult ever to suspend them, even if someone says, "It's just a play; lighten up." We are used to watching plays and applauding heroes and hissing villains. That is why melodrama is one of the most popular forms of entertainment and dominates television, whereas genuine tragedy is so rare. In daily life, we may have to take sides, but the unreality of drama (however realistic it may seem) allows us to look at both sides of an issue and give each its due. Shakespearean tragedy gives us a glimpse into the depths of characters and the ways that opposing values may clash in extraordinary individuals. Shakespeare's tragic heroes are dangerous figures, not because they threaten us in real life but because they challenge some of our most cherished assumptions. In a curious way, tragic heroes are like our modern superheroes. In the safe space of the imagination, they get to act out our fantasies of behaving transgressively. They thus allow us to explore vicariously the darker realms of human possibility. That is why tragedy is cathartic. In the imaginary world of the theater, tragedy allows us to indulge and perhaps to purge dangerous impulses that we normally have to suppress in order to live peacefully in everyday society. That is how tragedy can have a moral effect without being moralistic.

I hope that these considerations can serve to open up fresh perspectives on *Breaking Bad*. Vince Gilligan is no William Shakespeare. I would be the first to grant that *Macbeth* is a greater work of art than *Breaking Bad*. But still, I believe that Gilligan and his team are dealing with genuinely tragic material in the series and probably have come as close to Shakespeare's level as any show in television history. I want to turn now to analyzing *Breaking Bad,* bearing in mind what we have learned from *Macbeth*. At a minimum, I hope that we can come away from *Macbeth* with the understanding that we can be fascinated by the case of an ostensibly good character who goes on to commit evil. Even though we may lose much of our sympathy for him as he plunges deeper and deeper into a life of crime, we can still feel for his humanity, if only because we see how tormented he is by his own realization of the horror of what he has done. This is, I believe, a good characterization of our reaction to Macbeth, and it is also a good characterization of our reaction to Walter White. Only on these grounds can we explain the fact that puzzled Vince Gilligan—that a substantial portion of his audience continued to sympathize with and even to root for his Scarface. As the history of great literature has repeatedly demonstrated, the most interesting characters are not necessarily—or perhaps even typically—the most moral.[24] What great writers can do is precisely to show us that—on closer inspection—people who commit evil deeds may not be the monsters we at first think they are.[25] There may be no more gripping spectacle than a character with great potential for good who nevertheless turns to evil, or in Gilligan's terms, "breaks bad." Like Macbeth, Walter White is caught between antithetical ways of life, which draw him in opposite directions. We will see several ways in which *Macbeth* can illuminate *Breaking Bad*. In particular, we will see that the issue of manliness, so central to Shakespeare's play, resurfaces in *Breaking Bad* in a form we now call "masculinity," and it is an equally if not more problematic force in the contemporary world.[26]

Pursuing the American Dream

Breaking Bad is the story of a man who fails to achieve the American dream in two of the versions that we have been following in this book. He fails to create a happy home for himself and his family, and he fails in his entrepreneurial attempt to go into business for himself. When we meet him in the first episode, Walter White is slogging away at domestic life and might even seem to have achieved something of the American dream in one traditional sense. He is intelligent and well-educated, and works in the respectable if unglamorous profession of high school teaching.[27] He has a home in the suburbs with two cars and one child (with a second, we soon learn, on the way). He has a small circle of relatives and friends who care about him. Many would envy his circumstances. But the more we learn about Walt, even in just the first episode, we see that his apparent suburban happiness is an illusion. He eventually discovers that the foundation of his home is literally rotting away.

As for Walt's job, it is a source of frustration for him, rather than of pride. Most of his students treat him with indifference and sometimes contempt. They do not appreciate his remarkable knowledge of chemistry. All they want to know from him is, "Is this going to be on the midterm?" (1/2). That is why Walt never comes close to Mr. Chips status. Like many people overqualified for their jobs, he takes his frustration out on his students, speaking to them condescendingly and sarcastically, and he repays their contempt for him with nasty comments on their papers and exams.[28] A particular source of Walt's frustration is the fact that, because he is a high school teacher, he is not paid well, certainly not as well as his qualifications as a chemist would warrant (we learn in 2/3 that Walt makes $43,700 a year). To make ends meet, he is forced to take a second job even further below his dignity—in a car wash, where he is exposed to the humiliation of having to take guff from his crude boss and to behave obsequiously to some of his students when they show up as customers and take advantage of the role reversal.

Compounding Walt's frustration is the additional fact that, as we gradually learn, he could have been a very rich man. The high-tech company he cofounded has since gone public and reached a $2.16 billion capitalization. But for reasons that are never made fully clear in the series, Walt allowed himself to be bought out early in the history of Gray Matter Technology for a mere five thousand dollars.[29] Evidently Walt let personal feelings interfere with his business judgment and, in a fit of pique, missed out on the biggest financial opportunity of his life. Walt tells Gretchen Schwartz in 2/6, "My hard work, my research—you and Elliott made millions off it." It is not just the loss of money that bothers Walt. By his early exit from Gray Matter, he lost his chance to share in what has come to be one of the highest forms of glory in contemporary America—the new American dream is to become a star in the high-tech world. As Walt explains to a psychiatrist in 2/3, "I have watched all my colleagues and friends surpass me in every way imaginable."[30]

Breaking Bad thus exposes another fault line in the American dream. Financial success has always been one of its components, but the path to that success has been defined differently. Is it a matter of "a penny saved is a penny earned" or "strike it rich"? The standard middle-class vision of accumulating wealth gradually by means of hard work, steady saving, and prudent investment has always been at odds with the grander dream of making the one big killing in a business venture or hitting the jackpot in some form of gambling. Some of the most enduring images of the American dream have taken the form of quick paths to vast wealth—the California Gold Rush, the Wall Street bull market, or the dot-com boom in Silicon Valley. Some versions of the American dream focus on security and seek to avoid any form of risk taking, whereas other versions embrace risk taking as the only route to a big payoff. Walt's failure to succeed in business is never fully explained, but from what we see of his character, one element of it was probably a failure of nerve. He did not have enough faith in himself or his business plan and settled for an early buyout, leaving Elliott and Gretchen Schwartz to take the risks and reap the rewards of true entrepreneurship. Both financial versions of the American dream escape Walt. He cannot use a middle-class job to make the money patiently that he needs to support his family. But when he gets his one chance to strike it rich in one heroic enterprise, he gets cold feet and misses the opportunity to join the ranks of high-tech billionaires.

Having failed in financial terms, Walt falls back on his family for fulfillment—but he still does not find it. He has a loving relationship with his son, Walt Jr., and it would be wrong to say that his son is a disappointment to him. But Walt Jr. is unfortunately afflicted with cerebral palsy, and his physical limitations mean that the two do not get to share certain experiences that are usually thought of as basic to the father-son bond. Walt will never get to cheer on Walt Jr. at an athletic event, for example. Walt's relationship with his wife, Skyler, is also less than ideal. They love each other, but right from the beginning we sense a staleness in their marriage. They have settled into comfortable day-to-day routines, while all the passion, especially the sexual passion, seems to be drained from their lives. And we soon begin to wonder who wears the pants in the White household.[31] Skyler is a master of passive-aggressive behavior and knows how to manipulate Walt to get what she wants out of him.[32] She can be condescending to Walt and generally does more to tear down his ego than to build it up. At one particularly bitter moment, Walt says to Skyler: "You never believed in me. You were never grateful for anything I did for this family" (5/14). Walt's relatives, especially his brother-in-law Hank—a gruff DEA agent—also fail to treat him with the respect he thinks he deserves. A would-be alpha male, Hank is always calling Walt's manhood into question.

Walt's comfortable though stultifying existence is shattered by a diagnosis of lung cancer. This development sparks the existential crisis that gets the plot rolling in *Breaking Bad*. Walt is forced to face the fact of his own mortality, which reveals to him the meaningless of the life he has been leading. Has he accomplished anything in his life? What will be his legacy? In particular, will he be able to leave any money to his family? *Breaking Bad* is solidly grounded in the financial plight of its hero. The show mirrors the difficult financial circumstances of the American middle class during the Obama years. The series is not making a political statement and certainly not a partisan statement. But it does a remarkable job of portraying how hollow the economic "recovery" after the 2008 financial crisis seemed to be to a large portion of the American population, who felt that they had lost all chances to achieve the American dream.[33] There are several references in the show to the weakness of the economy. In explaining in 2/6 why Elliott and Gretchen cannot help him financially, Walt tells Skyler: "The economy's in the toilet, we all know that. All those big banks. Fannie Mae." In 2/11, Skyler's boss, Ted, says the same thing: "The economy's in the toilet. China's undercutting us at every turn."

Many of the economic problems that have emerged as political issues in recent years are evident in *Breaking Bad.* We see the development of an underclass that resorts to drugs out of the despair of poverty. We see the impact of globalization—specifically multinational corporations—on ordinary people's lives. Something sinister that happens in Germany or the Czech Republic has an impact on what happens in Albuquerque. In the midst of all the depressing economic trends, high-tech entrepreneurs like the owners of Gray Matter prosper beyond their wildest dreams, thus exacerbating the tensions between the haves and the have-nots and leaving Walt bitter about the economic system. Even the politically contentious issue of the Mexican border surfaces in *Breaking Bad.* Walt's conflict with the Mexican drug cartel puts him in great danger, an extreme example of how various forms of foreign competition have been threatening the American worker.

But the issue that truly marks *Breaking Bad* as the signature television series of the Obama years is health insurance.[34] In retrospect, there is something supremely appropriate in the fact that a show that ran from 2008 to 2013 really put to the test the principle, "If you like your doctor, you can keep your doctor." As the series opens, Walt is already having financial troubles paying Walt Jr.'s medical bills—hence his second job—and his cancer diagnosis is all the more troubling because his medical insurance will not cover the treatments he will need. Later in the series, Hank ends up in a wheelchair as a result of a gun battle, and he and his wife must fret over the fact that his government medical plan does not cover the kind of intensive physical therapy he wants (which may be the only way for him to walk again, at least quickly). It is remarkable how much of the drama in *Breaking Bad* turns on the quintessentially middle-class issue of the inadequacy of one's health insurance. Marie speaks for early twenty-first-century America when she says in 5/3 of Hank, "God knows where we'd be if we'd had to go through his health plan." The only organization in the series that has excellent health insurance is Gray Matter (1/5), thereby exacerbating the gap between the 1 percent and the 99 percent.

Thus Walter White is initiated into a life of crime out of financial considerations. Afraid that he will leave his family bankrupted by his medical bills, he would like to find a way to cover his hospital expenses and also to bequeath his family a substantial sum that would make them comfortable for life, and, in particular, pay for Walt Jr.'s medical treatment and also for both his children's educations. This initial obsession with the bottom line is very middle-class, not the sort of thing we associate with Scarface (who probably never worried about his medical coverage with the cocaine cartel). When Walt discovers the street value of crystal meth, he thinks that he has found a shortcut to accumulating large amounts of money. He can put his skills as a chemist to good use, synthesizing drugs to supply a lucrative market. Walt claims that he turns to crime for the sake of his family, to provide for his wife and children. His motives turn out to be much more complex, but in any overall judgment of his character, it is worth bearing in mind that, in the beginning, his motives were relatively innocent. He knows that what he will be doing is illegal, but he naively believes that he will be able to confine his activities to a laboratory, simply synthesizing chemicals just the way he does for his high school classes and leaving to other people the sordid and dangerous business of actually selling the drugs. Walt has no idea what drug dealing really involves and does not foresee the web of violent crime into which he is being drawn. It is fair to say that the Walter White of season 1 has no idea that by season 5 he will be involved in robbing a train and killing an innocent boy.

It is the genius of *Breaking Bad* that it comes up with a scenario that makes it plausible that a decent man like Walt would turn to meth manufacture, and we can sympathize with him because his family's good seems at first to be his only motive. He has spent his whole life on the right side of the law, unacquainted with criminals; in 1/6, Hank tells him, "You wouldn't know a criminal if he checked you for a hernia." It is precisely Walt's innocence, his unfamiliarity with crime, that makes him believe that he can dip into criminal activity and not have to change his way of life fundamentally. At first he believes that drug dealers can be dealt with rationally; he says of Jesse's drug distributor: "He's a businessman; it would therefore seem to follow that he's capable of acting out of mutual self-interest" (1/2). But events move swiftly in the criminal world, and Walt's education in how different it is to be on the wrong side of the law begins almost immediately. Already in the first episode, he finds himself having to kill people to protect his own life. Because he is dealing with hardened criminals, Walt can frame his actions as self-defense, but it should be a clear sign to him that he has gone down the wrong path. He learns that actions have consequences and that manufacturing crystal meth cannot be a mere sideline to supplement his income. At many points in the series, Walt tries to renounce his criminal activities, but for one reason or another—chiefly involving his fear and greed—he is drawn back in. He can say at many points that he is forced to commit crimes because he is dealing with criminals, but it was his choice to become involved in the criminal world in the first place. And as happens with Michael Corleone in the *Godfather* films, Walt's excuse that he is doing everything for his family begins to wear thin, especially when it becomes clear that his actions are harming his family rather than helping it.

As the series progresses, it becomes evident that Walt's motives go well beyond the good of his family. He takes pride in his new job—he is determined to manufacture the finest crystal meth in the world. In 3/4, he insists, "I am not going to lend my name to an inferior product." It is no mean feat to be able to produce crystal meth of almost 100 percent purity (99.1 percent, according to Hank in 1/4), and knowledgeable people in the drug trade appreciate the quality of the product Walt synthesizes as Heisenberg, not to mention its beautiful blue color. If there were a Nobel Prize for synthesizing crystal meth, Walter White would be on a plane to Stockholm to collect it. He is convinced that all his life he has been wasting his talent on cheap demonstrations for bored high school students. Now he is finally accomplishing something. The purity of his meth makes it safer to use and also gives it a bigger kick.[35] In the great tradition of the American entrepreneur, Walt is offering the public a superior product, and he thus beats out all his competition and is rewarded in the marketplace. Many people try to equal Walt's achievement as a chemist—Jesse, Gale, Todd, to name a few—but no one manages to do so. When he temporarily refuses to continue making meth, Saul Goodman says in 3/2: "Talent like that and he flushes it down the toilet. It's like Michelangelo won't paint." Walt can truly say that he is the world's greatest crystal meth manufacturer, and that gives him a kind of fulfillment that his career as a high school teacher never came close to equaling. As he says in 5/7, "Being the best at something is a very rare thing."

"I Am the Danger"

Walt's preeminence as an illegal drug manufacturer is surely a case where a human excellence is *not* a moral excellence. To its credit, unlike many movies and television shows, *Breaking Bad* does not glamorize the drug trade. In the story of Jesse Pinkman, Walt's former student and sometime "lab assistant," the show portrays the damage meth addiction can do to a decent young man who once had a promising future. The episode called "Peekaboo" (2/6), with its grim and gruesome portrayal of a grotesque meth-head family, offers perhaps the most powerful antidrug commercial ever created.[36] In contrast to what happens with cocaine use in De Palma's *Scarface*, *Breaking Bad* never presents meth use as enjoyable. That is one of the many reasons why Walter White never really becomes Scarface. The typical gangster movie tells the story of its protagonist's rise as well as his fall. We get to see Tony Montana at the top of his game, enjoying the fruits of his crimes, in orgies of sex and drugs.[37] Walt should be so lucky. His life as a criminal has a downward trajectory from the beginning. He is always working frantically and like a dog to meet his production quotas on time, and he never gets to take any pleasure from all the money he has earned. It becomes a literal burden to him when $11 million of it in cash ends up in a single barrel, which he must painstakingly roll across the desert, like the Sisyphus of the Southwest (5/14). Still, Walt does take pride in his work and finally has the satisfaction of being good at something, indeed the best. I would not say that we can unequivocally admire Heisenberg, but we can see why Walt cultivates his secret identity. His life was so devoid of accomplishment that we can understand why he seizes the opportunity to stand out in any way in the world.

But Walt's motives for a life of crime go even deeper, to the point where he gradually learns to embrace his inner criminal. The Walter White we meet at the beginning of the series is a hopeless and hapless nobody. Although he is intellectually superior to almost anyone he meets, he lets everyone push him around—his wife, his brother-in-law, his boss at the car wash, his students. It is a sad spectacle and makes us sympathize with Walt. He deserves better. The fundamental problem is that Walt is a coward, unwilling to stand up for himself and his rights. It is more a mental form of cowardice than a physical. The setbacks he has suffered over the years have made him lose faith in himself, and he is too ready to compromise, to make do with second- or third-best in life. He is just about the last person we would think is capable of succeeding as a criminal. If he cannot stand up to a car wash owner, how is he going to handle a vicious drug lord?

And indeed Walt does seem at times grotesquely out of his element in the criminal world. He and Jesse come across as the Three Stooges Minus Curly in some of their early bumbling efforts to execute their nefarious schemes (see especially 1/7).[38] Confronted with killers like Krazy-8 and Tuco, Walt is understandably overwhelmed with fear. From our first impressions of him, it is hard to believe that he could survive even a few days in the world of Krazy-8 and Tuco, let alone be able to deal with a criminal mastermind like Gus Fring and the entire Mexican drug cartel. And yet for all Walt's inadequacies, he eventually triumphs over his criminal opponents, including Gus, and he is able to keep the law enforcement officers out to get him at bay as well. It is partially Walt's intelligence that allows him to outfox his enemies on both sides of the law. Once again one of his excellences comes to his aid, as he thinks up ingenious schemes to defeat or neutralize the people who threaten him. There is more to Walter

White than we thought—more to Walter White than he himself thought. This seemingly pathetic pushover comes to surprise us with his resilience, resourcefulness, and sheer strength of character. He becomes a force to reckon with.[39] He not only outfoxes his opponents; he also outfaces them. Beginning as the mild-mannered Walter White, he becomes the implacable Heisenberg, who can transfix the most threatening criminals with an icy stare, not to mention a dash of fulminate of mercury.

This is Walt's real "achievement" in *Breaking Bad* and the way he can be said to become a "hero." I know that many would insist that this is the way that Walt becomes a *villain,* but there is one sense in which we can legitimately speak of Walt as a hero.[40] Once he becomes Heisenberg, he is no longer a coward. His transformation is about as magical as that of Clark Kent into Superman. A man who lets himself be bullied by the ordinary people around him learns to stand up to some genuinely dangerous criminals. He takes satisfaction in that. Walt's original turn to crime was purely instrumental. He surely was not seeking out a criminal way of life; he was just looking for a way to make a lot of money quickly. If anything, he regarded having to deal with criminals as the downside of his newly chosen profession. But gradually Walt comes to enjoy life among hardened criminals for its own sake. He enjoys the challenge, the competition, the chance to prove himself against other men. He takes pride in outsmarting them and outmaneuvering them. Walt comes to relish the pure act of transgression, of breaking the law to demonstrate his superior status, to show that he is above the law. Walt has built up many frustrations with society over the years; it has not given him the rewards he deserves, and it has denied him the American dream. His life as a criminal allows him to strike back against the conventional world that has held him back for decades from making a name for himself.

Walt's cancer plays a crucial role in his transformation into a would-be superman. At the beginning of the story, he is not afraid of dying; he is simply not thinking about dying at all. That is why he is wasting his life; he has no sense of urgency about making something of himself. But when Walt thinks that he is going to die—and not just in some vague, far-off future, but on a fast-approaching date—he is energized to leave a legacy behind. The threat of death paradoxically brings him to life. Moreover, knowing that he may be about to die liberates him from many of his normal fears. If he risks his life, he is thinking that he does not have that much time to live anyway. As Walt says in 2/8: "I have spent my whole life frightened of things that could happen, might happen, might not happen. . . . Ever since my diagnosis, I sleep just fine. I came to realize that fear—that's the worst of it, that's the real enemy."

Walt takes pride in his skill as a drug manufacturer, but he takes even greater pride in becoming master in the dangerous world of the drug trade. He responds to the many challenges he faces and does not back down from a fight. All his conflicts are highly personal—mano a mano, as several of his bitterest enemies would say. His great moment of recognition comes in 4/6, when Skyler is worried about all the threats to his life. In perhaps the most famous lines in the series, Walt responds to Skyler's concern: "You clearly don't know who you're talking to, so let me clue you in. I am not in danger, Skyler. I *am* the danger! A guy opens his door and gets shot and you think of me? No. I am the one who knocks!" This from a man who at the beginning of the series was afraid just to handle a gun, provoking Hank to say, "That's why they have men." Now instead of being the man who cowers in fear, Walt is the cause of fear in others.[41] Ultimately he proudly proclaims his superiority: "I'm the man who killed Gus Fring" (5/7)—the modern-day equivalent of the old Western's "man who shot Liberty Valance."

"I *am* the danger! . . . I am the one who knocks!"—that is the contemporary version of the traditional tragic hero's assertion of his greatness. Shakespeare's tragic heroes often die with a moment of self-affirmation on their lips, as witness Coriolanus:

> If you have writ your annals true, 'tis there
> That like an eagle in a dove-cote, I
> Flutter'd your Volscians in Corioles.
> Alone I did it. (5.6.113–16)

Walt has finally become a man in the sense of manliness we saw in *Macbeth* ("Dispute it like a man"). In the last episode (5/16), Walt is at last willing to admit that everything he did was not for the sake of his family but for himself, for his own ego. In another moment of tragic recognition, he confesses to Skyler to clear the air: "I did it for me. I liked it. I was good at it. And I was . . . really—I was alive."[42] The middle-class Walter White we see at the beginning of the series has to think of everything as instrumental. If he is manufacturing drugs, it must be to get money for his family. By the end of the series, Walt realizes that what he really wanted was to become a certain kind of man, a man who can stand tall in any company, a man who makes a difference. He was good at being a drug lord, and it made him for the first time feel alive. He has finally become the star of his story, no longer a bit player in his own life. When his family originally pressured Walt to seek treatment for his cancer in 1/5, he balked at having the decision made for him by others: "Sometimes I feel like I never actually make any of my own choices. . . . My entire life—it just seems I never . . . had a real say about any of it." As Heisenberg, Walt finally takes charge of his life. He is no longer the passive man to whom things happen; he is the active man who makes things happen.[43]

Walt comes to think of himself not in middle-class terms but on the model of great heroic figures out of the past. In the fifth season, he says to Jesse: "You asked me if I was in the meth business or the money business. Neither. I'm in the empire business." The idea of Walter White as the Napoleon of crime may be a stretch, but he can plausibly compare himself to the contemporary emperors of finance, the high-tech entrepreneurs of companies like Gray Matter. One of the reasons that Walt takes such satisfaction in his criminal career is that he looks upon himself as building a successful business. When he was young, he failed to take advantage of the entrepreneurial opportunity offered by Gray Matter. But as a drug kingpin, he hoped that he could rival Elliott Schwartz. Again, it is not so much the money that matters to Walt; it is what it represents. He pursues the American dream: owning his own business. Above all, he wants to be his own boss. He cannot stand having to work for someone else, including a drug lord like Gus.[44] In 4/6, he takes a special satisfaction in buying out the car wash he used to work at and reversing roles with the humbled ex-owner Bogdan, who has to admit, "So you're the boss now." In 5/6, Walt says proudly to Skyler: "Finally we're self-sufficient. And no one to answer to." He thinks that he has achieved his goal. He glories in what he actually accomplishes—by dint of his skill and hard work, and triumphing over all his competitors, he builds a business empire whose revenue would justify a NASDAQ listing (4/6). His business is of course illegal, but, as we saw with the criminal empire of the Corleones, developing it still requires many of the virtues that lead to success in any business.[45] Using technical business terms like distribution, infrastructure, high margin product, and risk/reward ratio, Walt often sounds like a conventional businessman, for example, when he tells Jesse in 2/7: "We're not charging enough. Corner the market, then raise the price. It's simple economics." Walt *is* a criminal, but he is not a run-of-the-mill criminal, not a petty thief. He is Heisenberg, and, as he shows in the episode "Say My Name" (5/7), that is a name to conjure with. Whatever else may be said for or against him, Walter White is impressive as a criminal, displaying several forms of human excellence that would redound to his credit in more conventional—and legal—endeavors.

Judging a Man by the Company He Keeps

Is Walter White a tragic hero? Someone who rejects this idea cannot simply point to the number of murders for which he is responsible. Hamlet—sweet, gentle Hamlet—is a tragic hero, and yet he is directly responsible for the deaths of Claudius (his uncle), Polonius (his almost father-in-law), Laertes (his almost brother-in-law), and Rosencrantz and Guildenstern (his college classmates), and he is indirectly responsible for the deaths of Ophelia (his beloved) and Gertrude (his mother). Walt has more in common with Shakespeare's tragic heroes than his murder record. Like them, Walt has many admirable qualities—his intelligence, his resourcefulness, his perseverance, his indefatigability, and his courage. He puts his virtues in the service of illegal and immoral causes, but that means that his evil deeds are bound up with his best qualities.[46] Contemplating his fate, we are confronted with the fundamental experience of tragedy—the sense of tragic waste, the disturbing insight that qualities we admire in people can be put to the wrong use. We want to say, "If only Walter White had put his virtues to good use!" In 4/5, Hank expresses just these sentiments with regard to Gale, when, finding him murdered, Hank thinks that he was Heisenberg: "He was a genius, plain and simple. If he had applied that big brain of his to something good, who knows how he could have helped humanity, or something like that? I mean, how many actual geniuses are there in this world? If he'd taken his life in a different direction, who knows?" Walt is so upset to hear Gale praised for what he himself accomplished that he tells Hank, "This genius of yours, maybe he's still out there." Hank was ready to close the case, and Walt might have been safe. But his pride overcomes his prudence (with the help of a little alcohol), and he goads Hank into continuing the search for Heisenberg. Walt values his reputation over his safety. His tragic fate is that only a diagnosis of cancer awakens him from his apathy, and a life of crime seems to him to be his only option for striking it rich quickly and obtaining the status he covets.

In evaluating Walt, we need to compare him to the other characters in the series. *Breaking Bad* does not offer us an ideal world filled with good people, among whom Walter White stands out as the epitome of evil. By comparison with many of the criminals he associates with, Walt comes across as a halfway decent human being. If you are looking for a psychotic killer, try Tuco Salamanca, or for a sociopath, consider Gus Fring.[47] Walt does not relish killing people the way Tuco does, and he never displays the cold-bloodedness of Gus. To see murder treated as a calculated business decision, we have to look at the way Gus kills Victor in 4/1. There is a steeliness in Gus's eyes at this moment that is truly chilling. People often say of sociopaths that one stares into their eyes and sees nothing—a total blank.[48] This is true of Gus, but it is not true of Walt. Many say that Walt's worst moment comes when he watches Jesse's girlfriend, Jane, die as she chokes on her own vomit during a heroin-induced stupor.[49] Just look at Walt's eyes during this scene and try to maintain that he is a sociopath. Of all Bryan Cranston's Emmy-award-winning acting in *Breaking Bad*, perhaps his greatest accomplishment is what he does with just his eyes alone in this scene to convey a sense of the inner torment Walt is going through as he watches Jane die. In his autobiography, Cranston revealed that he forced himself to think of his own daughter during this scene in order to nail the depth of Walt's feelings.[50] What Walt does in this scene is morally wrong, but he does not do it cold-bloodedly and without remorse; indeed this moment haunts him for the rest of his life, leading him, for example, to want to confess to Jesse what he did.

In several situations, Walt hesitates before murdering someone, and he has second thoughts about many of the crimes he commits. Like Macbeth, Walt never fully embraces evil as his good; to the bitter end, he remains conscious of the distinction between good and evil. To be sure, he constantly comes up with explanations and excuses for the evil he does, but he would not feel the need to defend his actions if he were not aware that they appear to be morally wrong. True sociopaths do not show regret or remorse or offer excuses for their crimes; they just do them. Walt, by contrast, feels uncomfortable with many of the criminals he has to work with, and he is wracked by remorse. He could say along with Lady Macbeth: "Nought's had, all's spent, / Where our desire is got without content" (3.2.4–5), or along with Macbeth: "To know my deed, 'twere best not know myself" (2.2.70). It takes the poetry of Shakespeare to capture the despairing mood of Walter White in the frozen wilderness of New Hampshire in season 5:

> I have liv'd long enough: my way of life
> Is fall'n into the sear, the yellow leaf,
> And that which should accompany old age,
> As honor, love, obedience, troops of friends,
> I must not look to have. (5.3.22–26)

With the words "tomorrow . . . tomorrow," *Breaking Bad* actually quotes *Macbeth* in 5/15, calling attention to the most famous speech in the play, which could well serve as a motto for Walter White's story:

> To-morrow, and to-morrow, and to-morrow
> Creeps in this petty pace from day to day,
> To the last syllable of recorded time;
> And all our yesterdays have lighted fools
> The way to dusty death. Out, out, brief candle!
> Life's but a walking shadow, a poor player
> That struts and frets his hour upon the stage
> And then is heard no more. It is a tale
> Told by an idiot, full of sound and fury
> Signifying nothing. (5.5.19–28)

It is a tribute to the quality of *Breaking Bad* and to the depth of Walter White as a character that it does not seem incongruous to quote these words of Macbeth in connection with him.[51]

Even the supposedly virtuous characters in *Breaking Bad* are not so perfectly good that they make Walt look like evil incarnate. Walt can certainly be criticized for his actions, but so can many of the people he harms. Viewers and commentators become very sentimental about Jane Margolis, but she is after all a heroin addict, and she seduces Jesse into trying heroin too. She has no compunctions about blackmailing Walt to get money to buy more drugs (2/12). For all of these failings, she does not deserve to die, but she is not exactly a paragon of virtue. Walt's main antagonist among the "good guys" is Hank, and he if anybody should stand for law and order in the show. But Hank proves willing to break the law in pursuit of his personal goals and vendettas, and he himself admits that he was wrong to beat Jesse as savagely as he does in 3/7 (when he takes all his pent-up frustrations out on the young man). In 3/7, Hank says, "What I did to Pinkman—that's not how I'm supposed to be, that's not me." And he admits further, "I'm not the man I thought I was." Moreover, Hank is a braggart and a blowhard. It would be wrong to set him up as a pure hero as opposed to Walt as villain.[52] In many ways, Walt is a better human being than Hank.[53] At the beginning of the series, Hank puffs himself up as courageous in opposition to the cowardly Walt, but their roles are reversed as the story develops. When the would-be cowboy Hank gets a glimpse of the real Wild West in El Paso, he ends up with a bad case of PTSD. Walt starts out looking cowardly but turns out to be courageous; Hank starts out looking courageous but turns out to be cowardly.[54]

One of the common criticisms of Walt is that he becomes a liar. But just about everybody in *Breaking Bad* lies, almost routinely, including Hank. He will not admit that his assignment in El Paso scared the daylights out of him. His wife, Marie, is a pathological liar. Gus's whole life is a lie, and, as we have seen, living a double life is epidemic in the series. The person who is most offended by Walt's lies and by the double life he is leading is Skyler. But she lies as frequently as Walt does and literally becomes his partner in crime. Like Banquo, she shows that a seemingly innocent character may be tempted by the fruits of crime when confronted with the option. Skyler has an affair behind Walt's back and becomes heavily involved in laundering the money he makes in the drug business. Her machinations almost get her boss, Ted, killed when she is trying to prevent having Walt's criminal career exposed. As Shakespeare does in *Macbeth*, Gilligan and his team avoid a sharp polarity of good and evil characters in *Breaking Bad*. They could easily have stacked the deck against Walt by making characters such as Skyler and Hank more attractive than they are. As it is, the show presents us with a spectrum in which very few characters are all the way over on the side of good, and most exist in the vast gray area between pure good and pure evil. Walt is not the most evil character in *Breaking Bad*. If he strikes us as a morally ambiguous figure, the reason is that he lives in a world rife with moral ambiguities.[55]

In Quest of a Tragic Ending

The consequences of Walt's decision to become Heisenberg are horrific—even for himself—but one can understand why he is tempted to make that choice. The original Walter White is a milquetoast, not much more of a man than the Hal of *Malcolm in the Middle*. In his all-around helplessness, he is pitiful and pathetic. He gets the idea of becoming a criminal when Hank takes him along on a drug bust with the injunction, "Get a little excitement in your life" (1/1). Walt desperately wants to be more of a man, even at the risk of exposing himself to high levels of danger. In that respect, the choice between the original Walter White and Walt/Heisenberg is a variant of the fundamental tragic choice. It goes all the way back to the *Iliad* and Achilles's choice. He can live to an old age but only in ignoble obscurity, or he can die young but achieve immortal fame for his noble actions. Walt's cancer diagnosis in effect forces a modern variant of Achilles's choice upon him. He can continue to eke out his safe life as a prudent middle-class man, or he can choose to break out of this rut and make something of himself.[56] Tragic heroes do *not* do the safe thing. They take chances; they are daring; they do not follow the ordinary rules. In one way or the other, this is true of all of Shakespeare's tragic heroes, from Romeo and Juliet to Antony and Cleopatra, from King Lear to Othello, from Macbeth to Coriolanus. If Romeo and Juliet were prudent, they would find partners more acceptable to their parents, enjoy big weddings in Verona, collect their gifts, and settle down to long, comfortable, and boring domestic lives. But then nobody would ever have heard of them. They would sink into the anonymity of all the happily married couples in Italy. Instead, Romeo and Juliet throw caution to the winds; they refuse to compromise with society's demands; and they sacrifice their lives for each other rather than accept a long-lasting but tepid marriage. Instead, they achieve everlasting glory as the noble archetype of true lovers. Their love burns brilliantly but briefly, as Juliet understands: "It is too rash, too unadvis'd, too sudden, / Too like the lightning, which does cease to be / Ere one can say it lightens" (2.2.118–20).

What makes a character tragic is that he or she stands for something out of the ordinary, however imprudent that may be. Nietzsche's "live dangerously" is the motto of tragedy.[57] Fortunately for the peace and survival of society, in real life most of us are unwilling to make such tragic choices. But tragedy appeals to us precisely because it allows us to experience vicariously and therefore safely what we cannot afford to do in our daily lives. Tragedy thereby expands our sense of human possibility, even as it reminds us why we ordinary people normally choose to live within a narrower range of practical options.

For most of his life, Walter White played by the rules, and look where it landed him. He accepted failure and wasted his potential. As Heisenberg, he finally tries to be somebody, and even though he ultimately fails in his goals— and chooses the wrong goals in the first place—at least he makes a name for himself and reveals his long-hidden potential. He is defeated in the end, but he goes down fighting; he could say, along with Macbeth, "Blow wind, come wrack! / At least we'll die with harness on our back" (5.5.50–51). That helps to explain why many viewers continued to side with Walter White and rooted for him to the end—not to succeed as a criminal but to die with dignity, like a tragic hero.[58]

And Walter White does die with dignity—Gilligan and his team made sure of that. As the *Breaking Bad* episodes began to count down to the finale, I started to worry about how it would all end. It was clear that Walt was going to have to die, but the question was, how? I could imagine several scenarios. Gilligan and his team could have had Walt go postal. He is compared to the Unabomber in the last episode (and looks like him). As a frustrated intellectual, Walt, like Ted Kaczynski, could have directed his hostility against the System at random targets or at society at large. He could have set off bombs in downtown Albuquerque (in fact he evokes that possibility as a way to keep the police preoccupied and off his trail).[59] As a terrorist, a Timothy McVeigh type, Walt would have left a truly tainted legacy. Or one can imagine an ending to the story in which Walt would have lost everything that mattered to him. Skyler, Walt Jr., and his little daughter, Holly, might have been killed in the crossfire of a gun battle with the police. That would have left Walt a complete and utter failure (perhaps to the satisfaction of some of his moral critics).

What I feared most was a sentimental ending to Walt's story. He would die, but before that he would be reconciled with Skyler and Walt Jr., tearfully reunited with his family, confessing his crimes, and begging for—and receiving—their forgiveness. Walt would renounce Heisenberg and return to his inner nerd. For me, that would have meant that Walt reembraced his mediocrity and repudiated everything that had made him heroic. All these endings were possible, and from what I know about the way Gilligan and his team worked, I am sure that they considered all of these and more.[60] By what they chose to reject and what they chose to use as the ending of the series, they revealed what they really thought about the Walter White character. In the process, they crafted what I regard as the perfect conclusion to *Breaking Bad* and a truly tragic ending.[61]

In "Felina" (5/16), Walt's violent impulses are still at work, but they are controlled and carefully targeted. He does not kill indiscriminately. In one of his clever technological schemes, he manages to take vengeance on the last of his enemies, gunning down the neo-Nazi gang with whom he got entangled (and who robbed him). In this case, his murders seem to be an act of justice.[62] He shows his decency by making sure to save Jesse's life and pointing him the way to freedom. Although Walt is not reunited with his family, in an earlier episode (5/14) he found a clever way to clear Skyler of all criminal charges, and, drawing once again on his cunning, he comes up with a scheme to intimidate Elliott and Gretchen Schwartz so that he knows that they will deliver $9,720,000 to his children when they come of age (5/16). Some of his ill-gotten gains will go to the good of his family after all. As it turns out, in shooting his last enemies, Walt fatally wounds himself. Like several of Shakespeare's tragic heroes, Walt in effect commits suicide. He does not have to suffer the humiliation of police arrest and a long trial in front of a hostile and uncomprehending public. He dies in the only place where he feels at home—in a chemical laboratory—and where he came closest to achieving fulfillment.[63]

This is not a happy ending to Walt's story, but it is, I believe, a truly satisfying one. I breathed a sigh of relief as the last episode unfolded and I saw that Gilligan and his team had found a way for Walt to die that would not diminish him in our eyes but that would in fact bring out some of his best qualities, including his resourcefulness and his genuine love for his family—and, above all, his willingness to take responsibility for all the harm he had done, just the way a tragic hero would.[64] I have faulted Vince Gilligan for analyzing his creation in terms of Mr. Chips and Scarface. Gilligan is not the best interpreter of his own work, perhaps because he does not have the concept of the *tragic hero* at his disposal.[65] But Gilligan the artist is far greater than Gilligan the commentator. As an author, Gilligan knows instinctively how to create a tragic hero, and above all he proved that he knows how a tragic hero *dies*. Several great television series have disappointed us with their final episode (*The Sopranos* is a case in point). But "Felina" is one of the greatest of all *Breaking Bad* episodes. Nothing reveals the tragic status of a hero as much as his death does, and Walter White dies like a tragic hero. As with any tragic hero, Walt's defeat is at the same time a triumph over his enemies and his own baser instincts and reminds us why we admire him.[66] In its portrayal of Walter White's death, *Breaking Bad* maintains the Shakespearean level of its drama to the very end.[67]

Crippled Masculinity

Having done my best to make a case for Walter White as a tragic hero, I can understand why many people would feel dissatisfied with my argument. There still seems to be something wrong with treating Walter White as a hero, tragic or otherwise. He displays certain virtues, but they are in the service of illegal and immoral activities. Is there anything genuinely noble about what he does? His main goal is making money, and his triumphs, such as they are, come over low-life types—mainly other criminals. Aristotle insists that the tragic hero be wellborn and his actions must have a "certain magnitude."[68] His conception of tragedy is aristocratic in nature, and Shakespeare seems to fulfill the ancient Greek criteria by choosing only kings and queens, princes and princesses, great generals and people of high rank as his tragic figures. What happens to them affects a whole kingdom, or, in the case of Romeo and Juliet, an entire civic community. As for Macbeth, he begins the play fighting bravely and nobly for his country. Manliness seems more admirable when it takes the form of public spiritedness and serves the common good. The tragic hero devotes himself to a cause, but can it be just any cause and not specifically a noble one?

This is one reason why it has become more difficult to set genuine tragedies in the modern, democratic world, where people's activities are generally confined to private life and lack the magnitude Aristotle expects of tragic action. Traditional forms of nobility are hard to find in a democracy, a form of government that fundamentally rejects the principle of aristocracy. Titles of nobility are in fact explicitly outlawed in the US Constitution (Article I, Section 9, Clause 8). As we saw in *Huckleberry Finn*, America's break with aristocracy left a void in its people's souls, which they tried to fill with imitations of or substitutes for traditional European nobility. Our American superheroes are one of democracy's substitutes for the aristocratic heroes of the past, who, like Achilles, were born to nobility, if not semi-divinity. By contrast, the superhero is typically an ordinary person who acquires a superpower only by virtue of an accident that could have happened to anyone—a stray blast of nuclear radiation, for example. In accordance with democratic principles, the American superhero is elevated to heroic status, not by noble birth but by something arbitrary—as if by lottery. That is why it is appropriate that Walter White/Heisenberg is a variant of the superhero myth. In a democracy, the heroic figure should be hidden in and spring out of an ordinary citizen.

Still, that emergence takes time, and Walter White starts off small and cuts an unimpressive figure initially. He and Jesse begin as small-time crooks, and in early episodes their behavior seems comic rather than tragic. Very little beyond the petty cash flow seems to be at stake in their initial drug deals. *Breaking Bad* does its best to elevate Walter White and give some gravitas to his story. He is of course not an aristocrat by birth, but he is a scientist, one of the new forms of aristocracy the modern world has produced (if you win the Nobel Prize in chemistry, you get to hobnob with Swedish royalty). As Walt's drug trade expands, his activities take on a certain magnitude. He ceases to be a petty criminal and becomes a drug lord, a drug kingpin.[69] The metaphors we commonly use to describe drug dealers lend a certain aristocratic aura to their activities. When Walt's meth manufacturing begins pulling in $80 million a year, we can start to talk of "serious money," and, as we have seen, he speaks of himself as building an empire and compares himself to another form of aristocracy in the contemporary world—the high-tech entrepreneur. As the plot progresses, Walt's actions begin to have national and even international repercussions. By the fifth season, his story generates headlines in the national media. Does this allow us finally to speak of him as a tragic hero, the Macbeth of Meth?

I confess that even I have my doubts about this and have trouble applying the word *noble* to Walter White. He is confined to a rather shabby world, with few if any outlets for what is traditionally viewed as heroism. Walt does not get to use his talents in the service of his country; he never thinks in terms of public service; he never goes to war, for example. The only form of war in *Breaking Bad* is the War on Drugs, and it is presented as a rather sordid business, with the DEA—especially Hank—disregarding the law, pursuing self-aggrandizing agendas, and often descending to the level of the criminals it is fighting. Can we really speak of any form of genuine nobility in *Breaking Bad*?

The absence of outlets for traditional heroism in the world of *Breaking Bad* may be the deepest theme of the series. If Walter White is heroic, his heroism seems to be twisted, bent out of shape, almost beyond the point of recognition. *Breaking Bad* is about the distorting and deforming of heroism in the contemporary world. The old heroic impulses are still present—the pride, the masculine aggressiveness, the drive to distinguish oneself, the overpowering urge to compete, especially against other males. But in the world Gilligan and his team have created, heroic impulses seem to go awry. They are unable to find healthy means of expressing themselves. In particular, what we discussed as the problem of manliness in *Macbeth* appears as the problem of masculinity in *Breaking Bad*, specifically what is now called "toxic masculinity." In a world in which masculinity is widely regarded as toxic, it becomes difficult for masculinity to develop properly and find the right outlets. Indeed, at its core *Breaking Bad* is a story of *crippled* masculinity—a motif that provides one of the central and pervasive symbols in the series.[70]

Walter White is crippled by his cancer. It lands him in a hospital bed and condemns him to a debilitating regimen of chemotherapy. His loss of hair is symbolic of a loss of masculinity. He worries that as his disease progresses, he will become an object of pity to his family. Walt Jr. is crippled by cerebral palsy. In a misguided effort to protect his sense of his masculinity, Hank attributes Walt Jr.'s need for crutches to a football injury and needlessly brags on his behalf, "He's got an arm like a howitzer" (1/2). Hank only succeeds in reminding Walt Jr. of what is missing from his teenage years, the chance to prove himself a man on an athletic field that most adolescent boys covet. For a good part of a season, Hank himself ends up crippled, in a wheelchair. Caught in a shootout with assassins from the Mexican cartel, Hank is paralyzed from the waist down, raising the dreaded specter of sexual impotence. Hank's sense of himself as a man is undermined by his confinement to a wheelchair and his inability to take care of himself in daily tasks. His injury infantilizes him as he allows his wife to nurse him and retreats into the childish world of his mineralogy hobby. Finally, *Breaking Bad* is haunted by the ominous figure of Hector "Tío" Salamanca, a former drug lord crippled by a stroke and condemned to life in a wheelchair. Once a potent figure in the drug world, Don Hector is reduced to a shell of his former self and must watch impotently as Gus Fring destroys his family one by one. Only through the help of Walter White is Hector able to weaponize his wheelchair, turning his weakness into strength and finally achieving his revenge on Gus, the opponent whose masculinity he questions by referring to him contemptuously as "chicken man."

These pervasive images of crippled men in *Breaking Bad* are telling us something—the world of the series is not a healthy one for males. Masculinity is not allowed to develop properly, and, even once developed, it tends to be deformed, prevented from full flourishing. We should sense that something is wrong when we realize that the most masculine men in *Breaking Bad* seem to be the criminals. We are troubled to see the traditional manly virtues perverted into criminal forms. Aggressive males like Tuco have hair-trigger responses to any threat or challenge to their authority, and they are likely to resort to violence at the slightest provocation. The Mexican and Mexican American drug dealers are involved in an ongoing blood feud, which leads to mounting violence among men anxious to prove their masculinity. There is an ethnic dimension to this development in the show. With their origins south of the border, the drug dealers are generally portrayed as having what has traditionally been regarded as Latin tempers.[71] They are obsessed with appearing macho and are unwilling to back down from a fight.

Like the mafia in the *Godfather* films, the Mexican drug cartel seems an atavism, a holdover from an earlier era, more primitive than modern America. Resembling the Sicilians, the Mexicans represent a more traditional kind of community than is typical of middle-class America. The Mexicans in *Breaking Bad* are clannish. The family is their fundamental unit of organization, and they are governed by the law of the vendetta. In Mafia style, they do not hesitate to take the law into their own hands. Deferring to the civil authorities in middle-class fashion is foreign to their way of life. There is even something lingeringly aristocratic about the Mexicans. Like the Sicilians, they still use the honorific title "Don." Moreover, the Mexicans are religious in a way that their American counterparts are not. Religion does not appear to be an important factor in the lives of Walter White and his family and friends. But the assassins who come up from Mexico to kill Walt first make a pilgrimage to a makeshift shrine to seek a blessing on their efforts in what seems like an archaic ceremony (3/1, 3/7). The Salamanca cousins seem to be a throwback to a more violent, less lawful past, when men settled their disputes on their own. They are displaced in genre. With their fancy boots, they seem to be stepping right out of an old-style Western and into a modern American suburb, where we would expect law and order to prevail. What might have been acceptable—and even heroic—on the legendary streets of Laredo seems both out of place and deeply threatening in a suburb of contemporary Albuquerque. The more archaic the characters in *Breaking Bad* seem and the more they embody traditional forms of masculinity, the more they seem dangerous and criminal. Masculinity is stigmatized as machismo in the series; it is presented as a force that is both foreign to and outdated in contemporary America.[72]

Borderlands

Breaking Bad thus turns on the same kind of historical and geographic contrasts as do the *Godfather* films and *Macbeth*. Albuquerque is presented as a borderland, poised between civilization and barbarism, between the present and the past. All the John Ford–style cinematography in *Breaking Bad* gives the series the feel of a Western.[73] The drug trade and its gang warfare, together with the War on Drugs, have returned New Mexico to the Wild West, complete with feuds, gun-fights, and vigilante justice. Albuquerque appears to be poised perilously on the boundary of civilization, surrounded by a hostile nature that cares nothing for human life.[74] And the border between Mexico and the United States functions the way the border between Scotland and England does in *Macbeth*, dividing barbarism from civilization. Mexico is the home of vicious drug cartels, run by quasi-feudal lords whose henchmen turn to bizarre religious rituals to carry out their criminal tasks. Albuquerque is the home of middle-class American suburban life, dotted with malls, car washes, law offices, and clinics.[75] El Paso is the place where these two worlds intersect, and going there is like a journey into the primitive past, into a Conradian heart of darkness. In 2/8, Hank says: "It's like *Apocalypse Now* there. Colonel Kurtz holed up in his jungle."

Like Macbeth, Walt is positioned between two different worlds, which embody antithetical codes of conduct and which pull him in opposite direc-tions. Walt comes from suburban America, where, as the story begins, he is leading a perfectly ordinary middle-class existence, absorbed in the typical bourgeois concerns of making a living and supporting his family—entirely legal and respectable activities, if a little dull. Through a strange sequence of events, Walt is suddenly exposed to a world of criminals who operate outside the law and make vast fortunes doing so. Walt is alternately attracted to and repelled by this criminal world. From this point on, he can never feel completely at home in either the middle-class world or the criminal. If he were simply loyal to his middle-class origins, Walt would not have embarked on a life of crime in the first place. If he could fully go over to the criminal world—if he truly became Scarface—Walt would become much crueler, but his life would also become much simpler. If it were not for the persistence of his middle-class moral scruples, he would, for example, have no problem with having Jesse or Hank killed, thereby eliminating many of his difficulties. In 3/12, Gus Fring's fixer, Mike Ehrmantraut, cautions Walt against half measures. In fact, Walt's divided nature means that he lives a life of half measures. For all his involvement in the drug trade, Walt views the criminal world as something foreign to him, something to be held at arm's length, never fully to be embraced.

Once again, it is important to stress that Walt never really becomes Scarface. He remains too middle-class for that. As much as he is drawn to a life of crime, Walt is never able to glory in it the way Scarface does (unlike, for example, the original Scarface, Al Capone, Walt never gets the prestige of being identified as Public Enemy #1). Walt is too cautious as a criminal ever to enjoy fully being one. Although Walt thrives on the danger of his criminal life, he comes across, like Hyman Roth in *The Godfather II*, as a curiously bourgeois gangster. He becomes obsessed with that most middle-class of concerns—security, and, as the witches say in *Macbeth*, "security / Is mortals' chiefest enemy" (3.5.32–33). If Walt were willing to live with the level of danger that is normally part of being a criminal, he would paradoxically be much more at ease. Instead, his perfectionism and his rational scientific worldview lead him to demand perfect security for himself. He wants to control all events and guarantee exactly the outcomes he desires. Ironically, Walt's Heisenberg will not accept the famous Heisenberg Uncertainty Principle.[76] To eliminate all possible threats to his safety, he has to forestall attacks from everyone he deals with, and that forces him to initiate preemptive strikes against all potential enemies, a mission that leads him into an endless cycle of violence that comes back to haunt him and condemns him to a life of perpetual anxiety.[77]

One could sum up Walt's problem by quoting Macbeth: "To be thus is nothing, / But to be safely thus" (3.1.47–48). Achilles would never put such an emphasis on his safety. He glories in his willingness to risk his life and scorns any concern with mere survival. Macbeth originally shares Achilles's form of heroism. At the beginning of the play, he is described as "disdaining Fortune" (1.2.17), and he is willing to take his chances on the battlefield, as any brave hero would. But the witches introduce Macbeth to the idea of a providential order in which his success is foreordained and thus assured. With their riddling prophecies, they convince Macbeth that he is invincible and invulnerable. In his quest for absolute security, he believes that he must anticipate all threats and eliminate all possible opponents. He is thus drawn, like Walter White, into a sequence of murders that eventually rebounds upon him and destroys him. Like Walt, Macbeth can never leave well enough alone. He is seeking a form of perfect security that no human being can ever achieve.

Macbeth is at heart a pagan warrior but one who paradoxically brings a Christian concern for the "eternal jewel" of his soul (3.1.67) to his criminal deeds, and thus he becomes even crueler in his attempt to control his fate. Similarly, when Walter White becomes a criminal, he brings along his middle-class concern for security and ends up trying to wipe all his enemies off the face of the earth. The ultimate toxic brew in *Breaking Bad* is a cocktail of middle-class anxiety mixed with would-be heroic criminal impulses. As in the *Godfather* films, the ethnic criminals in *Breaking Bad* come across as old-fashioned and out of place in contemporary middle-class America. But they are to some extent restrained by their antiquated sense of honor. They are destroyed in *Breaking Bad* by the forces of modernity—a new kind of criminal enterprise, bound up with and perhaps indistinguishable from multinational corporations like Madrigal. In some respects, Walt is more criminal than any of the Salamanca clan because he goes about his crimes with middle-class efficiency. In a world in which masculinity is viewed as alien and outmoded, all his aggressive impulses, which might have been channeled into noble activities, are diverted and distorted into crime.

Even the traditional masculine ideal of professionalism gets perverted in *Breaking Bad*. Gus Fring and Mike Ehrmantraut are ruthless murderers, especially Gus, but, unlike the many bumbling characters in *Breaking Bad* (including at times Walt and Jesse), at least Gus and Mike can be counted on to get the job done.[78] In a world filled with slackers, especially among the younger generation, we are forced to have a certain admiration for the characters who are not always waiting around for a free lunch. Beginning with its portrait of an American high school, *Breaking Bad* develops a very negative view of today's youth and its unjustified sense of entitlement. Characters like Jesse want to enjoy the American dream; they just do not want to have to do anything difficult to achieve it. Whatever else may be said against them, Gus and Mike do not think the world owes them a living. Mike is Gus's "cleaner."[79] If a crime scene needs to be scrubbed to baffle the police, Mike is Gus's go-to guy (also Saul Goodman's). Gus's professionalism is frightening. When he slits Victor's throat, he acts as if it is just another day at the office for him; he finally tells the stunned bystanders, "Well, get back to work" (4/1). But one has to be impressed by his ability to keep his cool, even in the most difficult circumstances, culminating in his final moment, when, with half his face blown off by Walt's bomb, he pauses to adjust his tie just before collapsing dead on the spot. Gus is evil, but the way he dresses, the way he maintains his calm demeanor, the way he never allows personal issues to cloud his business judgment—in all these respects, he is the epitome of professionalism.

Mike is a more attractive character than Gus, and in his own way even likable. In the *Breaking Bad* prequel, *Better Call Saul*, we hear more about Mike's origins and backstory and learn that he is a basically decent human being who has been drawn into the criminal world as a result of corruption in the Philadelphia police department and the death of his son.[80] Moreover, unlike Walt, Mike really is involved in crime for the sake of providing money for his family, in his case his widowed daughter-in-law and his granddaughter. Mike's forthrightness and gruff honesty are admirable qualities and make us sympathize with him. He is given an especially poignant death scene. It is very tempting to look at Mike Ehrmantraut and say: "*This* is a man." He is at least the sort of person one knows one can rely on. It is part of the overall tragic effect of *Breaking Bad* that Mike, perhaps its most manly character, is drawn into the criminal world for want of a more suitable outlet for his masculine virtues.

One might think that masculinity would be portrayed more positively among the "good guys" in *Breaking Bad*, the DEA and other law enforcement officials. After all, their masculine virtues ought to be in the noble service of the law.[81] There is a kind of male camaraderie among Hank and his fellow DEA officers, and they do rally to each other's aid in times of need. In that respect, they fit the standard pop culture model of cops on the buddy system. But in *Breaking Bad*, a dark side can be observed in the male bonding of its forces of law and order. The DEA officers in Albuquerque and even more so those in El Paso behave like adolescent males in a pissing contest. They are highly competitive and are always trying to outshine each other. They are visibly in contention for promotions, transfers, and other professional rewards. They tease and make fun of each other in ways that do not contribute to the success of their missions. In particular, they take delight in questioning each other's masculinity. In a typical moment, Hank says to his partner, Steve, "I didn't know you had balls" (5/10).

Hank is the worst of all the "good guys" in these respects. As we gradually learn, he is deeply insecure about his masculinity and overcompensates by constantly playing the glad-handing hail-fellow-well-met role. He is also continually bragging and showing off, both at home and at the office. He is the most obnoxious character in the series. His overconfidence and misplaced belief in his masculine virtues lead him to get in over his head in a dangerous border assignment in El Paso. When confronted with a spectacular example of the Mexican cartel's brutality—the head of an informant named Tortuga appropriately mounted on a tortoise's back—Hank shows his inexperience and weakness by promptly throwing up. The hardened DEA agents tease Hank mercilessly for his cowardice: "What's the matter, Schrader? You act like you never saw a severed human head on a tortoise before?" (2/7). They are killed when it turns out that the giant turtle conceals a bomb, and that explosion shatters what remains of Hank's self-confidence as a man. The agents of law and order in *Breaking Bad* mirror the criminals in the way that their masculinity puts them at odds with each other and at times interferes with their getting their job done properly.[82] Hank especially is a loose cannon, letting his personal feelings and, above all, his professional frustrations cloud his judgment as a law officer and lead him into highly unprofessional actions, such as beating up Jesse (3.7).

Hank's position as a representative of the law is further compromised by his own flirtations with illegality. We learn in 1/7 that he likes to smoke Cuban cigars, which at the time were banned in the United States. Defending himself in a conversation with Walt, Hank explains (sounding very much like a drug addict), "Yeah, well, sometimes forbidden fruit tastes the sweetest." This answer provokes Walt into raising the issue we saw explored in the *Godfather* films— whether something is outlawed because it is objectively wrong or regarded as wrong only because it is outlawed by the government. Walt obviously has a stake in this debate and presses the point: "What's legal—what's illegal. Cuban cigars, alcohol [pointing to the whiskey bottle]. You know if we were drinking this in 1930, you'd be breaking the law. Another year, you'd be okay. Huh, who knows what will be legal next year?" Hank wants to know if Walt has pot, cocaine, or heroin in mind, but he claims only to be making a general point: "I'm just saying it's arbitrary." As we saw in the *Godfather* films, the inconsistency with which governments ban various substances weakens their claim to be upholding anything other than their own arbitrary decrees.

The *Godfather* films have an easier time questioning the validity of Prohibition. Alcohol is widely consumed in the United States and accepted in polite society. Besides, by now, Prohibition is ancient history in America.[83] But the crystal meth epidemic is still making headlines today. The last thing *Breaking Bad* wanted to do was to mount a defense of the meth trade. Aside from the one moment when Gale offers his libertarian defense of his meth-making activities, the show is generally quiet on the subject and does not suggest at all that meth making is a victimless crime (indeed it makes a point of showing some of the victims). In fact, in 1/7, Hank thinks that the case of meth will clinch his argument against Walt's claims about the arbitrariness of the government's making certain substances illegal and not others: "Sometimes there is stuff that is legal that shouldn't be. I mean friggin' meth used to be legal. Used to sell it over every counter in every pharmacy in America. Thank God they came to their senses on that one, huh?" Most Americans would agree with Hank on this point, and yet he has raised an inconvenient fact: at one time meth was perfectly legal in the United States and widely prescribed by legitimate doctors.[84]

Thus even *Breaking Bad* raises some doubts about whether the government can claim the moral high ground when it comes to the meth issue. But the show never goes as far as the *Godfather* films in portraying government power in a negative light. There is no officer of the law in *Breaking Bad* who is as corrupt as Captain McCluskey in *The Godfather I* or a political figure as reprehensible as Senator Geary in *The Godfather II*. The forces of law and order in *Breaking Bad* may at times be incompetent or overzealous, or otherwise fail to measure up to the highest standards of professionalism. But generally the law officers are honest and devoted to duty. Yet *Breaking Bad* still does not feature a figure of the stature of Eliot Ness (even though Hank is treated like him by his colleagues in 2/3 after his successful drug bust). By the standards of a traditional TV cop show, Hank and his colleagues are not sterling representatives of their profession; they are not the Untouchables. Far from seeming noble, they often come across as petty, mainly concerned with stroking their own egos. They have a good deal of masculine aggressiveness, but they do not consistently and reliably channel it into noble forms of public service. The impression that something is wrong with masculinity in the world of *Breaking Bad* is not erased by the behavior of the representatives of the law.

Therapeutic Culture and the Death of Tragedy

Masculinity thus repeatedly appears as toxic in *Breaking Bad,* and it would be hard to find an example when it takes a purely healthy form. There are several reasons why masculinity is not properly nourished in the world of *Breaking Bad.* Masculinity is traditionally developed in the family, where a man gets to be treated like a man only if he accepts a responsible role as a husband and a father and learns to moderate his aggressive impulses. The family does not appear in a good light in *Breaking Bad.* At its heart, the series chronicles the story of two failed marriages, those of Walt and Skyler, and Hank and Marie.[85] Hank's frustration with needing Marie to take care of him when he is in a wheelchair is the response of a man who was never happy in the first place to become dependent on a woman in marriage. Marie's unhappiness with having to put up with Hank's male bravado and then with his sense of male inadequacy surfaces in her compulsive need to adopt fictional identities and to fantasize a better husband for herself (specifically a true hero, an astronaut).

Walt and Skyler both suffer from a case of failed expectations in marriage. Flashbacks reveal that, when younger, they expected to do much better in life, especially in financial and material terms. In a flashback in 3/13, we see them moving into their first house, and they are already thinking of something larger. Walt says, "We need to set our sights high" and adds, "Let's stretch our price range." They are in the grip of the version of the American dream that focuses on home ownership. As Walt says: "Why be cautious? We have nowhere to go but up." Although Walt never says so, one senses that he probably blames his family for holding him back from doing more with his scientific talents. Skyler's eagerness to get involved in Walt's criminal enterprise and her desire to take command of the finances indicate that she feels frustrated with her life as a suburban housewife (remember that she failed as a fiction writer). Skyler is constantly looking for ways to undercut Walt and his authority in the family, especially over Walt Jr. Far from nurturing Walt's masculinity, she works to emasculate him.[86] There are strong suggestions in *Breaking Bad* that when masculinity goes unnourished at home, it will express itself in distorted ways elsewhere. I am not saying that Skyler drives Walt into a life of crime, but the way that he seeks fulfillment as Heisenberg is related to the fact that he does not feel like a man at home. In W. C. Fields's films, we saw that a central comic motif is the henpecked husband, emasculated in his domestic life and driven to regain his lost dignity by pursuing dubious business schemes (Hal in *Malcolm in the Middle* experiences the same kind of indignities at home). This comic material is transformed into something tragic in *Breaking Bad*, when Walt's frustrations in his family lead him to try to express his masculinity in some other area, even in a life of crime.

Walt Jr. offers a good example of the way that masculinity goes unnourished in the world of *Breaking Bad*. Unfortunately because of his disability, he does not get to participate in the kinds of activities (mainly sports) that normally help adolescent males develop their sense of masculinity. Walt loves his son, but he is not a good father to him. In many respects, Hank—even with his false displays of masculinity—does a better job of being a father figure for Walt Jr. It is a sad commentary on Walt Jr.'s situation that, even as inadequate as Hank is as a man, he offers Walt Jr. a better male role model than his own father does. Walt is evidently upset that Walt Jr. is not growing up fast enough as a man. At one particularly ugly moment, a frustrated Walt forces tequila on Walt Jr.—over Hank's objections—to such an extent that his son throws up in the pool (2/10). Jesse also is searching for a proper father figure throughout *Breaking Bad*, since his own father lavishes his attention on Jesse's younger brother. Unfortunately for Jesse, he finds only criminals to mentor him, first Walt and then Mike. To the extent he mans up, it is only as a criminal. The lack of proper male role models in the world of *Breaking Bad* is emblematic of the way that masculinity does not get support from contemporary culture and is sometimes distorted into criminality.

One of the less noticed but brilliant achievements of *Breaking Bad* is the way that it portrays—and raises doubts about—the therapeutic culture of contemporary America. The story line is filled with twelve-step programs, all the way from Narcotics Anonymous to Gamblers Anonymous. With all the unhappiness, dissatisfaction, frustration, and insecurity the characters experience, addiction of various kinds is a widespread problem in *Breaking Bad*—and drugs are only part of a larger problem. Confined to his wheelchair, Hank even gets addicted to his mineral collection. Marie's kleptomania is a form of addiction, and she gets therapy for it. Jane undergoes therapy for her heroin addiction (unsuccessfully). Jesse undergoes therapy for his meth addiction (unsuccessfully). Walt undergoes therapy for his fictional addiction to gambling (4/4; successfully only because he was never addicted in the first place). Walt also goes to a cancer support group (1/6), and in 2/3 he undergoes a psychiatric exam. In 4/6, he speaks disparagingly of Dr. Joyce Brothers, who helped disseminate therapeutic culture on television. Saul Goodman brings up the king of TV therapists when, in 3/2, he speaks of "Dr. Phil." A hilarious scene early in the series (1/5) features one of the standbys of therapeutic culture—an intervention. Walt's family and friends stage one to get him to seek treatment for his cancer. As the characters pass around the "talking pillow," they mouth all the clichés of modern psychotherapy. In a scene of mass therapy, Walt's high school fills its gymnasium to try to come to terms with the students' grief over the air disaster at the end of season 2. Marie speaks for the whole world of therapeutic culture when, in 5/8, she tells Skyler reassuringly: "I'm so proud of you for going to therapy. It can be so helpful. Such a good tool."

In many respects, this therapeutic culture does more to undermine traditional notions of good and evil than anything Walter White does. Jesse is shocked when one of his therapists tells him that he has gotten over the guilt of having been responsible for the death of his own daughter (he accidentally ran her over with a car; 3/1). In 4/7, Jesse's therapist gives voice to the mantra of his profession: "We're not here to sit in judgment"—a position that undermines morality and the need to take responsibility for one's deeds. Walt does judge himself and at least on some level, he knows when he is doing something wrong. *Breaking Bad* portrays Walter White in a good light for finally owning up to his crimes and taking responsibility for them. In 4/6, Walt Jr., thinking that his father is suffering from an addiction to gambling, says that he has learned from reading online that this is a disease, like alcoholism. Therefore, Walt Jr. concludes, his mother is not entitled to be angry at Walt. Rejecting this cheap psychologizing and easy way out, Walt insists to his son: "What is going on with me is not about some disease. It's about choices, choices that I have made, choices I stand by." Therapeutic culture runs counter to this kind of tragic recognition as it frees people from the obligation to do what we mean when we tell someone to "man up." While the therapists in *Breaking Bad* let people off the hook when it comes to their responsibilities, it is paradoxically the most sinister character, Gus Fring, who, in 3/5, speaks the most moral words in the series (sounding remarkably like Vito Corleone), about the obligations of a man to his family: "A man provides for his family. . . . He does it even when he's not appreciated, or respected, or even loved. And he simply bears up and he does it. Because he's a man." Even the lone wolf Gus understands the connection between true manliness and the family.

Compounding the problem is the way that therapy is taking the place of traditional religion in contemporary America; arguably it has become the new religion.[87] At the high school group therapy session, one student is troubled about the plane crash: "Why did it happen if there's a God?" (3/1). "Could we just keep it secular?" is the impassioned plea of the aggressively agnostic school authorities, who feel compelled to keep religion out of the public sphere. Jesse's therapy sessions take place in a church. The implication is that therapy is substituting for traditional religious consolations and teachings. In *Breaking Bad,* religion maintains its power only south of the border. The cartel assassins still believe in saints. But not a single American character in the series experiences religion as a vibrant force in his or her life. *Breaking Bad* presents a contemporary America in which the churches are empty and the therapy sessions are full.[88]

The therapeutization of America does not bode well for the traditional masculine virtues. A principal form of contemporary therapy is anger management. One can think of several characters in *Breaking Bad* who might have benefited from an anger management session or two. But psychotherapy really seeks to eliminate anger, not to manage it. Therapeutic culture looks askance at impulses of anger, treating them as the source of conflict among human beings. The goal of therapy is to produce a peaceful, compliant world in which everybody will be nice to each other. That means that therapeutic culture is fundamentally at odds with masculine aggressiveness. It does not seek to channel masculinity into acceptable or even higher purposes.[89] It does not hope to use masculine aggressiveness to create soldiers, for example, to get them to direct their anger against the enemies of their country and thus to fight nobly for it, as Macbeth does initially. The aim of anger management is to get rid of it, or at least to suppress its manifestations, not to give it new and more suitable forms of expression.

Therapeutic culture is thus fundamentally at odds with the tragic view of life. Indeed, the complete triumph of therapeutic culture would mean the death of tragedy. Tragedy recognizes basic tensions in the human condition that cannot be eliminated without narrowing the range of what it is to be human. To do away with anger would make human beings more peaceful, but also less powerful. Aggressive impulses can lead to destructive conflict, but they can also fuel some of the most heroic achievements. Remember what we saw in Shakespeare's tragedies—the qualities a man may need in wartime may create problems for society in peacetime. The tragic insight is that not all forms of human excellence are compatible. *Breaking Bad* reveals the dangers of regarding masculinity as simply toxic, and not allowing it its legitimate place in human life. If you deny the value of masculinity and in effect criminalize it, you may drive especially masculine men to become criminals. That is, if you deny men legitimate outlets for their aggressive impulses, they may seek out illegitimate outlets. That is the story of Walter White. For his whole life, he has been forced to bottle up his aggressive impulses. When they are finally released, they go wild and are dangerous to him and everyone around him.

In the end, I would not insist on calling Walter White a tragic hero in the traditional sense. Perhaps his story might be best understood as a peculiarly modern form of tragedy, a kind of metatragedy. His tragedy is that traditional tragedy is no longer available to him because traditional masculine heroism is no longer available to him. Walt's tragedy is that he harbors genuinely heroic impulses, but in his society, with a therapeutic culture that denies the value of heroic virtue, he cannot find a way to give healthy expression to his masculinity. Faced with the choice of being a mild-mannered Clark Kent or to find some form of becoming Superman, Walt opts for the dangerous role of the criminal Heisenberg. He is destroyed as a result, but we are left wondering if he could ever have fulfilled himself in his original safe role as a peaceful but inconsequential human being. I am inclined to call Walter White a distinctively modern variant of the tragic hero, but I would settle for paying *Breaking Bad* this tribute: In a brilliant anatomy of contemporary America, Gilligan and his team lay bare the psychodynamics of a therapeutic culture that brands traditional masculine virtues as toxic and thereby deforms their expression into something ugly and criminal.

To sum up the achievement of *Breaking Bad*: Gilligan and his team found a way to refashion Shakespearean tragedy in the contemporary world, but by undertaking a comparison between that world and the heroic one of Shakespeare's tragedies, they exposed how ignoble modern existence threatens to become. The world of middle-class virtue, as admirable as it may be in itself, does not exhaust the full range of human possibilities or satisfy all the longings of the human soul. That is one reason why the American dream became problematic when it took a narrowly middle-class form in the twentieth century. At its roots, the American dream is a democratic idea and therefore an anti-aristocratic one. It is supposed to be equally available to all Americans, no matter the circumstances of their birth. And yet in some formulations, a component of the American dream is to distinguish oneself, to rise above the crowd, and that is an aristocratic notion. As we saw in *Huckleberry Finn*, memories of Europe haunt Americans, leading them to long to recapture an element of nobility and hence aristocracy in their democratic lives. That longing may lead them into imposture and even criminality. *Breaking Bad* tells the tragic story of a man who cannot achieve fulfillment in ordinary middle-class American life, but he cannot find a legitimate alternative to it either. In his quest to rise above the average American, Walter discovers that traditional modes of heroism are not open to him, and he is tempted into a criminal career to achieve his goals and make a name for himself. But to be a drug lord is not a genuine form of aristocracy, no matter how much money Walt makes, and his quest to achieve distinction proves to be self-defeating and self-destructive. In the way that Walter White gets tragically caught in the turbulent crosscurrents of democracy and aristocracy in American life, *Breaking Bad* provides a profound commentary on what we have been calling the dark side of the American dream.

5

THE APOCALYPTIC STRAIN IN POPULAR CULTURE

THE AMERICAN NIGHTMARE BECOMES THE AMERICAN DREAM

> The world of commerce and frivolous necessity has been replaced by a world of survival and responsibility.... In a matter of months society has crumbled—no government, no grocery stores, no mail delivery, no cable TV. In a world ruled by the dead, we are forced to finally start living.
>
> *The Walking Dead*

Dreams and Nightmares

American popular culture is overflowing with doomsday prophecies and end-of-the-world scenarios. According to film and television, vampires, werewolves, and zombies are storming across our landscape, and alien invaders, asteroids, and airborne toxic events threaten us from the skies. We might as well be living in the late Middle Ages. Our films and television shows seem locked into a perpetual and ever-more-frenzied Dance of Death. Whatever happened to the popular culture that used to offer up charming images of the American dream? Where are the happy households—the Andersons, the Nelsons, the Cleavers, the Petries—when we need them? Film and television today are more likely to present images of the American nightmare: our entire civilization reduced to rubble, and the few survivors forced to live a primitive existence in terror of monstrous forces unleashed throughout the land. Has the American nightmare paradoxically become the new American dream? Is there some weird kind of wish fulfillment at work in all these visions of near-universal death and destruction?

There are, of course, as many versions of the American dream as there are Americans, but by the middle of the twentieth century, one common pattern emerged in both reality and in popular culture.[1] This dream was very much embodied in material terms—a family happily ensconced in a spacious house, preferably in the suburbs, with the most up-to-date appliances and two or three cars in the garage. This dream was founded on faith in modern science and technology, which seemed to be continually improving the human and specifically the American condition. The path to achieving this American dream was clearly laid out. One got a good education in order to land a good job, which might or might not be fulfilling in itself but would in any case provide the financial means for buying all the material components that seemed essential to the American dream. As usually envisioned, the job—in order to pay enough—would be in one of the professions, chiefly law or medicine, or in some kind of business, probably a corporate position that would provide financial security. The notion of security was integral to this version of the American dream. One would find a job for life that included solid medical and retirement benefits. This model of happiness was often on view in film and television in the 1950s and 1960s, supplying the framework for television situation comedies, for example, or providing the happy endings in many Hollywood movies.

This vision of the American dream was bound up with trust in American institutions. The goal of long-term security rested on faith in financial institutions, such as banks, insurance companies, and the stock market. Medical institutions, such as hospitals, clinics, and the pharmaceutical industry, were supposed to keep extending our life expectancy. Americans also looked up to their educational institutions, from primary schools to universities. After all, they were relying on their schools to prepare them for the careers that would underwrite their financial prosperity. Universities could be counted on to do the kind of scientific research that makes technological progress possible. In short, Americans relied on their institutions to shape them properly in the first place; in many cases they looked forward to being employed by institutions such as corporations and the professions; and they trusted these institutions in turn to work for their benefit, providing, for example, health care and financial security.

Overarching all these institutions was the grandest institution of them all, American government: local, state, and above all the federal government. Especially during the Cold War era, Americans looked up to the Washington establishment because it was protecting them from foreign and domestic enemies. America had been the clear winner in World War II, emerging from the conflict relatively unscarred and assuming an uncontested place as the most productive and powerful nation in the world. America had triumphed over its enemies because of its superior economic and scientific power. It is no accident that the particular conception of the American dream we have been examining crystallized right after World War II. Given the widespread faith in technical expertise in the wake of America's victory in World War II, Americans generally trusted their government to regulate the economy and produce the prosperity that would make the American dream possible. In the second half of the twentieth century, the American government kept expanding its scope as a welfare state, with the goal of ensuring the security of all aspects of its citizens' lives. Moreover, the federal government steadily increased its role in financially supporting and regulating the various institutions that were woven into the fabric of the American dream, especially educational and medical institutions. In sum, for decades the American dream came boxed in an institutional framework, and most Americans, without thinking much about it, assumed that they could not realize their dreams without these institutions.

But even at the peak of this conception of the American dream in the 1950s, this faith in institutions did not go unchallenged. Dissenting voices charged that Americans were being increasingly "institutionalized," sacrificing their freedom in their quest for comfort and security. Talk of the "organization man" (the title of a 1956 book by William Whyte) reflected fears that Americans were selling their souls to corporations, giving up their individuality and autonomy to work in bureaucratic organizations.[2] Skeptics also voiced concerns that the standard conception of the American dream might be self-defeating. In the course of trying to provide material benefits to their families, men—and later women—were losing touch with the very spouses and children they claimed to cherish. The notion of the happy, close-knit family was at the core of the American dream, and yet career values often seemed to conflict with family values. Working hard at the office left men—and later women—with little or no time for their children. Everywhere institutions seemed to be coming between people, preventing them from interacting in face-to-face situations. The very institutions that Americans had turned to in order to achieve and secure their dreams seemed to have trapped them in a vast impersonal system that by its nature was inimical to personal fulfillment. These anxieties about the American dream sometimes surfaced in popular culture in the middle of the twentieth century.[3] Movies such as the 1957 *The Man in the Gray Flannel Suit* portrayed corporate life as empty and stultifying. And the immense popularity of Westerns during this era, in film and especially on television, signaled dissatisfaction with comfortable suburban life. Dramas set in the Wild West provided an imaginative escape from the safe and boring world of modern institutions—an image of a rugged frontier existence in which earlier Americans, especially men, were on their own and could act heroically in their struggle with hostile and dangerous environments.

Disenchantment with the mid-twentieth-century formulation of the American dream gradually increased and became widespread at the turn of the twenty-first century, as people lost their confidence in American institutions. A series of bubbles and meltdowns led people to doubt the fundamental honesty and integrity of financial institutions, above all, their ability to provide long-term economic security. Confidence in the competence and caring nature of the medical establishment began to erode, as witness the alternative-medicine movement, the return to traditional home remedies, skepticism about vaccination programs, and the proliferation of medical malpractice suits. Whether these doubts are scientifically justified is irrelevant to the larger cultural issue. The fact is that doctors and the medical profession in general are no longer held in the high esteem they once enjoyed in America. Educational institutions are also being challenged on a wide range of fronts, with critics complaining that they fail to deliver on their promises and charge exorbitant rates in the process. The home-schooling movement offers concrete proof that many Americans have become disillusioned with the educational establishment. As for government institutions, with one "-gate" scandal after another, polling suggests that Americans' faith in institutions such as Congress and the presidency is at all-time lows. Looking at the world around them, Americans may be excused for concluding that the financial-medical-educational-government complex that was supposed to help them achieve their dreams has failed them. At this point, it becomes tempting for Americans to wish away their banks, their hospitals, their schools, and their government. Perhaps life might be easier and more fulfilling without all these institutions.

Popular culture has stepped forward to offer Americans a chance to explore these possibilities imaginatively and to rethink the American dream. Films and television shows have allowed Americans to imagine what life would be like in the absence of all the institutions they have been told they cannot do without, but which they now suspect may be thwarting their self-fulfillment. We are dealing with a wide variety of fantasies here, mainly in the horror and science-fiction genres, but the pattern is strikingly consistent, cutting across generic distinctions. In the television show *Revolution,* for example, some mysterious event causes all electrical devices around the world to cease functioning. The result is catastrophic and involves a huge loss of life, as airborne planes crash to earth, for example. All social institutions dissolve, and people are forced to rely only on their personal survival skills. Governments around the world collapse, and the United States divides up into a number of smaller political units. This development runs contrary to everything we have been taught to believe about "one nation, indivisible." Yet it is characteristic of almost all these shows that the federal government is among the first casualties of the apocalyptic event, and—strange as it may at first sound—there is a strong element of wish fulfillment in this event. It is as if these shows are saying: "We've lost everything, but at least we're rid of the federal government. Maybe we can run our own lives now." The thrust of these end-of-the-world scenarios is precisely for government to grow smaller or to disappear entirely. These shows seem to reflect a sense that government has grown too big, and too remote from the concerns of ordinary citizens and unresponsive to their needs and demands. If Congress and the president are unable to shrink the size of government, perhaps a plague or cosmic catastrophe can do some real budget cutting for a change.

One might even describe these shows as a return to the original spirit of federalism (which was, after all, conceived as an antidote to a powerful central government). The aim seems to be to reduce the size of government radically and thereby to bring it closer to the people. Cut back to regional or local units, government becomes manageable again, and ordinary people get to participate in it actively, recovering a say in the decisions that affect their lives. In cases where the apocalyptic event dissolves all government, these shows in effect return people to what political theorists call the state of nature. As if we were reading Thomas Hobbes, John Locke, or Jean-Jacques Rousseau, we get to see how people form a social contract. No longer locked into institutions already in place, the public gets to assess their value and see if it really needs them or might be better off under other arrangements or perhaps no government at all.

The Return of the Minutemen

In the television show *Falling Skies*, it is invading aliens who destroy civilization as we know it, and they are quick to eliminate governments around the world. Set in and around Boston, the show revives the tradition of the New England town meeting, as the characters get to deliberate on their own affairs and debate courses of action in the absence of any higher political authority. The characters have been left to their own devices, because, in a decisive blow to civilization, the aliens have destroyed communication circuits and in particular the internet. The internet is a perfect example of the kind of technological advance that has usually been featured in the formulation of the American dream. The characters in *Falling Skies* of course miss the internet, but they learn to live without it and develop more intimate, and perhaps more satisfactory, modes of communication. The loss of modern technology is characteristic of all these apocalyptic scenarios and reflects Americans' love-hate relationship with their machines, appliances, and devices. These shows display an ambivalent attitude toward modernity in general, perhaps a genuine disillusionment with it, a sense that all the technological progress upon which we pride ourselves has not made us happier and may, on the contrary, have made us miserable by depersonalizing our relationships and limiting our freedom.

To be sure, the characters in *Falling Skies* lament the loss of the benefits of modern civilization. Many of them wish that they still had access to the advanced medical technology that used to be available in Boston's world-class hospitals.

Several of the episodes take place in an abandoned school, which points to the loss of modern educational institutions. But the show portrays major compensations for the destruction of modern medical and educational facilities. The featured band of survivors includes a female pediatrician. As she herself admits, she cannot provide the services of a big-city, hospital-based physician, but she makes up for her lack of scientific expertise with her personal concern for the welfare of her patients, who are also her friends. Deprived of urban hospitals, our survivors now have access to a genuine family doctor who, unlike modern physicians, makes old-fashioned house calls. Similarly, all the children are now home-schooled. Their teachers are their parents, and in the absence of professional educators, the students seem to thrive, actually enjoying their lessons for a change. They are now being taught by people who know them and care about them as individuals. Perhaps there is something dreamlike about this nightmare after all.

The way that the relationships between parents and children have changed in light of the apocalyptic events goes right to the emotional core of *Falling Skies*. The characters have lost everything that used to make up the American dream— all their material possessions, their social status, their professional careers, and of course their three-bedroom houses. But that means that they can now focus on each other. Careers no longer distract them from their family obligations. For the adults, parenting becomes their full-time job. They used to put their careers ahead of their family life; now they will sacrifice anything for the sake of their children. As a typical Steven Spielberg production, *Falling Skies* dwells obsessively on the father-son relationship. The main character is a father who gets to bond with his sons in a way that was not possible when he was pursuing his career as a history professor at Boston University. Now he spends all his time with his sons at his side and gets to watch them grow up under his guidance. This logic takes us to the heart of these end-of-the-world narratives. The characters have lost everything that used to make their lives seem worthwhile, but they discover that those elements of the American dream were at best distractions from, and at worst obstacles to, their true happiness and sense of fulfillment. Liberated from material concerns and impersonal institutions, the characters have the opportunity to search for what makes life truly meaningful, and that turns out to be devotion to friends and especially family. These apocalyptic fantasies seem to reflect the guilt feelings of perpetually overachieving American dreamers, who discover that, in their drive for success, they have betrayed their families.[4] Secretly they wish that the institutions they work so hard in might be dissolved so that they could get back in touch with their families.

With its setting in Massachusetts and its main character a history professor, *Falling Skies* frequently refers to the American Revolution. The names of

Lexington and Concord keep coming up, and our heroes become latter-day Minutemen. Their resistance to the alien invaders is repeatedly compared to the American colonists' resistance to British tyranny.[5] The Spirit of '76 thus comes to prevail in *Falling Skies*. The characters have lost their material possessions and the security that institutions used to give them, but they have regained their independence and self-reliance. In the midst of a nightmarish existence, an older conception of the American dream comes back to life. The characters grow in self-respect because they learn that they can rely on their own resources to deal with the challenges they face. They do not need a whole network of impersonal institutions to preserve their lives and to take care of their welfare—and in particular they do not need the federal government. In the spirit of the American Revolution, they form militias and become citizen-soldiers, defending themselves. As do many of these apocalyptic narratives, *Falling Skies* features boys who have to grow quickly into men, a process epitomized by their learning to use weapons and thus assuming the adult role of protecting their loved ones. Taking pride in their maturation, these boys reveal what these shows stand for—they champion people who assume responsibility for their lives rather than passively accepting a role as wards of institutions or the state.

Zombies and the CDC

If alien invaders are temporarily unavailable, fortunately American pop culture can supply us with all the zombies we need to reexamine the meaning of our lives. A zombie narrative such as the television show *The Walking Dead* embodies the same patterns we have just seen operating in an alien invasion narrative such as *Falling Skies*.[6] In *The Walking Dead* a zombie plague has quickly spread around the world, annihilating all but a remnant of the human population. In these end-of-the-world scenarios, whatever triggers the apocalypse tends to affect the entire Earth more or less simultaneously. The fear of modernity in all these narratives is specifically a fear of global modernity. What upsets people is the sense that they are losing control of their lives in a world of impersonal and unresponsive institutions, and the fact that all this is happening on a global scale is especially unnerving. If people are disturbed by the remoteness of the authorities that control their lives, then globalization is the ultimate nightmare.

Among their many meanings, zombies have come to symbolize the force of globalization.[7] National borders cannot stop the zombie plague from spreading, and it evidently dissolves all cultural distinctions. The zombies lose their individuality, freedom of will, and everything that makes them human beings. With their herd mentality, they are precisely the kind of mass-men that impersonal institutions seek to produce, and in a curious way they represent the docile subjects that governments secretly—or not so secretly—desire. Zombification is a power-ful image of what governments try to do to their citizens—to create a uniform, homogeneous population, incapable of acting independently.[8] It is no accident that zombies sometimes are portrayed as the products of scientific experiments and specifically of government projects gone awry (or gone all too well).

In *The Walking Dead*, it is not clear what force produced the zombies, but in any event they set off the typical end-of-the-world scenario. Governments have fallen everywhere, and in the power vacuum that results, the characters are plunged back into the state of nature, with a decidedly Hobbesian empha-sis on the war of all against all. Chased by relentless if plodding zombies and also by marauding gangs of the remaining humans, the main characters at first think of turning to traditional authorities to protect them. Coming from rural Georgia, they head for Atlanta, assuming that a big city will have the resources to keep them safe. But the city, with its concentration of zombies, proves to be even more dangerous than the countryside. The characters keep thinking of the federal government as their ultimate protector. Pinning their hopes on the military, they talk about going to Fort Benning for security, although they never get there and are warned away from it by other fugitives they encounter.[9]

Season 1 culminates in a quest to find safety with a well-known federal agency, the Centers for Disease Control and Prevention (CDC), conveniently located in Atlanta and a seemingly ideal refuge from a plague. But the characters' relief at reaching their goal proves to be short-lived. Viewing the CDC as their salvation, our band of survivors finds instead that it is a source of destruction. The gleaming modernistic edifice is a deathtrap, run by a sole survivor, Dr. Edward Jenner, who seems borderline sane and fast approaching a pop culture stereotype of the mad scientist. Far from finding a cure for the zombie plague, the CDC may be the source of the infection. We learn in the sixth episode that the CDC weaponized smallpox. It is holding so many deadly germs and viruses that the building is programmed to self-destruct once its generators fail. Remi-niscent of HAL in Stanley Kubrick's *2001*, the CDC computer has taken control away from the one scientist remaining in the headquarters. Blindly following its protocols and standard operating procedures, the computerized containment system destroys the most important zombie specimen the CDC possesses and then goes for the whole facility. As portrayed in the series, the CDC represents science at its most inhuman and frightening, an overwhelming force on auto-matic pilot, indifferent to ordinary people's feelings and their fate. Our heroes and heroines barely have time to escape before the building blows up, taking the last of the CDC scientists with it.[10] If the CDC functions as a symbol of the federal government in *The Walking Dead*, then the medical-military-industrial complex proves to be a dangerous and self-destructive force.

As federal agencies go, the CDC is one of the more respected ones. It is, therefore, a measure of the antigovernment spirit of *The Walking Dead* that it portrays the CDC so negatively. Evidently the agency was not about to see its reputation tarnished without putting up a fight. Perhaps in direct response to *The Walking Dead*, the real CDC created its own zombie narrative in the form of a graphic novel on its official website.[11] Called *Zombie Pandemic*, it is generously provided free of charge by the CDC to anyone "looking for an entertaining way to introduce emergency preparedness."[12] Unsurprisingly, in the CDC's own narrative, the organization comes across as looking pretty good; it responds quickly and effectively to the zombie plague. *Zombie Pandemic* thus belongs to a different category of apocalyptic narratives—those with a progovernment bias. In contrast to what we have been examining thus far, some apocalyptic narratives insist on portraying ordinary people as helpless in the face of disaster. They are shown to panic or to freeze or to despair, thus only making matters worse for themselves. Of course this happens with some of the characters even in *The Walking Dead*, but the keynote of the series is human self-reliance and resilience. By contrast, in some zombie stories, such as the film *World War Z*, ordinary people are presented as incompetent. They are forced to rely on elites to save them, often a combination of scientific experts and military special forces, sponsored and directed by national governments or even the UN.[13] In this type of narrative, individual human beings, dwarfed and overwhelmed by a global or a cosmic catastrophe, must turn to the government to save them.

The CDC's *Zombie Pandemic* follows this kind of script. The story is told largely from the perspective of an ordinary couple named Todd and Julie, who listen to the news of a zombie plague unfold in public service announcements from the CDC. The government orders people to remain passive in the face of disaster. Todd and Julie dutifully obey the CDC's instructions: "Stay in your home. Do not go outside." Their reliance on government action to save them promises to be rewarded, because the CDC makes remarkably swift progress in dealing with the zombie plague. Only a few days later, one of its doctors proclaims: "Yes, the health department sent it in Monday and we've managed to map the virus's DNA. It appears to be a highly mutated form of the flu. They've labeled it Z5N1." Working around the clock, the CDC soon comes up with the needed countermeasure for the zombie outbreak. As one doctor announces, "We're using the same type of vaccine that we use for the seasonal flu." Despite the spotty effectiveness record of flu vaccines, apparently this news is meant to reassure the public. One week later, the CDC is ready to distribute the vaccine, as an official from the "Strategic National Stockpile" reports.

Todd and Julie continue to follow the directives they receive from the CDC's broadcasts, and accordingly they head for what is called a "safe zone" at a nearby elementary school. County Health Department officials carefully monitor their entrance into the safe zone, where they are assured that the vaccine is on its way. Unfortunately, just as it seems that Todd and Julie will be saved, a horde of zombies converges on the school building. Faced with being overrun by zombies, the military guards balk at using their weapons: "We can't just shoot them. These are our fellow citizens!" Apparently a government agency like the CDC draws the line at portraying the US military being used to mow down Americans, however zombified. The CDC could proudly annotate its website: "No zombies were harmed in the making of this graphic novel." Unopposed, the zombies smash their way into the gym where the people thought they were safe, and "mass panic ensues as everyone realizes there's no place to run."

Just when things are beginning to look truly grim, Todd wakes up and discovers that all this was just a nightmare, brought on by his having recently watched a horror movie. But the experience has not been in vain. As the story ends, Todd tells Julie: "I've been thinking. . . . We should really make an emergency kit in case something happened. What if we were stuck in the house or had to evacuate? We need to have a plan!" With its use of the "it was all a bad dream" cliché, *Zombie Pandemic* is not going to win any awards at a comic book convention. But it does get across the progovernment message the CDC wishes to promote. Faced with any major disaster, ordinary citizens need to rely on government authorities and institutions to save them, and in particular they must docilely follow official orders. Government scientists will quickly come up with the solution to any catastrophic problem and make sure that it is quickly made available to all citizens. Central planning, especially by government experts, and centralized models of control are the proper response to any crisis. We seem to have traveled back in time to the 1950s, when the faith of Americans in their government was unbounded.

By contrast, in *The Walking Dead,* the characters learn to be skeptical about any orders they receive from people in authority, and they refuse to accept their fate passively. Their first impulse is to fend for themselves and to practice the venerable art of self-defense. As for central planning, season 1 reveals that "the government's plan to herd everyone into the cities was a failure. All it did was provide food for the undead, turning everyone within the city into these creatures."[14] The government's first impulse is always to centralize things, to bring everyone under its control and come up with a single master plan to solve the problem. At first glance, this would seem to be the only way to handle a large-scale disaster. As in *Zombie Pandemic,* a government institution, in this case the CDC, gathers together all the data on the zombie outbreak and scientifically analyzes it in order to come up with the right vaccine. Then the population will be brought together to be inoculated. Only a response centralized at all levels and at all stages seems capable of dealing with the crisis as a whole, and indeed the goal is to find a single, comprehensive solution to the total problem. This certainly sounds like the right idea, but this approach rests on a number of questionable assumptions—that a cure for the plague can be found and found quickly, that production and distribution delays will not prevent the vaccine from being properly administered on time, that the general population will follow the CDC's instructions to the letter and present themselves in an orderly fashion for inoculation, and so on. If any of these assumptions proves to be incorrect, the centralized government approach could make matters much worse and run the risk of exposing the whole population much faster to the zombie virus, as indeed happens in the story *The Walking Dead* tells. Even the CDC's own graphic novel culminates in disaster when the zombies break into the inoculation center. In a strangely candid moment, the CDC admits that even the best of government plans may misfire when put to the test in the real world, with all its unpredictable and uncontrollable elements.[15] The government's "all-or-nothing," "one-size-fits-all" approach becomes a matter of "putting all your eggs in one basket."[16] If the strategy fails, then all is lost, and we are left with a complete disaster.

The Walking Dead suggests that dispersing people rather than concentrating them is the better way to respond to the zombie plague. When scattered into small groups, people are able to pursue a variety of survival strategies and find out which ones work rather than pinning all their hopes on a single plan dictated by the government, which may fail catastrophically. To use a technical term, nomadic existence is antifragile—it makes people more resilient and capable of adapting better to changing conditions.[17] The decentralized response to the zombie plague at first glance might seem not to be a genuine response at all. This approach does not attempt to deal with the problem as a whole or to seek a total solution for it. But if there were a coherent theory behind what amounts to an improvised and instinctive response to the crisis, it might run something like this: "We do not know what caused this plague or what might cure it. All we can do is to survive as long as we can. Maybe the plague will run its course, or maybe a cure will be found someday. The main thing is to stay alive so that some remnant of humanity will be available to repopulate the Earth if it becomes feasible. We must each pursue our own survival strategies, alone or in small groups. The greater the variety of strategies we pursue, the more it is likely that at least some of us will survive. But if we adopt a single, uniform strategy, we risk losing everything." This is the logic that underlies the decision our heroes and heroines in *The Walking Dead* make to take to their RVs, SUVs, motorbikes, and Dale's camper and hit the road.[18] Over the seasons, *The Walking*

Dead has developed a rhythm of episodes of nomadism alternating with episodes of attempted settlement.[19] The show thus follows a pattern familiar in human history. Whenever the characters settle down, they turn to farming to secure for themselves a reliable food supply, but as soon as they have any success, they become prey to roaming bands of predators. These "barbarians" (think of the Saviors) seize their produce and demand more, and they may also try to take over their settlement or destroy it. It says something about *The Walking Dead* that the attempts at settlement always fail and the characters are thrown back upon a nomadic existence to save their lives.[20]

Farms, Prisons, and Gated Communities

In season 2 of *The Walking Dead*, the characters find a refuge, but it is in an isolated farmhouse, presided over by a sort of biblical patriarch. The solution to the crisis seems to be to get as far away as possible from the modern world and all its complex interrelations and institutions. Cut off from interaction with the larger world and retreating into the narrow realm of the nuclear family, the survivors find a momentary peace and even a degree of safety. Given the primitive conditions under which they live, it is almost as if they have journeyed back in time, to the simpler and happier age of nineteenth-century America, when living on a self-contained farm was the typical way of life and an early incarnation of the American dream. As in *Falling Skies*, medicine becomes a marker of where *The Walking Dead* stands on the issue of modernity. The characters of course miss modern medicine and often have to go scavenging in cities for stores of drugs and other medical supplies. But when a boy in the group named Carl is shot, they look to the patriarch, Hershel, to save him. To their shock, Hershel turns out to be a veterinarian, not a board-certified surgeon. But as in *Falling Skies*, the fact that the old man genuinely cares about his patient and is willing to sit up with him all night by his bedside trumps his lack of medical expertise. Once again home medicine beats the big-city hospital. In fact, we see in flashbacks that when the main hero, Sheriff's Deputy Rick Grimes, wakes up from a coma, he finds himself in a hospital at its most hideous, portrayed as a prison-like containment facility for zombies being slaughtered by military forces. In *The Walking Dead*, public health institutions seem to be devoted to imprisoning and annihilating their patients, not curing them. Far from being safe refuges, hospitals appear to be among the most dangerous places to be in *The Walking Dead*.[21]

Zombies eventually overrun the pastoral retreat at the end of season 2 of *The Walking Dead*, and in season 3 the band of survivors (much reduced) finds a new refuge—this time in a prison. An institution originally designed to keep criminals in turns into the best way to keep the zombies out. Season 3 deals with various efforts to move beyond the nuclear family and restore order to society, but they are not portrayed in positive terms. At the end of season 2, Grimes ominously proclaims, "This isn't a democracy anymore," and the specter of autocracy haunts season 3.[22] A prison is obviously not an attractive model of social order; it suggests that the overriding concern for security requires locking down everything and allowing no scope for freedom. Later in season 3, we encounter an alternate model of order, the town of Woodbury, presided over by a character named simply the Governor, the epitome of a smooth-talking southern politician. At first Woodbury seems nice enough, indeed the very model of small-town America. With its southern atmosphere—barbecues on holidays—Woodbury comes across as a re-creation of Andy Griffith's Mayberry. In the third episode of season 3, the Governor says with some pride: "People here have homes, medical care, kids go to school. . . . And people here have jobs. It's a sense of purpose. We have community." It sounds as if government institutions have been reconstituted to good effect, and people are recapturing the old American dream. But we soon discover that Woodbury is a gated community in the bad sense of the term, basically just a prison with a Main Street, USA facade. The armed guards posted to keep the zombies out are also tasked with keeping Woodbury's citizens in, thus maintaining their subjugation to the Governor's arbitrary commands. Once again the price of security is freedom, and the more we learn about the Governor, the more he appears to be a tyrant and a crazed one at that. His obsession with imposing his plans on everybody leads him to kill almost all the people in the town when they fail to carry out his orders to attack Grimes and his associates in the prison. It is the planned community of Woodbury that turns out to be the real prison in season 3 of *The Walking Dead*—and another deathtrap. The character of the Governor reflects the skepticism about governments in *The Walking Dead*—in the name of protecting their citizens, they have a nasty habit of annihilating them.

All attempts to turn to institutions to solve problems in *The Walking Dead* seem to fail. The show suggests that its characters must ultimately rely on themselves and their own resources. Challenging the conventional wisdom that government central planning is the only way to deal with a crisis, the show suggests that, in the face of disaster, even on a massive scale, individual initiative and self-reliance offer the best chance of survival. Our heroes and heroines figure out how best to protect themselves, often improvising solutions, and they become urban explorers, foraging for what they need in abandoned buildings. Their local knowledge stands them in good stead. A young pizza delivery boy named Glenn, who had no status whatsoever in the pre-apocalypse world, becomes the man of the hour. His knowledge of the streets of Atlanta makes him a hero when he skillfully navigates urban environments during resupply missions. In various flashbacks, we learn that, prior to the zombie plague, many of the characters seemed inadequate and unable to take care of themselves. They had all sorts of problems in their relationships. The husbands and wives were generally unhappy in their marriages, with soap opera consequences.[23] Again as in *Falling Skies,* a disaster in material terms proves to have some good results in emotional terms. Under the pressure of the zombie threat, family bonds grow tighter and people learn who their real friends are. On one level, the zombies represent the absence of true humanity, a mass of beings who are brain-dead. They go through the mere motions of living, but their existence is completely meaningless. By contrast, life has become meaningful for the surviving human beings.

As shown in several episodes, the characters have had to make conscious choices to go on living, and thereby they recover a strong sense of purpose in their struggle for survival. Andrew Lincoln, the actor who plays Rick Grimes, commented on his upcoming struggle in season 8 with his archenemy Negan: "Crazy as it sounds, war means hope. Everyone may end up dead, but there's something wonderful and empowering about taking matters into our own hands."[24] With a revitalized sense of purpose, the characters rediscover their sense of community and band together in small units to fight for their survival. As often happens with natural disasters, the zombie apocalypse proves to be the catalyst for ordinary people to become heroes. As executive producer David Alpert said of the role of catastrophe: "Sometimes it brings out the best in people. When people sort of rally together and support each other and come to each other's aid."[25] Again and again, *The Walking Dead* pays tribute to the ability of Americans to work together to deal with the challenges facing them. In his *Democracy in America,* the great French political thinker Alexis de Tocqueville argued that what distinguishes Americans from their Old World forbears is their ability to form associations among themselves that can solve problems in the absence of government intervention. The way the characters in *The Walking Dead* keep forming and reforming alliances against the zombies and their human enemies makes the show deeply Tocquevillian in spirit.[26]

Clinging to Their Guns

Given the survivalist ethic in all of these end-of-the-world shows, they are probably not popular with gun control advocates. One of the most striking motifs they have in common—evident in *Revolution, Falling Skies, The Walking Dead,* and many other such shows—is the loving care with which they depict an astonishing array of weaponry. *The Walking Dead* features an Amazon warrior named

Michonne, who is adept with a samurai sword, as well as a southern redneck named Daryl Dixon, who specializes in a crossbow. The dwindling supply of ammunition puts a premium on weapons that do not require bullets.[27] That is not to say, however, that *The Walking Dead* has no place for modern firearms and indeed the very latest in automatic weapons.[28] Both the heroes and the villains in the series—difficult to tell apart in this respect—are as well armed as the typical municipal SWAT team in contemporary America. The heavy armament in these series goes hand in hand with the militia spirit they embody. In the absence of municipal or state police, as well as the US military, the characters have to protect themselves and need weapons to do so. They band together to secure and patrol their own territories, and whatever order they achieve must be self-imposed.

To some of the characters, clinging to their memories of pre-apocalyptic peaceful times, guns are an unfortunate and last resort. But it is more characteristic of these shows to celebrate the role of guns in the survivors' lives. Being able to use a weapon is the chief marker of status in *The Walking Dead*. At first the need to go armed restores the men to positions of unchallenged leadership, overcoming feminist tendencies in the pre-apocalyptic world (suggested in several flashbacks). In a throwback in human evolution, the men again become the hunter-gatherers, while the women return to household chores.[29] But the gun is actually a great equalizer and is particularly effective in overcoming women's usual disadvantage in physical strength vis-à-vis men. A character named Andrea starts off as a stereotypically weak, dependent woman, but once she learns to shoot—more specifically to *kill* zombies—she is completely transformed into a powerful figure who can take command in difficult situations, even over aggressive males (the same process takes place with several women in the series, including Carol and Maggie). Andrea is emblematic of the overall tendency of *The Walking Dead* to show ordinary people moving from situations of dependence (relying on other people and institutions to save them) to genuine independence (relying only on themselves and each other).

This tendency applies even to children in *The Walking Dead* (as it also does in *Falling Skies*). The young boy Carl wants nothing more than to learn how to shoot a gun, and, although his mother and father are at first hesitant, they allow a family friend to initiate the young boy into the company of trained marksmen. Carl graduates from shooting zombies to taking out fellow human beings, and, in one of the more shocking developments in a series that thrives on shock value, the youngster eventually reaches an elite plateau of cold-bloodedness when he shoots his own mother rather than let her turn into a zombie. Carl is the ultimate example of how the characters in *The Walking Dead* must toughen up or fall by the wayside.

Home on the Firing Range

Carl's father is Rick Grimes, and earlier in the series he gives the boy his lawman's hat. In the February 17, 2013, episode of *The Talking Dead,* a fan discussion show that follows the weekly broadcasts of *The Walking Dead* on AMC, actor-director Kevin Smith cleverly referred to Carl as "Wyatt Twerp." Smith's evocation of a classic Western hero is right on the mark. Beneath all the horror-story gore in *The Walking Dead* beats the heart of a good old-fashioned Western.[30] The show transposes the Wild West to a contemporary setting, reviving the spirit of rugged individualism that Westerns promoted as an antidote to the overly comfortable version of the American dream in the middle of the twentieth century. By stripping away all the institutions that constitute modern civilization, *The Walking Dead* gives us what the Western has traditionally provided in American pop culture—an image of frontier existence, of living on the edge, of seeing what it is like to manage without a settled government, of facing the challenge of protecting oneself and one's family on one's own, of learning the meaning of independence and self-reliance.

The zombies play the stereotypical role traditionally assigned to Indians in Westerns—the barbarian hordes lurking on the borders of the civilized community and threatening to annihilate it. Just like the Indians in many Westerns, the zombies are nameless and virtually faceless, they never speak, and they may be killed indiscriminately. The odyssey of the characters in *The Walking Dead* through the shattered landscape of Georgia and beyond resembles the wagon trains of Westerns, navigating through one danger after another, fighting or negotiating with rival groups, troubled by dwindling supplies, searching in vain for refuge in military outposts that turn out to have been overrun and abandoned, slowed down by stragglers and delayed by searches for lost comrades, torn by disputes over their destination and other challenges to their leaders, dealing with childbirth or other medical emergencies on the fly—the list of parallels goes on and on. As for the vicious assortment of robbers, rapists, and murderers who repeatedly assail our heroes and heroines in *The Walking Dead,* they correspond to the bad guys who populate Westerns. People have been lamenting the closing of the frontier throughout American history. Zombie tales and other apocalyptic scenarios turn out to be a way of imaginatively reopening the frontier in twenty-first-century popular culture.[31]

In the end, then, all these apocalyptic shows are re-creations of that most basic of American genres, the Western. The "Westernization" of end-of-the-world narratives is made clear by their use of the central symbol of the genre: the horse. In an iconic moment—arguably the money shot of the whole series—Sheriff's Deputy Rick Grimes rides into plague-ravaged Atlanta alone on a horse.[32] More generally, horses become a frequent mode of transportation in *The Walking Dead*, as well as in other apocalyptic series, such as *Revolution*. As professional survivalists have pointed out, this makes no sense. In a postapocalyptic world, in the absence of readily available and gassed-up automobiles, the logical mode of transportation becomes the bicycle. Horses represent a net loss in a postapocalyptic economy with its severely reduced food supplies. Horses have to be fed, thus diverting resources from human consumption, and they could become food themselves for their hungry owners (this is something that the otherwise dumb zombies quickly realize—unlike humans, they eat horses rather than try to ride them). There is no economic logic to the continued use of horses in the world of *The Walking Dead*, but of course it has a powerful symbolic value as a sign that the characters have returned to a premodern and frontier existence, which is to say a Western one. A character in *Falling Skies* says of the postapocalyptic environment: "It's the Wild West out there." The 2011 film *Cowboys and Aliens* explicitly unites the Western and the alien invasion narrative. Once we realize that contemporary end-of-the-world scenarios share with Westerns the goal of imaginatively returning their characters to the state of nature, we can see how the American nightmare can turn into the American dream when rampaging aliens or zombies descend upon a quiet American suburb. The dream of material prosperity and security is shattered, but a different ideal comes back to life—the all-American ideal of rugged individualism—the spirit of freedom, independence, and self-reliance.[33]

The Rehabilitation of the Redneck

The "Western" character of these end-of-the-world narratives is reflected in the fact that the apocalypse generally returns people to a rural setting, or at least uproots them from the urban setting in which they grew up. The popularity of the Western in mid-twentieth-century popular culture was a reaction to the increasing urbanization of America during this period. In the nineteenth century, the family farm had been at the center of the American dream, and twentieth-century Westerns drew their power from nostalgia, from an urge to go back vicariously to an earlier and simpler time, when American life was based on frontier values. In the twentieth century, much of popular culture, including gangster movies and crime dramas, embodied rural suspicions about the new urban way of life. When the Western exhausted itself as a genre—if for no other reason than overproduction—popular culture turned to variants of it— the zombie narrative, for example, as we have seen in the case of *The Walking Dead*. The series champions rural values over urban values. It suggests that life is healthier, safer, and just better all around when people are living dispersed, and human existence is at its worst when people are crammed together in big cities.³⁴ The main characters are constantly tempted to aggregate into larger groupings, but every community they are drawn to turns out to be a hellish trap. In season 4, they seek salvation at a place called "Terminus," but when they finally arrive there, they discover that they have been lured by the promise of safety into a community of cannibals, and they are on the menu. Later the main characters encounter a group of people who call themselves the Saviors, led by a deranged tyrant named Negan. In their efforts to restore normalcy, the Saviors have reinstituted industrialization, putting enslaved people to work in a factory. In *The Walking Dead,* every step away from isolated rural life to congregated urban life is presented as a disaster. Evil appears to dwell in the city, and good flourishes only in the country.

It is no accident, then, that one of the most popular characters in *The Walking Dead* is the redneck Daryl—he of the crossbow and the motorbike. *The Walking Dead* is the anti-*Deliverance.* For decades the rural South has been the butt of Hollywood jokes or the site of its most gruesome horror stories. It was not always that way. For roughly the first half of the twentieth century, Hollywood had catered to Middle America, and in particular had romanticized the rural South (think, *Gone with the Wind* or Disney's *Song of the South*). Movies and then television shows celebrated the small town and its middle-class virtues, while often picturing cities as riddled with crime and corruption. A TV show like *Mayberry RFD* presented southerners as the best neighbors in the world. The sitcom *Beverly Hillbillies* dealt with hicks from the South moving to the heart of the entertainment industry in Los Angeles, and they were portrayed as moral innocents at the mercy of city slickers, although the country people, with their folk wisdom, tended to outwit the urban sophisticates who tried to take advantage of them.

This positive view of the rural South in popular culture began to change, in some cases as early as the 1940s and 1950s, as a result of many developments, chief among them the civil rights movement. The South began to be viewed as the most backward and unenlightened region of the United States, the home of ignorance, racial prejudice, religious bigotry, and superstition. In popular culture, the lynch mob became a potent image of the South.³⁵ If southerners were not taken seriously as the greatest threat to the civil rights of minorities and generally presented as living in the Dark Ages, they were ridiculed as country bumpkins, incapable of dealing with the complexities of modern life. Even as ethnic stereotypes in humor were being proscribed as politically incorrect, redneck jokes began to flourish, as witness Jeff Foxworthy and his "You Might Be a Redneck If" routines. *Deliverance* was only the most powerful exemplar of Hollywood's dark vision of the rural South. Four men from Atlanta leave the safety of the city and civilization and enter the world of dueling banjos, only to find that they have undertaken a nightmarish journey into the heart of darkness, Georgia-style. By contrast, in *The Walking Dead*, the heart of darkness is in Atlanta, and the shining light is Hershel's farm in the remote Georgia countryside.

The Walking Dead is thus part of a reaction to an earlier reaction against the South, and might be viewed as an attempt to restore balance to the portrayal of the rural South—and rural America in general—in popular culture. To be sure, Daryl's brother Merle looks as if he had just stepped out of *Deliverance*. He is Daryl's evil twin—violent, cruel, vicious, and bigoted. But Merle is generally the odd man out among the cast of *The Walking Dead*, and even he earns some sympathy eventually and redeems himself at the time of his death. The show participates in a general rehabilitation of the redneck in American popular culture. This development has been evident in perhaps the oddest corner of popular culture, reality TV. In this category, one show after another has centered on a rural subculture: *Duck Dynasty, Mountain Men, Swamp People, Ax Men, Ice Road Truckers, Gold Rush,* and my favorite in terms of title, *Gods, Guns, and Automobiles* (the redneck's holy trinity).[36] These programs dramatize ways of life quite foreign to the urban sophisticates who generally create movies and TV shows. They celebrate such politically incorrect virtues as manliness, marksmanship, and the ability to fix a car engine with one's bare hands.

These shows may well have been developed by urban sophisticates to make fun of the rural subcultures ("Look how ridiculous these rubes are!"), but their surprising success with audiences and their endless proliferation indicate something quite different. Americans evidently like what they see on these shows, responding favorably to contemporary versions of the old frontier virtues traditionally chronicled in Westerns. Reality TV offers viewers a dramatic alternative to the comfortable but boring lives they lead in middle-class America. Pent up in their office cubicles, leading a nine-to-five existence, people enjoy watching Americans in remote and exotic places like the Louisiana bayou or the Bering Strait. These intrepid characters confront nature in all its wildness, battling the elements, as well as alligators or grizzly bears. When your biggest challenge is combating a computer virus, watching someone struggling with something a little more elemental provides a vicarious thrill. These shows generally portray the very opposite of urban sophisticates—they give us people down on their luck, often trying to eke out a bare living, armed only with traditional family values and religious beliefs (and perhaps a couple of guns). The heroes and heroines are often rugged individualists, proving that they can be self-reliant and live off the grid, doing without the sophisticated technologies that have come to seem necessary in the modern world. The technology that does appear in these shows seems positively archaic by contemporary standards: chain saws, drill bits, fishing nets, backhoes, and tractor trailers. This is technology that requires more brawn than brains to operate it. One reason we secretly admire the characters on these shows is that they can make real machines work and most of us could not. In any kind of postapocalyptic scenario, most human beings would be at a loss to keep all the machines on which their lives ultimately depend in working order. On both reality TV shows and programs like *The Walking* Dead, urban sophisticates see their world turned upside down—the working-class types they normally disdain becomes objects of awe for their competence in the material world.[37] There is something almost archaeological about these programs, as if they were offering fleeting glimpses of corners of the old America that are fast vanishing in the wake of modernity.

Red States versus Blue States

This group of reality shows, together with all the postapocalyptic narratives, embodies important political trends in contemporary America as well. The shows reflect the great political divide that has opened up in America, encapsulated in such terms as "Red States versus Blue States" or "Flyover America versus Coastal America." From their command posts in New York and Los Angeles, urban elites have been in charge of the entertainment industry for many decades. A show such as *The Walking Dead* represents a pushback against the entertainment establishment, even if it had to be produced by elements within that establishment.[38] Television needs to appeal to a mass audience, and evidently there is still a market in Middle America for a show that celebrates Middle American values, especially independence rather than dependence on government. We have seen that people began to lose faith in the American dream when they came to lose faith in the elites who were supposed to guide them to the fulfillment of that dream. *The Walking Dead* is deeply suspicious of elites, of anyone who claims the right to rule over the mass of ordinary people, whether it be scientists at the CDC or would-be autocratic politicians such as the Governor or Negan.

In season 5, *The Walking Dead* found an effective way to dramatize the conflict between the elites and the masses in contemporary America. Having escaped Terminus, and still looking to the federal government to solve their problems, our heroes and heroines set their sights on Washington, DC, in the belief that surely their wise rulers must by now have found a cure for the zombie plague.[39] Just as they get a glimpse of the Washington Monument and the Capitol Building, the band is sidetracked into another possible safe haven—Alexandria, Virginia. They are invited into a literally gated community in this DC suburb, and they join it in the hope of being protected from the zombie-infected countryside around them. Renamed the Alexandria Safe-Zone, this suburban town is the perfect Blue State community—it has gun control, a gay couple, solar power, and no capital punishment. When the zombie apocalypse broke out, the army directed a group of federal government insiders to safety in this suburban redoubt. Alexandria offers a powerful image of the isolation of the DC elite, the way these government functionaries are insulated from the problems affecting the heartland of the country. They live in a world of privilege, far beyond the means of the average citizen—homes in this planned community were advertised as "starting in the low $800,000s." Shielded from the threats the average American faces, the Washington elite are able to continue to live their lives the way they did before the apocalypse. While ordinary Americans are out battling zombies just to stay alive, these members of the elite still hold cocktail parties, where they serve white wine and exchange gourmet recipes. When one of our heroines goes out to hunt wild boar, one of the Alexandrians asks her if she can have a leg from which to make prosciutto.

Alexandria is presided over by a woman named Deanna Monroe, who is very different from the autocratic types who rule elsewhere, such as the Governor or Negan. At least she is a democratically elected official, a congressperson, she explains, from the Fifteenth District in Ohio. Although it is never specified, she seems to be an Obama Democrat. When she interviews our band of survivors, she films the proceedings, reassuring them, "We're about transparency here," and thus echoing President Obama's promise to run the most transparent administration in history.[40] Deanna sees the zombie apocalypse as an opportunity to initiate her political plans for the future. She describes Alexandria as environmentally friendly: "This is the start of sustainability." The town is now operating on a solar grid, and it has instituted ecobase sewage filtration. When Rick remarks on the fact that Deanna has given jobs to everyone in his group, she shows her true colors by laughing and saying, "It looks like the Communists won after all." Alexandria is very progressive. Looking beyond the zombie apocalypse, Deanna has a vision of the future. She is sure that "there's going to be a government here one day," and she adds, "I see a vibrant community here" with "industry, commerce, civilization." Undoubtedly, she intends to regulate all three.

Naturally Deanna has instituted a strict gun control policy within the borders of Alexandria. As repeatedly happens with our heroes and heroines, the first thing they have to do when they enter this new community is to turn over their guns, the very weapons that have so often saved their lives in the world of the zombie apocalypse. Deanna reassures them, "They're still your guns," and adds, "We store them for safety," but how can Rick and the crew be sure of that? Soon even the warrior Michonne is hanging up her trusty samurai sword on the wall above her fireplace as an ornament. Our band of survivors is nervous about giving up their weapons, and they worry that their new comfortable surroundings will make them grow soft. The intrepid Carol, one of the toughest of the survivors, expresses her fear: "If we get comfortable here, let our guard down, this place is gonna make us weak." But despite these reservations, our survivors are seduced by the material benefits of modern civilization. As Rick Grimes says, "Electricity, showers, haircuts: I never thought I'd see those again." He recalls the days when he and his wife used to drive through upscale neighborhoods like Alexandria and imagine that one day they might live in such opulence. Enchanted again by the American dream of suburban life, our heroes and heroines are willing to trade their independence and self-reliance—represented by their guns—for tract houses with all the latest appliances in a gated community. They have been living in the Wild West, and now they are settling down in a community where the children name a horse "Buttons."

The Alexandria sequence portrays what amounts to the culture clash between Red State and Blue State America. Having lived through a Hobbesian war of all against all in the outside world, our survivors have a hard time adjusting to a peaceful life within the DC Beltway. Alexandria is a marvelous image for what has been called the Beltway Bubble, the cocoon within which the Washington elite live in isolation from the troubles with which most ordinary Americans have to deal. The actress who plays Deanna (Tovah Feldshuh) captures perfectly the smugness, self-righteousness, and "holier-than-thou" attitude of elitist politicians in DC. Despite her liberal convictions, she is quick to shut down any opinions that dissent from her orthodoxy: "That sort of thinking doesn't belong in here." Our survivors have a hard time coping with their new conditions. Suffering from varying degrees of PTSD, they look bewildered when they have to make small talk at a standard Beltway cocktail party. It is as if they have wandered into a completely different world, and in a way they have. They keep wondering which of the two worlds is the real one. Indeed, the Alexandria sequence suggests that Americans are now living in two different worlds, one for the elites, one for the masses.

The show sets up the greatest culture clash of all when redneck Daryl teams up with a gay couple named Aaron and Eric. Their encounter is presented evenhandedly and subtly. Gay couples are of course in theory accepted in liberal Alexandria, but Aaron tells Daryl, "Eric and I—we're still looked at as outsiders." Daryl may never have met an openly gay couple before, but he does not react the way a stereotypical redneck would. Instead, Aaron's confession creates a bond between Daryl and his new neighbors. As a redneck, he is equally an outsider in the world of urban sophistication. He might as well be from an alien planet. When Daryl says, "I ride bikes," Aaron replies, "I take it you don't mean ten-speeds." Here is the culture clash in miniature: Daryl would be a fan of Motocross; Aaron and Eric would follow the Tour de France. Finally,

Aaron invites Daryl to dinner. In the most awkward and yet poignant moment in the sequence, Aaron and Eric look on with amused condescension as Daryl slurps up the spaghetti and wipes his mouth on his sleeve. This is a complex moment. We share the mild contempt these urban sophisticates cannot help feeling for the uncouth Daryl, who for once shows up, even to us viewers, as a stereotypically crude redneck. But we must remember that it is tough men like Daryl who survive in this postapocalyptic world, and it is tough men like Daryl who are needed to protect the civilized but helpless citizens of Alexandria.[41] Indeed, moments later, Aaron asks Daryl to assemble a motorbike from parts he has been collecting. Shades of reality TV—the urban sophisticate has no idea how the parts fit together and must rely on a redneck grease monkey to do the job for him.

The Alexandrians may be politically progressive, but they are unable to protect themselves. Safe behind their walls, they have not had to come to terms with what the zombie apocalypse really means, and they are too quick to look beyond a dangerous situation that shows no signs of ending soon. They just do not know how cruel the outside world has become and what challenges they now face. As the gruff soldier, Sgt. Abraham Ford, tells the townspeople, "There's a vast ocean of shit that you people don't know shit about." Even young Carl sees what is lacking in the Alexandrians and worries about joining the community; he tells his father, "They're weak—and I don't want us to get weak too." Rick sees the advantages of settling in Alexandria and is willing to make compromises to do so, but he has no illusions about the situation. He tells his followers, "If [the Alexandrians] can't make it, then we'll just take this place." And in the Hobbesian world of *The Walking Dead,* that is just what happens. Rick gets into a vicious fight with the town doctor, Peter Anderson, because the doctor has been abusing his wife (with whom Rick has grown friendly). Deanna and the Alexandrians take the doctor's side, partly because they need his services and partly because Rick is just too belligerent for them. Deanna's husband, Reg, expresses the typical prejudice of city dwellers against the rural population—they are throwbacks to a violent past. Reacting to Rick, Reg rejects nomadism in the name of civilization: "The cavemen—they were all nomads and they all died; then we evolved into this and we lived. Civilization starts when we stop running—when we live together." The Alexandrians in effect put Rick on trial and are on the verge of exiling him, when the doctor goes berserk, and in an attempt to get at Rick, kills Deanna's husband instead.

Fortunately, Rick has violated the town's gun control regulations and is armed and ready to deal with the murderous doctor. Abandoning her liberal principles, Deanna says simply, "Rick, do it," and he executes Anderson on the spot. In the terms of the series, this is a cathartic moment. The DC elites have proven unable to keep the peace in their own community, and they must yield authority to the sheriff's deputy from the backwoods of Georgia. In the end, in *The Walking Dead* the spirit of the Wild West triumphs over the spirit of Beltway liberalism. The federal government elite cannot save the common citizen; the common citizen is needed to save the federal government elite. That may be the ultimate fantasy in the zombie apocalypse narrative, a fantasy of the empowerment of the ordinary citizen in a world long dominated—and poorly run—by a government elite. If you are wondering why a macabre series like *The Walking Dead* has become so popular, consider this possibility: the show managed to capture and express the frustration of the American people in the second decade of the twenty-first century. Wherever they look, the American people think they are seeing their world going to hell in a handbasket, and when they turn to their leaders for aid and comfort—their cultural, scientific, and above all their political leaders—they are met with deaf ears. The elites seem content to remain in their comfortable bubbles, enjoying their privileged lifestyle and congratulating themselves on their cultural superiority, while ordinary Americans have to deal with the genuine problems of the everyday world. *The Walking Dead* evidently strikes a responsive chord in its audience when it celebrates the resilience and self-reliance of ordinary Americans who are not turning to anyone else to solve their problems but instead taking their destiny into their own hands.

The way that American popular culture has increasingly turned to nightmarish end-of-the-world scenarios seems at first truly odd, especially the persistent fantasy of the disappearance of the federal government. One might have thought that the Civil War had settled the issue of secession once and for all in the United States. It is, then, very strange that the dissolution of the nation-state into smaller units has become a common nightmare/dream scenario in American popular culture. Several years before secession emerged as a serious issue in states like California, it surfaced in popular culture. In *Revolution,* for example, postapocalyptic America is divided into rival republics, and the series culminates in the ultimate battle between the Red States and the Blue States, as the Republic of Texas manages to defeat the Republic of California. Another variant of this motif was provided by the short-lived TV series *Last Resort,* in which an American navy submarine in effect secedes from the United States when it disobeys suspicious orders from Washington.[42] With its full complement of nuclear weapons, the sub possesses one of the chief components of national sovereignty these days and indeed uses its armament to maintain its independence in the face of all the forces arrayed against it (finally succumbing only to the ultimate power in the television universe—network cancellation). Perhaps it now takes the likes of rogue nuclear subs, inhuman aliens, and implacable zombies to shake us out of our complacency and suggest that we may have been sacrificing fundamental American values in our quest for material goods and security. In our rush to achieve these goals, we may have surrendered our freedom to the shackles of a web of institutions, the prison house of the administered world. *The Walking Dead, Falling Skies,* and other postapocalyptic narratives may be warning us against a graver danger than mere zombies and alien invaders.

NOTES

Introduction

Epigraph: James Truslow Adams, "America Faces 1933's Realities," *New York Times,* January 1, 1933, SM1, qtd. in Lawrence R. Samuel, *The American Dream: A Cultural History* (Syracuse: Syracuse University Press, 2012), 13. Adams offers as good a definition of the "American dream" as anybody. As surprising as it may sound, his 1931 book *The Epic of America* introduced the phrase "American dream" into public discourse.

1. The American dream is at least as old as the Declaration of Independence, with its talk of "life, liberty, and the pursuit of happiness." For good and compact surveys of the various meanings and incarnations of the "American dream," see Samuel, *American Dream;* and Jim Cullen, *The American Dream: A Short History of an Idea That Shaped a Nation* (New York: Oxford University Press, 2003). For a good bibliography of writings on the subject, see Lawrence R. Samuel, "The American Dream: A Bibliographical Review," *Hedgehog Review* 15, no. 2 (Summer 2013): 57–65. For the specific issue of the "self-made man" and the American dream, see Jim Cullen, "Problems and Promises of the Self-Made Man Myth" in the same issue, 23–33.

2. I am aware of the irony that *Shark Tank,* however all-American it presents itself, is based on foreign models; it began as *Tigers of Money* in Japan and then turned into *Dragons' Den* in Britain and Canada, before finally coming to the United States under its new name in 2009.

3. For this understanding of the Western, see especially the chapter "Order Out of the Mud: *Deadwood* and the State of Nature" in my book *The Invisible Hand in Popular Culture: Liberty vs. Authority in American Film and TV* (Lexington: University Press of Kentucky, 2012), 97–127, 381–88. For a thought-provoking essay that relates *Breaking Bad* to Hobbes, "state of nature" thinking, the Western, and Mafia stories, see James Bowman, "Criminal Elements," *New Atlantis* 38 (Winter/Spring 2013): 163–73.

4. For Milch, see the *Deadwood* chapter, and for Ford, see the chapter "The Western and Western Drama: John Ford's *The Searchers* and the *Oresteia*," in Cantor, *Invisible Hand,* 31–57, 364–72.

5. See the chapter "The Original Frontier: Gene Roddenberry's Apprenticeship for *Star Trek* in *Have Gun—Will Travel*" in Cantor, *Invisible Hand,* 59–95, 373–81.

6. See the chapters "*Mars Attacks!* Tim Burton and the Ideology of the Flying Saucer Movie" and "Un-American Gothic: The Alien Invasion Narrative and Global Modernity" in Cantor, *Invisible Hand,* 137–66, 388–95, 299–347, 419–33.

7. Qtd. in Dennis Thompson, ed., *Breaking Bad: The Official Book* (New York: Sterling, 2015), 23.

8. Alan Sepinwall gives a moral reading of *Breaking Bad* in his book on the subject. Yet at one point he lets slips a very different reaction to the show, involving the moment when Jesse kills Gale and thereby frustrates Gus and Mike's scheme to replace Walt as the meth manufacturer (the complicated details of this situation will become clearer in chapter 5): "Watching it the first time, I was so damn happy to see someone finally wipe that look of bland certainty off of Mike's face that I briefly put aside the moral implications of what Jesse was being sent to do" (Alan Sepinwall, *Breaking Bad 101: The Complete Critical Companion* [New York: Abrams, 2017], 139). Why does Sepinwall simply dismiss his initial—and honest—reaction to Jesse's helping Walt outfox his opponents? I had the same reaction, as I am sure many viewers did. Television shows do *not* simply engage our moral faculties; they also engage our aesthetic and intellectual faculties, and we can react to these shows on several levels simultaneously. We take pleasure in a good *plot* in both senses of the term ("story" and "criminal scheme"). In real life, we may have to let morality settle all issues for us, but one function of fiction is to allow us to indulge our nonmoral reactions for a change. We may rejoice when we watch a fictional criminal get away with something; perhaps it is a case of, "I wish I could get rid of my problems so easily." Sepinwall provides a cautionary tale—we should not simply replace our immediate gut reactions to a show with later, more abstract, critical reflections. The gut reaction is probably the reason why we watched the show in the first place—and the reason why we enjoy it. The gut reaction is integral to a full understanding of the impact and meaning of the show. You can bet that the show's creators set out to produce that gut reaction; whether they had any moral conclusions in mind is another question.

9. This was, for example, a theme of the television series *Fantasy Island,* in which, week after week, people would get to act out their lifelong fantasies, only to realize that they would be better off back in their everyday existence.

1. Aristocracy in America

Epigraph: Qtd. in Catherine Zuckert, *Natural Right and the American Imagination: Political Philosophy in Novel Form* (Savage, MD: Rowman and Littlefield, 1990), 152 (this passage is from Twain's *Autobiography*).

1. Mark Twain, *Adventures of Huckleberry Finn,* ed. Sculley Bradley, Richmond Croom Beatty, and E. Hudson Long, eds. (New York: Norton, 1961), 307. The passage is from Pritchett's essay "*Huckleberry Finn*: The Cruelty of American Humor" (originally published in 1941 in *New Statesman and Nation*).

2. Mark Twain, *Adventures of Huckleberry Finn,* ed. Emory Elliott (Oxford: Oxford University Press, 1999), 92. Hereafter page citations to this work will be given parenthetically in the chapter text.

3. Twain, *Huckleberry Finn,* ed. Bradley, Beatty, and Long, 307.

4. In chapter 2 we will see how W. C. Fields dealt with this issue in his brief film *The Fatal Glass of Beer.*

5. Twain develops this idea in *A Connecticut Yankee in King Arthur's Court.* Confronted with the power of the Catholic Church in medieval England, the Yankee condemns the idea of an established church and wants to break it up to create a free market in religion: "My idea is to have it cut up into forty free sects, so that they will police each other, as had been the case in the United States in my time. Concentration of power in a political machine is bad; and an Established Church is only a political machine" (Mark Twain, *A Connecticut Yankee in King Arthur's Court,* ed. M. Thomas Inge [Oxford: Oxford University Press, 1997], 216).

6. Twain was an entrepreneur himself, and not just in his successful career as a literary celebrity, in which he exploited all the advantages offered by the modern media. Even before he became Mark Twain, he was involved in a number of nineteenth-century America's booming businesses, including the Mississippi riverboat industry (he was a successful riverboat pilot) and the Nevada silver rush (he was an unsuccessful prospector and miner). Twain was fascinated by inventions and even patented a few himself. He made millions of dollars over the years, but unfortunately he lost millions investing in a mechanical typesetter called the Paige Compositor. His career as a publisher also followed a rags-to-riches-back-to-rags pattern. He made a fortune publishing *Huckleberry Finn* with his own company and also had a gigantic bestseller with Ulysses S. Grant's memoirs. Unfortunately, a number of publishing failures forced Twain to declare bankruptcy in 1894. In sum, in his own life Twain experienced both the bright side and the dark side of the American dream. With his long and varied career and his manifold achievements, Twain might lay claim to being *the* representative American of the nineteenth century.

7. Twain's own family was not immune to this fascination: "Both his father, John Marshall Clemens, and his mother, Jane Lampton Clemens, were third-generation Americans whose families had arrived in the colonies by the mid-18th century. Like many Americans, they proudly claimed an aristocratic heritage, including membership in the tribunal that sentenced Charles I to death, earls of Dunham, and first families of Virginia. Their actual relations to these figures were dubious at best" (Ranjit S. Dighe, ed., *The Historian's Huck Finn* [Santa Barbara, CA: Praeger, 2016], 1).

8. See Zuckert, *Natural Right,* 131, on "the ridicule of aristocratic pretensions" as the goal of *Huckleberry Finn.* For Twain's attack on "the pseudo-aristocratic society of the antebellum South," see Richard F. Adams, "The Unity and Coherence of *Huckleberry Finn,*" in *Huckleberry Finn,* ed. Bradley, Beatty, and Long, 342–57.

9. See Zuckert, *Natural Right,* 144: "like their feudal Scottish ancestors—these 'aristocrats' prefer clan loyalty to civic justice."

10. Twain's critique of Scott appears in chapters 40 and 46 of his *Life on the Mississippi* (Mineola, NY: Dover, 2000): "Then comes Sir Walter Scott with his enchantments, and by his single might checks this wave of progress, and even turns it back, sets the world in love with dreams and phantoms, with decayed and degraded systems of government; with the silliness and emptiness, sham grandeurs, sham gauds, and sham

chivalries of brainless and worthless long-vanished societies" (208). Condemning Scott's "maudlin Middle-Age romanticism" (105), Twain held the British novelist "in great measure responsible for the [American Civil] war" (209). For Twain's critique of Walter Scott and aristocracy, and their connections to the issue of slavery, see also David Foster, "Reason, Sentiment, and Equality in *Adventures of Huckleberry Finn*," *American Political Thought* 6 (2017): 404–6.

11. Zuckert draws a contrast between Tom and Huck in this regard: "Tom's antics parody aristocratic romances; Huck speaks of down-to-earth democratic skepticism" (*Natural Right,* 137). For the final sequence of *Huckleberry Finn* as Twain's effort "to 'kill' romanticism," see Thomas Arthur Gullason, "The 'Fatal' Ending of *Huckleberry Finn*," in *Huckleberry Finn,* ed. Bradley, Beatty, and Long, 357–61.

12. For further discussion of Twain's views on democracy versus aristocracy and on the relation of America to England, see my essay "Yankee Go Home: Twain's Postcolonial Romance," in *Democracy's Literature: Politics and Fiction in America,* ed. Patrick J. Deneen and Joseph Romance (Lanham, MD: Rowman and Littlefield, 2005), 31–60.

13. Mark Twain, *The Mysterious Stranger,* ed. William M. Gibson (Berkeley: University of California Press, 1969), 165. *The Chronicle of Young Satan* is one of the manuscript fragments published after Twain's death as part of *The Mysterious Stranger;* it was written between 1897 and 1900. For an explanation of the complicated status of this manuscript, see Gibson's introduction, 1–11.

14. Twain, *Mysterious Stranger,* ed. Gibson, 165–66.

2. The Talented Mr. Dukenfield

Epigraph: Variants of this quotation have been attributed to George Burns, Groucho Marx, Samuel Goldwyn, Jean Giraudoux, and many others. The ultimate source is unknown. But it sounds like something W. C. Fields could have said (see www.reddit .com/r/quotes/comments/4rtyva/the_most_important_thing_in_show_businesss_is/ and https://quoteinvestigator.com/2011/12/05/fake-honesty/).

1. For an analysis of how this logic plays out in the nineteenth-century novel, see René Girard, *Deceit, Desire, and the Novel,* trans. Yvonne Freccero (Baltimore: Johns Hopkins University Press, 1965). Girard's theory of "mimetic desire" is perfectly illustrated by *Being John Malkovich.* We look up to our celebrity idols so much that we want to be them in the most ordinary details of their lives, or, rather, the ordinary details of their lives become extraordinary to us because they are celebrities. On the connections between postmodernism and democracy, see my essay "*Waiting for Godot* and the End of History: Postmodernism as a Democratic Aesthetic," in *Democracy and the Arts,* ed. Arthur Melzer, Jerry Weinberger, and Richard Zinman (Ithaca: Cornell University Press, 1999), 172–92, 201–6.

2. Qtd. in Simon Louvish, *Man on the Flying Trapeze: The Life and Times of W. C. Fields* (New York: Norton, 1997), 468. Portions of this chapter were originally published in a review of Louvish's book in the *Weekly Standard,* February 21, 2000, 29–33. I have relied heavily on Louvish's excellent biography for the facts of Fields's life, as well as

on Louvish's central thesis that Fields "was forever inventing and re-inventing himself" (10); his life is "an actor's tale, the story of a creative artist whose greatest creation was himself, a fully achieved, imaginary person, who completely subsumed his creator" (12).

3. See, in particular, the chapter "The Culture Industry: Enlightenment as Mass Deception" in Max Horkheimer and Theodor W. Adorno, *Dialectic of Enlightenment*, trans. John Cumming (New York: Continuum, 1986).

4. Louvish, *Flying Trapeze*, 28.

5. Louvish, *Flying Trapeze*, 9, 15, 474.

6. Louvish, *Flying Trapeze*, 34.

7. Louvish, *Flying Trapeze*, 51.

8. As we saw in *Huckleberry Finn*, Mark Twain also satirized con men who use stories of moral reformation to extract money from a gullible public.

9. Louvish, *Flying Trapeze*, 343.

10. Louvish, *Flying Trapeze*, 282.

11. On this point, see Simon Louvish, *It's a Gift* (London: British Film Institute, 1994), 20. Louvish points out that, in the true spirit of the American entrepreneur, Fields "actually patented his own original sketches, such as his golf skit, listed as 'Copyright Number 109' on 4 November 1918" (25).

12. We can see how carefully Fields worked on the final cut of *The Bank Dick* by examining his notes to the studio concerning the preview of the film, printed in the volume of his writings assembled by his grandson, Ronald Fields, *W. C. Fields by Himself* (New York: Warner, 1974). After detailing which scenes needed to be cut and which restored, Fields ends with a not-so-veiled threat to the studio: "However, if some kind of adjustment cannot be arrived at I shall reluctantly insist upon the clause where it is agreed we each pick a judge and mutually agree upon a third person to decide" (467).

13. Louvish, *Flying Trapeze*, 451.

14. I have transcribed all quotations from Fields's films from the DVD versions.

15. Louvish aptly describes Bissonette: "Inside the small-town failure, J. P. Morgan struggles to spring out, to realize the American dream" (Louvish, *It's a Gift*, 47).

16. Fields enjoyed making fun of any sort of aristocratic pretension, which he, like Twain, associates with claiming European roots. We have already seen that Egbert Sousé insists on a French pronunciation of his name. In *It's a Gift*, the social-climbing Mrs. Bissonette similarly points out to everybody that her name should be pronounced "BissoNAY."

17. With their hope springing eternal, Fields's heroes resemble the character of Mr. Micawber in Dickens's *David Copperfield* and his principle of "something will turn up." An avid reader of Dickens, Fields to some extent modeled his comic persona on Mr. Micawber (Louvish, *Flying Trapeze*, 122–23). He was thus perfectly positioned to play the role in the 1935 George Cukor film of *David Copperfield*, and he delivered one of his greatest performances on screen. Louvish points out: "His only regret in the part was Dickens' foolish omission of a poolroom scene" (389). Once again we are faced with a vertiginous postmodern spiral—a real man, W. C. Fields, is playing the cinematic reproduction of a character out of a book, a character on whom he had based his stage persona in the first place.

18. In his notes on the preview, Fields immodestly said, "The chase I thought the best I have ever seen" (Ronald Fields, *Fields by Himself,* 467).

19. Ever ahead of his time, Fields thus anticipated the faux presidential runs of comedian Pat Paulsen in 1968, 1972, 1980, 1988, 1992, and 1996.

20. W. C. Fields, *Fields for President,* with commentary by Michael M. Taylor (New York: Dodd, Mead, 1973), 23.

21. Louvish, *Flying Trapeze,* 431.

22. Fields, *President,* 10–12.

23. Fields, *President,* 20.

24. Fields, *President,* 47.

25. Louvish, *Flying Trapeze,* 103–4.

26. Louvish, *Flying Trapeze,* 350–51.

27. Fields, *President,* 45.

28. Louvish, *Flying Trapeze,* 351.

29. See Louvish, *Flying Trapeze,* 411–13, for more on Fields's making fun of the New Deal and labor unions. In a more serious context, the threat of a union shutting down a Hollywood production comes up again in Coppola's *The Godfather I,* as part of Don Corleone's plot to get Johnny Fontane a part in a movie.

30. Louvish, *Flying Trapeze,* 312–13.

31. Louvish, *Flying Trapeze,* 308–9. For what purports to be a transcript of Fields's trial for avicide, see Ronald Fields, *Fields by Himself,* 94–117.

32. Louvish, *Flying Trapeze,* 439. For Fields's full letter to Breen, see Ronald Fields, *Fields by Himself,* 447.

33. Louvish, *Flying Trapeze,* 461.

34. Louvish, *Flying Trapeze,* 461.

3. "I Believe in America"

Epigraph: Qtd. in Tom Santopietro, *The Godfather Effect: Changing Hollywood, America, and Me* (New York: St. Martin's, 2012), 58–59.

1. All quotation from the *Godfather* films, including deleted scenes, have been transcribed from the DVDs, and sometimes checked against other sources.

2. For an excellent and extended analysis of this opening scene along similar lines, see Paul A. Rahe, "Don Corleone, Multiculturalist," *Business & Professional Ethics Journal* 16 (1997): 133–39.

3. This contrast was formulated by Ferdinand Tönnies in his 1887 book *Gemeinschaft und Gesellschaft.* For an English translation, see *Community and Society,* trans. Charles P. Loomis (East Lansing: Michigan State University Press, 1957). Fredric Jameson brings up the *Gemeinschaft/Gesellschaft* contrast in his discussion of the *Godfather* films in his famous essay "Reification and Utopia in Mass Culture," *Signatures of the Visible* (London: Routledge, 1992), 44.

4. The idea of the "movement from Status to Contract" was first formulated by Sir Henry Maine at the end of chapter 5 of his famous book *Ancient Law* (1861).

5. In a review of the return of *The Godfather I* to movie theaters in 1997, Edward Rothstein summed up its core theme: "*The Godfather* hit upon one of the great themes of American life in this century, the challenge of becoming American. . . . How is the passage to be made from family to society, from ethnic culture to American life, from the bonds of blood to bonds of citizenship?" ("Chilling Balance of Love and Evil," *New York Times,* March 23, 1997).

6. On this point, see Carl Freedman, *Versions of Hollywood Crime Cinema: Studies in Ford, Wilder, Coppola, Scorsese and Others* (Bristol, UK: Intellect, 2013), 30–31.

7. See Jon Lewis, *The Godfather* (London: Palgrave Macmillan, 2010), 68; and Thomas J. Ferraro, *Ethnic Passages: Literary Immigrants in Twentieth-Century America* (Chicago: University of Chicago Press, 1993), 31–32.

8. On the chaperones' importance, see Santopietro, *Godfather Effect,* 57.

9. The shooting script describes this scene as a ritual moment: "There is a bridal procession into the street of the village, the same in feeling and texture as it might have been five hundred years ago. . . . We present the entire bridal procession and ceremony with all the ritual and pageantry as it has always been in Sicily" (Jenny M. Jones, *The Annotated Godfather: The Complete Screenplay* [New York: Black Dog and Lewenthal, 2007], 107).

10. The Mario Puzo novel on which the *Godfather* films are based can be helpful in analyzing them (for more on this subject, see the appendix to this chapter). In Puzo's novel, Michael comes to understand his father's destiny only when he visits Sicily and observes the horrific conditions there: "For in Sicily he saw what they would have been if they had chosen *not* to struggle against their fate" (Mario Puzo, *The Godfather* [Greenwich, CT: Fawcett, 1969], 324).

11. In its heyday, Little Italy consisted of "two dozen square blocks" in Lower Manhattan (Santopietro, *Godfather Effect,* 78).

12. These questions are answered in summary fashion in book 3 of Puzo's novel, which, among other matters, goes into Vito's successful gang war with Salvatore Maranzano and even his relations with Al Capone. The picture of Vito's career given in the novel is as a result much darker than what is shown in the films.

13. Vito also tries to appeal to Roberto as a fellow Sicilian, only to learn that the landlord is from the Calabria region of Italy. Earlier, Don Fanucci complains to a theater manager that his shows feature Neapolitan rather than Sicilian songs. In the minds of these Italian Americans, Italy is not a nation-state; they are still in the grip of their Old World regional loyalties.

14. See Lewis, *Godfather,* 39. For an overview of the history of the gangster movie, with detailed plot summaries of the major examples, see Marilyn Yaquinto, *Pump 'Em Full of Lead: A Look at Gangsters on Film* (New York: Twayne, 1998). For *Little Caesar, Public Enemy,* and *Scarface* specifically, see 26–47. For a more analytic study of the gangster movie as a genre, see Thomas Schatz, *Hollywood Genres: Formulas, Filmmaking, and the Studio System* (Boston: McGraw Hill, 1981), 81–110; for the "big three" films specifically, see 86–95. See also Santopietro, *Godfather Effect,* 101–3. For a broader treatment of the Mafia in popular culture—from opera to movies to television—even to

video games, see Roberto M. Dainotto, *The Mafia: A Cultural History* (London: Reaktion, 2015). Dainotto goes beyond American popular culture to study Italian representations of the Mafia as well.

15. Given the pressure of public opinion and even government censorship at the time, these 1930s mob movies make a point of denying that they are glamorizing the gangsters they portray. They typically call explicitly for greater efforts by the government to fight organized crime. In an unusually self-conscious moment, *Scarface* actually reflects on the genre of the gangster story and compares it unfavorably in moral terms with the Western. At a police station, a reporter asks for more news of the mobster Tony Camonte, insisting: "The public's interested in him. He's a colorful character." The reporter could be speaking for the audience of the film; he is sharply rebuked by the police representative: "Colorful? What color is a crawling louse? . . . That's the attitude of too many morons in this country. . . . They think those big hoodlums are some sort of demigods. What do they do about a guy like Camonte? They sentimentalize him. Romance. Make jokes about him. They had some excuse for glorifying our old western bad men. They met in the middle of the street—high noon—and waited for each other to draw. But these things sneak up and shoot someone in the back and then run away." Rarely has a movie audience been so rebuked by the very film they were watching. For the parallels between gangster movies and Westerns, see also Clarence Darrow's comment: "Gang pictures are action pictures. The screen has played them for years. It called them westerns when they stole horses instead of booze" (qtd. in Lewis, *Godfather,* 41). For more on the condemnation of gangsters in these films, see Dainotto, *Mafia,* 57–58. For a good discussion of *Scarface* and the American dream, see Marilyn Roberts, "'Scarface,' 'The Great Gatsby,' and the American Dream," *Literature/ Film Quarterly* 34 (2006): 71–78. For more on this subject, see Dainotto, *Mafia,* 73–80.

16. Coppola used a striking analogy to explain this point: "If you were taken inside Adolf Hitler's home, went to his parties and heard his stories, you'd probably have liked him. My point is that you can't make a movie about what it's like inside a Mafia family without their seeming to be quite human" (qtd. in Peter Biskind, *The Godfather Companion* [New York: HarperPerennial, 1990], 117).

17. As Roger Ebert wrote: "The Don seems more like a precinct captain than a gangster, intervening on behalf of a poor widow who is being evicted from her apartment" (qtd. in Yaquinto, *Gangsters on Film,* 142).

18. In an early review of *The Godfather I,* William Pechter identified Coppola's strategy for creating sympathy for Vito: "Even were we given some more detailed picture of what the Corleones' business entailed, it must surely modify our admiration for their success that it involves, if it is not actually based on, killing people, but, fascinating as is a depiction of how the family's fortune was acquired and how its businesses are run might be, virtually nothing of this sort is presented (aside from the family's unlikely decision not to become involved in heroin traffic, the effect of which—like that of the family's victims being only other gangsters—is merely to make the Corleones more acceptable to us)" (William Pechter, "Keeping up with the Corleones," in *Francis Ford Coppola: The Godfather Trilogy,* ed. Nick Browne [Cambridge: Cambridge University Press, 2000], 169; this review originally appeared in *Commentary,* July 1972).

19. For Francis Ford Coppola, the *Godfather* films became a family business. In a deleted scene in *The Godfather II*, Coppola had originally thought of inserting his own father into the grand *Godfather* narrative. Vito, together with Clemenza and Tessio, seek aid from a gunsmith named Augustino Coppola. He asks his son Carmine to play his flute for the proto-gangsters, thus displaying the musical talent that was to propel the director's father into a career as a successful orchestra musician and composer. The real Carmine Coppola actually appears in *The Godfather I* playing the piano in the gang war montage sequence. Although Nino Rota wrote most of the music for the *Godfather* films, Carmine contributed to the score. The director's newborn daughter, Sofia Coppola, appears for Michael Francis Rizzio in the baptism scene at the end of *The Godfather I*. For a complete list of Coppola's relatives who were involved in the films in one capacity or another, see Biskind, *Godfather Companion*, 44–45. See also Santopietro, *Godfather Effect*, 188.

20. On how the Corleone family "re-creates southern Italian village life in the New World," see Santopietro, *Godfather Effect*, 86.

21. Similarly, when Sollozzo kidnaps Tom Hagen in *The Godfather I*, he reassures him that he will not be harmed: "I know you're not in the muscle end of the family."

22. Without delving too deeply into the complicated issue of the actual history of the Mafia, it is fair to say that Puzo and Coppola invented the notion that, as late as the 1940s, gangsters were still debating whether to go into the drug trade. Evidence shows that Joseph Profaci, one of the models for Vito Corleone, was involved in drugs as early as the 1930s (see Dainotto, *Mafia*, 123–24). Perhaps the greatest romanticizing of the Mafia in the *Godfather* stories is the claim that it was initially reluctant to deal in drugs. In defense of Puzo and Coppola, they were under no obligation to produce a truthful documentary about the Mafia. The changes they made in Mafia history are of the kind that Shakespeare made in English history in his plays. For the record, Joseph Profaci was in fact in the olive oil business and was known as the "Olive-Oil King." For those who find implausible Michael Corleone's hope to turn his family's operations into a legitimate business, it is worth noting that Joseph Profaci's son, John J. Profaci, eventually partnered in 1978 in founding the well-known (and legitimate) Colavita Olive Oil Company. In 2009, he was inducted into the Hall of Fame of the Culinary Institute of America. His Harvard-educated son Joseph R. Profaci was named the executive director of the North American Olive Oil Association in 2017 (see www.oliveoiltimes.com/olive-oil-business/north-america/olive-oil-importers-name-new-director/59006). Joseph R. Profaci's brother, John Profaci Jr., as an executive in Colavita Olive Oil, never sponsored anything more violent than a well-known and successful women's cycling team, which featured such stars as multiple-time National Champion Tina Pic, Jamaican Olympian Iona Wynter-Parks, and Route de France stage winner Andrea Dvorak. According to a 2010 *New York Post* story, law-enforcement sources confirmed John Jr.'s claim: "We've gone so far, our family has, since those days. We all went to good colleges and got good educations. We are businessmen. . . . That's so far removed from our past" (see https://nypost.com/2010/12/12/godmother-of-real-estate/). In a notable case of truth being stranger than fiction, in the real world at least, part of the family that served as models for the Corleones did succeed in becoming legitimate and respected businessmen.

23. This idea is expressed in slightly varying form by Don Barzini to the mob syndicate and by Don Tomassino to Michael in Sicily in *The Godfather I* and by Michael to his mother in *The Godfather II*. The point is also made in Puzo's novel by Sollozzo in his conversation with Michael in the restaurant: "Your father is an old-fashioned man. He stands in the way of progress. The business I am in is the coming thing, the wave of the future. . . . But your father stands in the way because of certain unrealistic scruples" (Puzo, *Godfather,* 149). The novel indicates that Sollozzo is speaking here in "rapid Sicilian," and that is how some of this speech appears, without subtitles, in *The Godfather I*.

24. Don Corleone expands this argument at a later meeting of the mob syndicate: "I believe this drug business is gonna destroy us in the years to come. I mean, it's not like gambling or liquor. Even women, which is something that most people want nowadays and is, too, forbidden to them by the pezzonovante of the Church. Even the police departments that've helped us in the past with gambling and other things are gonna refuse to help us when it comes to narcotics."

25. Puzo's novel portrays Vito as morally conservative and attributes his unwillingness to go into business with Sollozzo to an aversion to his involvement in prostitution: "He was notoriously straitlaced in matters of sex" (Puzo, *Godfather,* 73). Later the novel attributes Vito's displeasure with his middle son's behavior in Las Vegas to similar reasons: "The Don was straitlaced about sex. He would consider such cavorting by his son Freddie, two girls at a time, as degeneracy" (389).

26. In Puzo's novel, Michael makes this point about his father in a conversation with Kay: "He doesn't accept the rules of the society we live in because those rules would have condemned him to a life not suitable to a man like himself, a man of extraordinary force and character. . . . He refused to live by rules set up by others, rules which condemn him to a defeated life" (Puzo, *Godfather,* 365).

27. Qtd. in Lewis, *Godfather,* 36.

28. In an essay entitled "Crime & the American Dream," Norman Podhoretz offers an interesting twist on the idea that stories like *The Godfather* identify businessmen with gangsters. He argues that such gangster stories actually celebrate capitalism, or at least the capitalist virtues that used to be celebrated in America. He speculates that in an intellectual climate that has become increasingly hostile to capitalism, popular culture can no longer offer old-style Horatio Alger stories, in which hard work and entrepreneurism are rewarded with substantial wealth. Wondering why gangster novels and movies have been so successful, Podhoretz writes: "The delight we take in this literature is very similar to the delight people used to take in biographies of successful businessmen and in romantic novels about them. For the gangsters who fascinate us today are not the straightforward thugs [of the 1930s]. . . . They claim our attention not primarily by virtue of their brutality but by virtue of their worldly success; they are self-made men who have started from nowhere and managed to climb to the top. . . . We still want to read about self-made men with the will, the energy, the daring, the boldness, and the ruthlessness to claw their way to the top. But so powerful has the animus against business and commerce become in our culture—and, by now, every level of our culture—that no legitimate businessman could possibly serve as the hero of any such story. Only an

illegitimate businessman could; which is to say a gangster. . . . We grant them heroic status because they are in a certain sense rebels against society" (*Commentary,* January 1, 1972). This is a highly speculative argument but a fascinating one.

29. Even in the case of a minor character—the policeman on his beat who interrupts the murder of Frankie Pentangeli in *The Godfather II*—his good deed is just an accident of timing. For the absence of any good representatives of the law in the *Godfather* films, see Vera Dika, "The Representation of Ethnicity in *The Godfather*" in *Godfather Trilogy,* ed. Browne, 90–91.

30. For an excellent overview of crony capitalism in recent years, see Hunter Lewis, *Crony Capitalism in America, 2008–2012* (Edinburgh, VA: AC2, 2013).

31. Alessandro Camon argues that the Mafia portrayed in the *Godfather* films is not an example of capitalism: "From a socio-economic standpoint, the Mafia represents in fact a confluence of aristocratic and proletarian interests. The organization flourished in Sicily, which was at the time a distinctly non-industrialized, precapitalist area where the economy (and the social struggle) revolved around the land. . . . And owning the land, rather than owning stock or commercial concerns is what drives both the peasant and the aristocrat" ("*The Godfather* and the Mythology of Mafia," in *Godfather Trilogy,* ed. Browne, 167).

32. To see the difference between the operation of a free market and the operation of the mob in the *Godfather* films, one need only look at Don Corleone's signature line: "I'm gonna make him an offer he can't refuse." In a free market, an "offer you can't refuse" involves a product that is priced to move—the quality is so high and the cost so low that people rush to buy it. Don Corleone means something entirely different when he speaks of an "offer you can't refuse"—he means putting a gun to someone's head until he signs a contract. Despite the claims of Marxist critics of capitalism, this is *not* how markets routinely work. Although some force and fraud are occasionally involved in market transactions, in the overwhelming majority of cases, free markets operate on the principle of exchange, in which both parties in their own perception profit from the bargain; otherwise the exchange would not take place. In the ordinary course of business, nobody puts a gun to your head; that is why the gangster stands out and is of such dramatic interest. Marxists will no doubt accuse me of naiveté, but I do not see them feeling compelled to carry guns with them when they go to their local supermarkets.

33. Another revealing point of contrast with Vito Corleone in *The Godfather I* is provided by the movie studio head, Jack Woltz. Many of the men who founded the great Hollywood studios were Jewish immigrants (or their sons). Thus Woltz is another example of the immigrant pursuing the American dream. From presumably humble beginnings (suggested by his coarse manner of speech), he has built himself into one of the most powerful figures in Hollywood. In typical American fashion, he has used his great wealth to imitate European aristocracy. When Tom Hagen visits Woltz's estate— a junior version of William Randolph Hearst's San Simeon—the Hollywood big shot immodestly says of one of the statues in his garden: "It used to decorate the palace of a king." He then shows off to Hagen a prize horse he bought for six hundred thousand dollars, adding, "I'll bet Russian czars never paid that kinda dough for a single horse." Puzo's

novel adds the fact that Woltz has achieved a social status high enough for his children to wed into European aristocracy: "His daughter had married an English lord, his son an Italian princess" (Puzo, *Godfather,* 56). Woltz seems to have achieved the American dream—an immigrant becoming the modern-day equivalent of a European aristocrat.

A crack in Woltz's aristocratic facade is that no true aristocrat would show off his possessions to brag about his aristocratic status. In fact, *The Godfather I* portrays Woltz as a low-minded, mean-spirited vulgarian. He is prejudiced against Italian Americans, speaking of "dago, guinea, wop, grease-ball goombahs" and referring specifically to Johnny Fontane's "olive-oil voice and guinea charm." In many respects Woltz seems morally inferior to Don Corleone. At a time when Vito is hesitating to go into the drug business, Woltz's studio is already deeply involved. Tom Hagen points out, "One of your top stars has just moved from marijuana to heroin." Woltz exercises tyrannical power at his studio and is trying to run Fontane out of the entertainment business. Woltz is so morally obtuse that he thinks that he can justify his actions to Hagen by claiming that sexual jealousy is the motive behind his vendetta against Fontane. He blames Fontane for seducing a studio starlet when Woltz was enjoying her favors: "She was the greatest piece of ass I ever had, and I've had 'em all over the world!" Woltz turns out to be a sexual predator, exploiting his power at the studio to prey on underage actresses. In a deleted scene, we learn that even while Hagen is visiting Woltz's home, a sixteen-year-old actress is living with him (with the consent of her mother). In another deleted scene, when Vito learns this fact from Hagen, he is deeply disgusted and calls it an "infamia." The *Godfather* films are largely confined to the corrupt world of crime, police, and politics, and we see little of alternate ways of life. But when we do get a glimpse of an alternative—the supposedly glamorous world of Hollywood—it turns out to be more corrupt than anything we see of the Mafia.

34. Roger Jellinek said something similar of Puzo's novel in his *New York Times* review: "The victims of the Corleone 'family' are hoods, or corrupt cops—nobody you or I would actually want to know. . . . You never glimpse regular people in the book, let alone meet them, so there is no opportunity to sympathize with anyone but the old patriarch, as he makes the world safe for his beloved 'family'" (qtd. in Harlan Lebo, *The Godfather Legacy* [New York: Fireside, 1997], 6). Strictly speaking, this claim is untrue, since we do see ordinary people in characters like the undertaker Bonasera, the baker Enzo, and the widow Colombo. But of course it is precisely these people whom Vito helps, thus earning our sympathy.

35. On Castellano's improvisation, see Jones, *Annotated Godfather,* 98.

36. Puzo's novel goes further, imputing to Michael the opinion: "If the Families had been running the State Department there would never have been World War II" (Puzo, *The Godfather,* 142). On the war theme in the *Godfather* films, see Dainotto, *Mafia.* 131.

37. On this development in the actual history of the Mafia, see Dainotto, *Mafia,* 62.

38. Jones, *Annotated Godfather,* 182.

39. Puzo's novel raises this issue concretely in terms of Benito Mussolini's famous war on the Italian Mafia in his determination to impose the will of his fascist central government on any recalcitrant elements in the polity: "The dictator had known that

the Mafia would be a threat to his regime, forming what amounted to a separate authority from his own. He gave full power to a high police official, who promptly solved the problem by throwing everybody into jail or deporting them to penal work islands. In a few short years he had broken the power of the Mafia" (Puzo, *Godfather*, 277–78). Totalitarian regimes carry the logic of the nation-state to its ultimate conclusion, trying to eradicate any prepolitical forces that seek to resist their power, including the family. Puzo concludes his account of Mussolini's crackdown on the Mafia: "[He] also brought ruin to a great many innocent families."

40. The issue of family versus country is so important in the *Godfather* story that it surfaces at several stages of the project. The dialogue between Michael and Sonny that ends *The Godfather II* was originally supposed to take place between Michael and Vito. Paramount had hoped to get Marlon Brando to reprise his signature role for a brief moment at the end of *The Godfather II*, but he wanted too much money and the scene had to be rewritten with Sonny substituting for his father. As originally written, Don Corleone was supposed to show up on-screen for the birthday party and challenge Michael's decision to enlist: "You would risk your life for strangers?" Michael replies, "Not for strangers; for my country." Vito remains true to his village ethic and expresses his contempt for the nation-state: "Anyone not in your family is a stranger. Believe me, when trouble comes, your country won't take care of you." It is a shame that this dialogue never made it to the screen, because Michael's reply to his father goes right to the heart of the matter: "That's how it was in the Old World, Pop, but this is not Sicily" (Biskind, *Godfather Companion*, 115). A variant of this dialogue did make it into *The Godfather I*, but only as part of Genco Abbandonando's macabre deathbed scene—which means that it was deleted from the final cut. Waiting in the corridor to enter Genco's hospital room, Vito questions Michael's medal-bedecked military uniform: "What are all these Christmas ribbons for?" Michael answers, "For bravery." Vito replies, "What miracles you do for strangers" (Jones, *Annotated Godfather*, 55). In yet another scene deleted from *The Godfather I*, Vito in conversation with Michael gets to develop further his argument for family and against the nation-state: "Believe in family. Can you believe in your country? Those pezzonovante of the state who decide what we should do with our lives? Who declare wars they wish us to fight in to protect what they own? Do you put your faith in the hands of men whose only talent is that they tricked a bloc of people to vote for them? . . . Believe in a family; believe in a code of honor, older and higher. Believe in roots that go back thousands of years in your race" (Jones, *Annotated Godfather*, 181). One sees from all these deleted scenes how deeply rooted the *Godfather* films are in the contrast between *Gemeinschaft* and *Gesellschaft*, between family and the nation-state, between a community of neighbors and a community of strangers.

41. This point is explicit in Puzo's novel, when it discusses a prewar agreement Don Corleone secured among the mob families: "Like the Constitution of the United States this agreement respected fully the internal authority of each member in his state or city" (Puzo, *Godfather*, 224).

42. As shown in this scene, the Mafia is more like a cartel than a corporation operating in a free market. Today we constantly speak of drug cartels.

43. The Cold War threat of communism hovers in the background of the *Godfather* films. In a deleted scene in *The Godfather I*, we get a brief glimpse of Italian communists marching behind a red banner in Sicily. And of course Fidel Castro's communist revolt in Cuba plays an important role in the plot of *The Godfather II*. In his Marxist interpretation of the films, Fredric Jameson makes much of the spectral presence of communism, especially in the appearance of the Cuban Revolution (*Signatures of the Visible*, 45). On the importance of Cuba, see also Freedman, *Hollywood Crime Cinema*, 36–37.

44. In a deleted scene, Michael worries about the way Vito has peacefully acquiesced in the gangsters' agreement: "Won't they take that as a sign of weakness?" Still acute in his ability to assess a situation, Vito replies, "It *is* a sign of weakness." In Puzo's novel, in a conversation just before his death with Michael and Tom Hagen, Vito says, "I'm old-fashioned, you're the modern generation, don't listen to me" (Puzo, *Godfather*, 404). The novel draws the contrast between Don Corleone and Don Barzini on just this issue: "He was a man much like Don Corleone, but more modern, more sophisticated, more businesslike. He would never be called an old Moustache Pete and he had the confidence of the newer, younger brasher leaders on their way up" (285).

45. This point is made explicit in Puzo's novel by Mama Corleone when she describes the aging Vito working in his garden "as if he were some peasant still" (Puzo, *Godfather*, 393). Later the novel says of Vito's garden: "It brought back his childhood in Sicily sixty years ago" (408).

46. William Pechter writes: "The one single thing that most distinguishes *The Godfather* from other gangster films is that Don Corleone is not a doomed over-reacher but a man who dies, in effect, in bed" (Browne, *Godfather Trilogy*, 170). *Little Caesar* provides the standard arc of the gangster's story; a policeman says of its protagonist, "Meteoric as was Rico's rise from the gutter, it was inevitable that he should return there."

47. These words are part of the magnificent scene between Vito and Michael written by Robert Towne, who was called in at the last minute as a script doctor to give father and son an appropriate last moment together. Vito's words are based on an eloquent speech he gives in Puzo's novel at the Mafia board meeting: "We are all men who have refused to be fools, who have refused to be puppets dancing on a string pulled by the men on high" (Puzo, *Godfather*, 292). This long speech, only small sections of which appear at the corresponding moment in the film, is worth studying as a whole—it goes to the thematic heart of the *Godfather* story in all its incarnations. On Towne's role in the scripting of *The Godfather I*, see Jones, *Annotated Godfather*, 204–5; Lewis, *Godfather*, 24–28; and Lebo, *Godfather Legacy*, 161–68.

48. All speculation on this subject goes back to the pioneering essay by Robert Warshow, "The Gangster as Tragic Hero" in the collection of his writings *The Immediate Experience: Movies, Comics, Theatre & Other Aspects of Popular Culture* (Cambridge: Harvard University Press, 2001), 97–103. Writing in 1948, Warshow of course does not discuss the *Godfather* films; he focuses on earlier cinematic incarnations of the gangster, such as *Little Caesar* and *Scarface*.

49. Qtd. in Jones, *Annotated Godfather*, 133.

50. In *The Godfather III,* this movement is reversed. Retracing his family's steps, Michael moves back to New York and finally back to Sicily. The wheel has come full circle. On this point, see Santopietro, *Godfather Effect,* 255.

51. This issue does come up explicitly in Puzo's novel. When Vito sends friends to Nevada to check out the background of his daughter's fiancé, "they also came back with detailed information on legal gambling in Nevada which greatly interested the Don" (Puzo, *Godfather,* 19). Later in the novel, a character is unconcerned about any conflict breaking out when Michael starts to muscle in on the casino business: "He knew there was no chance of any violence, not in Vegas itself. That was strictly forbidden as fatal to the whole project of making Vegas the legal sanctuary of American gamblers" (387).

52. Al Capone said something similar of his illicit distilling operations: "Everybody calls me a racketeer. I call myself a businessman. When I sell liquor, it's bootlegging. When my patron serves it on a silver tray on Lake Shore Drive, it's hospitality" (qtd. in Dainotto, *Mafia,* 72).

53. When confronted by Michael Corleone's claim that Greene's casino is losing money, Moe says defensively: "You think I'm skimming off the top, Mike?"

54. On this point, see Lewis, *Godfather,* 44.

55. The difference between Vito and Michael shows up in their contrasting attitudes toward the principle of contract. To the Old World Vito, contracts mean nothing. He makes people offers they can't refuse. He successfully breaks Johnny Fontane's service contract with a bandleader by having Luca Brasi threaten him with death. The New World Michael has more respect for contracts. When he shows up in Las Vegas to get Fontane to enter into a service agreement with the mob's casinos, Michael has a briefcase full of written contracts for Johnny and his show-business friends to sign—contracts drawn up, no doubt, by the fine lawyerly hand of Tom Hagen. The movement from status to contract is often offered as a measure of the civilizing process, but the *Godfather* films raise doubts about preferring the modern principle of contract. Jon Lewis provides an excellent formulation of the movement from Vito to Michael Corleone: "Coppola offers a capitalist parable expansive enough to chronicle a transition from the 30s-era entrepreneurial gangster to a more refined version of the post-war corporate capitalist, from Vito, who is essentially a shake-down artist (making offers one dare not refuse) to his son Michael, who is a takeover artist, a corporate raider who offers to buy out his rivals before he reaches for the heavy artillery" (Lewis, *Godfather,* 43–44).

56. For more on the cultural significance of Las Vegas, see my essay "Postmodern Prophet: Tocqueville Visits Vegas," *Journal of Democracy* 11 (2000): 111–18. For Las Vegas and the American dream, see Jim Cullen, *The American Dream: A Short History of an Idea That Shaped America* (New York: Oxford University Press, 2003), 164–67.

57. In Roth's speech, Moe Greene emerges as another embodiment of the American dream, another rags-to-riches tale. Roth tells the story of a younger Jewish gangster being mentored by an older: "There was a kid I grew up with; he was younger than me. Sorta looked up to me, you know. We did our first work together—worked our way out of the streets. Things were good, we made the most of it. During Prohibition, we ran molasses into Canada—made a fortune. . . . Later on he had an idea—to build a city

out of a desert stopover for GIs on the way to the West Coast. That kid's name was Moe Greene, and the city he invented was Las Vegas. This was a great man, a man of vision and guts. And there isn't even a plaque, or a signpost, or a statue of him in that town!" In Roth's telling, Moe Greene becomes the archetypal American entrepreneur, whose creative efforts went unrewarded and unrecognized by the very community he brought into existence. Once again, the American dream takes a tragic turn. Note the absence of a sense of history in America. Italy is littered with monuments, but Las Vegas has no marker even for its founder.

58. For a good analysis of this juxtaposition, see Freedman, *Hollywood Crime Cinema,* 33–34.

59. Here is how Coppola explained his intentions in this scene: "People tell me that they like the opening wedding party in the original film better than the opening (First Communion) party for Michael's son in the sequel. Well, so do I. That was my point. I was trying to show how the family had lost its authenticity. I wanted to have scenes that would remind you of the first film and to show by their altered shape how much the family had changed" (qtd. in Lebo, *Godfather Legacy,* 244). Lewis speaks of Michael's "modern rootlessness, a loss of ethnicity that is for him and his family the price of assimilation"(Lewis, *Godfather,* 70). On this loss of ethnicity, see also Biskind, *Godfather Companion,* 113; and David Denby, "The Two Godfathers," in *Godfather Trilogy,* ed. Browne, 178–79.

60. As a sign of the Corleones' newfound respectability, at this party the police are assisting in the parking lot rather than taking down license plate numbers as they do in *The Godfather I.* This time the police are almost guests at the party—they are handed drinks in the parking lot. A deleted scene provides additional evidence for the higher social status of the Corleone family under Michael. They can now marry into the upper echelons of the social world in America. Michael gives his blessing for one of his nieces to marry a very WASPy preppie-type. To explain why Michael need not worry about his niece's financial future, the young man says: "I'm a major stockholder in the family corporation" (a neat parallel to the Corleone family). Michael has to tell the young man, "You shouldn't be embarrassed by your wealth," and goes on to recommend that he take a course in business administration in college to supplement his art history major. We keep seeing signs of how the Corleones have entered the mainstream of American business life. At the congressional hearings, Michael tells the committee that he owns stock in IBM and IT&T.

61. As Naomi Greene points out: "The bonds of family love and duty are disintegrating: Fredo, married to a blonde floozy, drinks; Connie ignores her children as she flits from one husband to another; Michael neither feels nor inspires the love for family that governed his father's life" ("Family Ceremonies: or, Opera in *The Godfather Trilogy*" in *Godfather Trilogy,* ed. Browne, 138).

62. In accordance with the transition to a modern economy in *The Godfather II,* gifts become less important. Connie has brought a gift for her mother to Anthony's party, but Mama Corleone virtually ignores it. In *The Godfather I,* Michael does his own Christmas shopping along with Kay, but in *The Godfather II,* he delegates that task to Tom Hagen.

Returning from Cuba, Michael has to ask Tom about "his" Christmas present to his son: "What was it, so I know?" Not gifts but money is what binds the mobsters together in *The Godfather II*. To praise his boss, Johnny Ola need only say, "Hyman Roth always makes money for his partners." Frankie Pentangeli shows how old-fashioned he is when he is insulted by the fact that the Rosato brothers slip him a hundred-dollar bill in confirmation of the deal they have made. Similarly in *The Godfather I*, Don Fanucci is willing to take less money from Vito as long as he shows him more respect.

63. The one glimpse we get of Kay's hometown is almost straight out of Currier & Ives. Michael has come to ask her to marry him. It is a crisp autumn day in New Hampshire (actually the scene was shot in Mill Valley, California; see Jones, *Annotated Godfather*, 187). Kay, who is now a teacher, appears shepherding a group of WASPy children. We see a dog running down the street and then a boy riding by on a bicycle, saying, "Hi, Miss Adams." He might as well be Wally from *Leave It to Beaver* or Bud from *Father Knows Best*. This is not a Sicilian small town. In Puzo's novel, Kay's father is "the pastor of the town Baptist church" (Puzo, *Godfather*, 231).

64. In a deleted scene, the band is playing not Old World traditional Italian music but patriotic American numbers, such as "Yankee Doodle Dandy" and "Columbia the Gem of the Ocean."

65. This kind of distance is characteristic of modern society. In *The Godfather II*, Pat Geary laments at the Corleone party, "We see Nevada so seldom," an odd statement from a senator from Nevada, but par for the course in modern politics. In Corleone and Little Italy, the oppressed people at least know who their oppressors are and can see them every day. In a modern nation-state, the big shots become increasingly remote from the people whose lives they affect. That is one price people pay for vastly extending the bounds of the communities they live in.

66. See Freedman, *Hollywood Crime Cinema*, 34–35.

67. Puzo's novel puts more emphasis on Michael's desire to Americanize his family. When he is trying to persuade Kay to marry him, he insists that he will make the Corleone family legitimate for the sake of the children he and Kay will have: "I want them to grow up to be All-American kids, real All-Americans, the whole works. Maybe they or their grandchildren will go into politics. . . . But I'll settle for my kids being doctors or musicians or teachers. They'll never be in the Family business. . . . And you and I will be part of some country club crowd, the good simple life of well-to-do Americans" (Puzo, *Godfather*, 363). Michael is so obsessed with Americanizing his children that he is upset when Kay converts to Catholicism: "He would have preferred the children to be Protestant, it was more American" (441). That may have been the basis of Michael's attraction to WASPy Kay in the first place.

68. In *The Godfather I*, Sonny in effect gives up his life because he will not tolerate a man striking his wife in the case of his sister, Connie, and her husband, Carlo.

69. We learn in *The Godfather III* that, of all Michael's sins and crimes, he regards having Fredo murdered as the most heinous and the most unforgivable.

70. On the subject of violence against women in the *Godfather* films, see Dika, "Representation of Ethnicity," 90–91.

4. The Macbeth of Meth

Epigraph 1: William Blake, *The Complete Poetry and Prose of William Blake,* ed. David V. Erdman (Berkeley: University of California Press, 1962), 252 (*Jerusalem,* plate 91, lines 54–55).

    Epigraph 2: Friedrich Nietzsche, *The Will to Power,* trans. Walter Kaufmann and R. J. Hollingdale (New York: Vintage, 1967), 485 (#918).

    1. Qtd. in Alan Sepinwall, *The Revolution Was Televised* (New York: Simon and Schuster, 2012), 340.

    2. For references in *Breaking Bad* to the Brian De Palma film *Scarface* (1983), see season 1, episode 6 (hereafter season and episode numbers are cited in the form 1/6) and 4/5. In 5/3, we see the *Breaking Bad* characters actually watching a scene from *Scarface* on television. Walter and his son bond by repeating together the famous line, "Say hello to my little friend." Ominously and prophetically, Walt observes, "Everyone dies in this movie." All quotations from *Breaking Bad* have been transcribed from the DVDs of the series. On the importance of the De Palma *Scarface* in *Breaking Bad,* see Dennis Thompson, ed., *Breaking Bad: The Official Book* (New York: Sterling, 2015), 76.

    3. As the actor who played Walter White—Bryan Cranston—said of the series: "One of the things that made the show so compelling was this lack of bright moral lines. No indispensable turning points. No easy answers. We put the moral burden as much on the audience as it was on Walt" (Bryan Cranston, *A Life in Parts* [New York: Scribner, 2016], 205). On this point, see Lara C. Stache, *Breaking Bad: A Cultural History* (Lanham, MD: Rowman and Littlefield, 2017), 16. Throughout these notes, I grant a certain authority to comments from both Bryan Cranston and Vince Gilligan as the two people most responsible for creating the character of Walter White. But I do not offer them as the ultimate authority on the subject. As they would both agree, what they say about Walter White is not the absolute truth, and, for that matter, they often disagree about the character.

    4. In response to the claim that "for some viewers [Walter White] remains the unquestionable hero of the piece, the guy they like and root for no matter what," Gilligan responded: "I have to say it does surprise me. . . . I thought it'd be interesting as an experiment to create a television show where a major point of the show was change—to see a good man transform into a bad man. I figured what would happen is that we would lose sympathy for Walt with every subsequent episode we produced—that people would start to sympathize less and less with Walt. . . . But there are some people who, come hell or high water, will never lose sympathy for Walt. Some lost sympathy way back in Season 1, and bell-curve-wise, the average person lost sympathy around when he watched Jane die and didn't intervene" (Sepinwall, *Revolution Was Televised,* 359–60).

    5. See Dustin Freeley, "The Economy of Time and Multiple Existences in *Breaking Bad,*" in *Breaking Bad: Critical Essays on the Contexts, Politics, Style, and Reception of the Television Series,* ed. David P. Pierson (Lanham, MD: Lexington, 2014), 43.

    6. In 3/4, Skyler's boss, Ted, actually refers to Walt as "mild-mannered." As for the fly, in 4/10, Walt spends a whole episode trying to kill one and fails (Walt's sidekick Jesse has to do it).

7. Others have made this point. See, for example, Thompson, *Breaking Bad*, 76, who refers to the show as "a monster-mash of different genres, drawing on horror, crime drama, Western, coming-of-age narratives, and even superhero stories."

8. See Brett Martin, *Difficult Men: Behind the Scenes of a Creative Revolution* (New York: Penguin, 2013): "[Walter White's] journey becomes a grotesque magnification of the American ethos of self-actualization, Oprah Winfrey's exhortation that all must find and 'live your best life'" (268).

9. Cranston, *Life in Parts*, 196, 201.

10. Cranston, *Life in Parts*, 198–99.

11. For other parallels between *Malcolm in the Middle* and *Breaking Bad*, see Alan Sepinwall and Matt Zoller Seitz, *TV (The Book)* (New York: Grand Central, 2016), 202. Uncannily, in "season 3's 'Health Scare,'" "Hal becomes convinced he has cancer." Bryan Cranston discusses the parallels between the two series in his 2015 interview with James Lipton on *Inside the Actors Studio* (season 19, episode 20).

12. See Sepinwall and Seitz, *TV (The Book)*, 49, who talk about Walt "as a wish-fulfillment fantasy for generations of middle-aged, married white men"; the show "does feel like a fantasy/nightmare of the American patriarchy in decline."

13. In her opening chapter, Lara Stache raises the question of whether Walter White is a hero, a villain, or an antihero. After surveying a wide range of critical opinion on the subject, she concludes, "To me, Walter White dies not as an antihero or a villain, but as a tragic and complex human figure" (Stache, *Breaking Bad*, 16).

14. Since this is a book on popular culture, I do not wish to burden it with much in the way of literary theory. For the record, the concept of tragedy I am operating with is a synthesis of the ideas of the Greek philosopher Aristotle and the German philosopher Georg Wilhelm Friedrich Hegel. Aristotle's view of tragedy can be found in his *Poetics*. Hegel's scattered writings on tragedy have been conveniently collected in English translation in *Hegel: On Tragedy*, ed. Anne Paolucci and Henry Paolucci (New York: Harper Torchbooks, 1975). This volume also contains A. C. Bradley's essay "Hegel's Theory of Tragedy," which is perhaps the best introduction to the subject. For more on this subject, see Mark William Roche, *Tragedy and Comedy: A Systematic Study and a Critique of Hegel* (Albany: State University of New York Press, 1988). Hegel's theory of tragedy is particularly important for the way it cautions us against a strictly moral analysis of *Breaking Bad*. For Hegel, tragedy occurs when two legitimate principles come into conflict, and there is no way out of the situation without incurring some form of guilt. The prototype of tragedy for Hegel is Sophocles's *Antigone*, in which Antigone, standing up for her brother Polynices's right to a decent burial, represents the principle of the family, while her uncle Creon, forbidding the burial of Polynices because he was a traitor to Thebes, represents the principle of the city or the political community. Hegel locates tragedy precisely at the point where two different moralities come into conflict, or morality comes into conflict with another principle, such as political necessity. Thus, for Hegel, tragedy involves the conflict of two goods, and in truly tragic situations, there are never simple moral answers to the dramatic dilemma. That is why tragedy can be so unnerving and upsetting to our conventional notions but also why it lays bare the profound complexity of the human condition.

15. Qtd. in David Bianculli, *The Platinum Age of Television* (New York: Double-day, 2016), 203. In talking about his choice of Bryan Cranston to play Walter White, Gilligan said, "We needed an actor the audience could sympathize with, even in his darker moments" (203). On some level, Gilligan realized that even a dark character like Walter White can maintain an audience's sympathy.

16. For another attempt to understand *Breaking Bad* in terms of *Macbeth*, see Ray Bossert, "*Macbeth* on Ice," in *Breaking Bad and Philosophy: Badder Living through Chemistry*, ed. David R. Koepsell and Robert Arp (Chicago: Open Court, 2012), 65–77. Many others have noted parallels between *Breaking Bad* and *Macbeth*. Indeed, as Walter White grew more sinister, the topic erupted on the internet. Google "Breaking Bad and Macbeth" to see the range of responses, which vary from insightful to amusing to quirky. *Macbeth* has been used in another television crime story, HBO's dark comedy *Barry*, in which Bill Hader plays a hit man who improbably finds himself acting in a small-time production of *Macbeth* in the Los Angeles area.

17. The great Shakespeare critic A. C. Bradley understood that *Macbeth* is the ulti-mate test case of Shakespearean tragedy and hence tragedy in general. In his essay on "Hegel's Theory of Tragedy," he argues that Macbeth is not a criminal (or at least not simply a criminal), but a character caught in the kind of conflict between two goods that Hegel saw as the cornerstone of tragedy (see A. C. Bradley, *Oxford Lectures on Poetry* [London: Macmillan, 1909], 87–90).

18. All quotations from Shakespeare are taken from *The Riverside Shakespeare*, ed. G. Blakemore Evans (Boston: Houghton Mifflin, 1974) and are cited in the text by act, scene, and line numbers.

19. Bossert writes, "These all seem good enough values to hold in medieval Scotland where King Duncan describes Macbeth's ability to cut a man in half as making him a 'gentleman,' but they also end up being the things that turn Macbeth into a monster" ("*Macbeth* on Ice," 68).

20. For a systematic exploration of this theme in *Macbeth*, see José A. Benardete, "Macbeth's Last Words," *Interpretation* 1 (1970): 63–75.

21. For a fuller development of my interpretation of *Macbeth*, see my essay "*Macbeth* and the Gospelling of Scotland," in *Shakespeare as Political Thinker*, ed. John E. Alvis and Thomas G. West (Wilmington, DE: ISI, 2000), 315–51. For the larger context of this interpretation, see my book *Shakespeare's Roman Trilogy: The Twilight of the Ancient World* (Chicago: University of Chicago Press, 2017), 148–55.

22. Bradley clearly articulates this point in his analysis of *Macbeth*: "It is not a question merely of moral goodness, but of good. . . . And such bravery and skill in war as win the enthusiasm of everyone about him; such an imagination as few but poets possess; . . . a determination so tremendous and a courage so appalling that, for all his torment, he never dreams of turning back, . . . are not those things, in themselves, good, and gloriously good? Do they not make you, for all your horrors, admire Macbeth, sym-pathise with his agony, pity him, and see in him the waste of forces on which you place a spiritual value? It is simply on this account that he is for you, not the abstraction called a criminal who merely 'gets what he deserves' . . . but a tragic hero" (*Oxford Lectures*

on Poetry, 87–88). As we will see, with the necessary adjustments, Bradley's analysis of Macbeth can be applied to Walter White.

23. Bradley specifically cautions against this move: "It is dangerous to describe tragedy in terms that even appear to exclude *Macbeth*, or to describe *Macbeth* . . . in terms which imply that it portrays a conflict of mere evil with mere good" (*Oxford Lectures on Poetry*, 90). For Bradley, any definition of "tragedy" that does not allow for including *Macbeth* in the category must be wrong.

24. This principle is enunciated in *Breaking Bad* when Walt's brother-in-law Hank gives his son the book *Killing Pablo* (about the infamous Colombian drug lord). In 3/8, Walt Jr. comments: "Uncle Hank says 'everybody knows who Pablo Escobar is, but nobody knows about the guys who brought him down. . . . Good guys never get the ink like the bad guys do.'" Hank is no doubt thinking of himself compared to Heisenberg.

25. To the people of Scotland, Macbeth and Lady Macbeth at the end appear to be a "butcher" and a "fiend-like queen." That is very much an external view of them. By giving us access to a deeply interior view, Shakespeare makes us see that they are something much more than mere monsters, something much more complex. We will see that Gilligan does something similar in *Breaking Bad*. Had Walter White been brought to trial, we can imagine how the press would have treated him; they would have reduced his complex story to the simple headline: "Crazed High School Teacher Is Evil Drug Lord Heisenberg." In the course of the five-season series, we come to know a lot more than this about Walter White, thanks to the Shakespearean scripts Gilligan and his team produced, and he becomes a human being for us, not a mere monster.

26. Bossert sees that the problem of "masculinity" links *Macbeth* and *Breaking Bad*; see especially his comment about Walt's "deep, troubled insecurity about his own lost masculinity" ("*Macbeth* on Ice," 71). For more on the problem of masculinity in *Breaking Bad*, see Brian Faucette, "Taking Control: Male Angst and the Re-Emergence of Hegemonic Masculinity in *Breaking Bad*," in *Breaking Bad*, ed. Pierson, 73–86.

27. At a birthday party for Elliott Schwartz in 1/5, Walt explains why he is no longer with Gray Matter Technology: "I went into education." Someone asks immediately: "What university?," assuming that no one with Walt's credentials would go into high school teaching. For an insightful analysis of why Walt may have gone into teaching high school, see Cranston, *Life in Parts*, 199–200.

28. See Sepinwall and Seitz, *TV* (*The Book*), 48: "Walt exudes the specific resentment of a man who thinks himself entitled to more than he already has and hates every instant spent in the company of those he deems intellectual or moral inferiors."

29. Walt's fullest explanation of the Gray Matter business comes late in the series in 5/6: "I cofounded Gray Matter. Actually I named it. We were going to take the world by storm. Something happened. For personal reasons I decided to leave the company. I took a buyout for five thousand dollars. $2.16 billion as of last Friday. I look it up every week. I sold my kid's birthright for a few months' rent." Walt turns out to be more obsessed with the loss of his stake in Gray Matter than he at first appears to be. Walt's bitterness is only increased when, in the penultimate episode (5/15), he accidentally sees Elliott and Gretchen on *The Charlie Rose Show* on a barroom television. Faced with all

the bad publicity of being associated with the criminal Walter White, Elliott, trying to shore up Gray Matter's falling stock price, denies that Walt ever had a significant role in the company, describing him as "a person who was there early on but had virtually nothing to do with the creation of the company and still less to do with growing it into what it is today." This statement confirms Walt's conviction that he has never gotten the credit he deserves in life. For yet another explanation of what really happened among Walt, Elliott, and Gretchen, from Vince Gilligan himself, see Stache, *Breaking Bad,* 14.

30. In 2/6, Walt lectures his class about a chemist named H. Tracey Hall at General Electric who came up with a process for producing synthetic diamonds, which made the company an "incalculable" fortune. As for Hall, GE rewarded him with only a ten-dollar bond. Walt obviously identifies with Hall as a mistreated genius. For more on Tracey Hall, see Ensley F. Guffey and K. Dale Koontz, *Wanna Cook? The Complete, Unofficial Companion to* Breaking Bad (Toronto: ECW, 2014), 95–96.

31. In 1/2, Walt's former student and criminal sidekick, Jesse Pinkman, sarcastically compliments Walt: "Good job on wearing the pants in the family."

32. In 4/3, Walt says to Skyler, "This is so passive-aggressive."

33. Sepinwall refers to Walter White as "the recession era's everyman" (*Revolution Was Televised,* 357). On the way that *Breaking Bad* mirrors the financial crisis that began in 2008, see also Thompson, *Breaking Bad,* 1–3; and Camille Fojas, *Zombies, Migrants, and Queers: Race and Crisis Capitalism in Pop Culture* (Urbana: University of Illinois Press, 2017), 32–40. Martin, *Difficult Men,* 272, observes that the recession left "many previously secure middle-class Americans suddenly feeling like desperate outlaws in their own suburbs" (this mood was reflected in Showtime's dark drug comedy, *Weeds,* which in many respects parallels *Breaking Bad*).

34. The main rival for the "signature television series of the Obama years" would be *The Walking Dead,* which provides another bleak picture of this time period. For a detailed analysis of this series, see chapter 5, which shows that in its own way this series also raises the issue of health care. The chapter also analyzes the way *The Walking Dead* portrays the conflict between the haves and the have-nots in America. For more on the issue of health insurance in *Breaking Bad,* see Guffey and Koontz, *Wanna Cook?,* 32–33; and Stache, *Breaking Bad,* 56.

35. In 3/6, Walt's lab assistant Gale tries to defend their criminal activities on the grounds of the quality of the product they manufacture: "I'm definitely a libertarian. Consenting adults want what they want, and if I'm not supplying it, they will get it somewhere else. At least with me, they're getting exactly what they pay for. No added toxins or adulterants." Gale provides an illuminating mirror to help us understand Walt. Similar frustrations about an academic career drove him to crime, as he tells Walt: "I was doing it the way you are supposed. I was doing my doctorate at Colorado, NSF research grant. I was on my way, jumping through hoops, kissing the proper behinds, tending to all the nonchemistry that one finds oneself occupied with. You know that world—that is not what I signed up for. I love the lab. Because it's still magic." When Walt agrees with Gale about the magic of chemistry, we get a glimpse of why he did not pursue a conventional academic career at a research university.

36. For details, see Guffey and Koontz, *Wanna Cook?*, 92–93. For more on the depiction of drug use in *Breaking Bad*, see Stache, *Breaking Bad*, 70–73.

37. The character in *Breaking Bad* who most resembles Tony Montana is Don Eliado, the head of the Mexican drug cartel. His pool is the site for parties almost as sybaritic as Montana's. In a link to the Brian De Palma film, Don Eliado is played by Stephen Bauer, who played Montana's best friend, Manny Ribera, in the 1983 classic. Mark Margolis, the actor who plays Hector Salamanca in *Breaking Bad*, also appeared in *Scarface*.

38. We see a shot of the Three Stooges on television in 1/2 and then again in 5/3. Walt and Jesse are referred to as the "Two Stooges" in 2/3. In 5/7, Saul Goodman speaks of "the law firm of Moe, Larry, and Shemp." The frequency with which the Three Stooges appear in a dark show like *Breaking Bad* may seem strange, but it actually reflects Vince Gilligan's instinctive understanding of tragic form. Like Shakespeare, Gilligan realizes the need for comic relief in a tragedy (see Thompson, *Breaking Bad*, 80). *Breaking Bad* is filled with moments of comedy that help set off the pathos of its moments of tragedy. The Three Stooges serve as Gilligan's equivalent of the famous drunken porter in *Macbeth*. For more on comedy in *Breaking Bad*, see Thompson, *Breaking Bad*, 80, 150 (he points out that a number of the actors in the series also have careers as standup comedians, including Bob Odenkirk, who plays Saul Goodman). For a highly theorized discussion of comedy in *Breaking Bad*, see Gertrud Koch, *Breaking Bad, Breaking Out, Breaking Even*, trans. Daniel Hendrickson (Zürich and Berlin: Diaphanes, 2017), 45–55. Koch appears to overstate the comic nature of the series: "Not just at the end, but throughout White has also been a comedic figure" (47).

39. For a similar view of Walt as a "twenty-first-century *geek* hero," see "A Fine Meth," the introduction Koepsell and Arp wrote to the collection of essays they edited, *Breaking Bad and Philosophy*, vii–ix. They compare Walt to traditional literary—and tragic—heroes, such as Macbeth, Faust, and Milton's Satan (a hero at least in William Blake's interpretation of him).

40. For a concise and effective statement of the opposing view, that Walter White is just a villain, see Jonah Goldberg, "Life and Death on Basic Cable," *National Review*, August 19, 2013, 39–42.

41. Walt reveals his thinking about himself when he tells Jesse in 1/7: "Today is the first day of the rest of your life. But what kind of life will it be? A life of fear? . . . of never once believing in yourself?"

42. For a thorough discussion of these few words, see Alan Sepinwall, *Breaking Bad 101: The Complete Critical Companion* (New York: Abrams, 2017), 267–68.

43. Cranston perceptively speaks of Walt's "wanting to feel like he'd really lived, like he'd really been a man" (*Life in Parts*, 206). In his *Inside the Actors Studio* interview, he says of Walt: "For a man who was once a milquetoast to be able to spread his chest and feel the sense of intimidation upon others, that's a very powerful, intoxicating feeling."

44. Vince Gilligan said of Walt: "He prefers to think of himself as the master. That is what chafed so much in the season where Walt was under Gus Fring's thumb" (qtd. in Stache, *Breaking Bad*, 151).

45. Gale blurs the line between legal and illegal businesses when, in 4/1, he says of Gus's spanking-new drug lab equipment, "At Pfizer, at Merck, that would be right at home."

46. Compare what Bradley says about Macbeth: "The tragic effect depends . . . on our feeling that the elements in the man's nature are so inextricably blended that the good in him, that which we admire, instead of simply opposing the evil, reinforces it. Macbeth's imagination deters him from murder, but it also makes the vision of a crown irresistibly bright. If he had been less determined, nay, if his conscience had been less maddening in its insistence that he had thrown the precious jewel of his soul irretrievably away, he might have paused after his first deed, might even have repented. Yet his imagination, his determination, and his conscience were things good" (*Oxford Lectures on Poetry*, 88–89).

47. On Gus as sociopath, see Jeffrey A. Hinzmann, "The Riddle of Godfather Gus," in *Breaking Bad and Philosophy*, ed. Koepsell and Arp, 105–7.

48. Giancarlo Esposito, the actor who played Gus, says, "The moments when Gus is really demonstratively powerful and frightening are when his eyes go dead" (qtd. in Stache, *Breaking Bad*, 124).

49. See, for example, Guffey and Koontz, *Wanna Cook?*, 129–32.

50. See Cranston, *Life in Parts*, 1–3. Having created the part of Walter White, Cranston is arguably the world's greatest authority on the character, and thus this whole passage is fascinating because it reveals the complex thoughts that were going through Cranston's mind as he played the scene of Walt watching Jane die. Indeed, Cranston chose to open his autobiography with three pages devoted just to this moment, which he calls the "the most harrowing" scene he has ever acted (3). Playing the scene was evidently so difficult for Cranston that he comes back to it later in his autobiography and gives an even more detailed analysis of this scene. Cranston reveals that, as originally written, it painted Walt in a darker light: "Vince Gilligan originally thought of Walt as a more active, aggressive murderer" (202). The original script called for Walt to push Jane over on her back deliberately and thereby to cause her to choke on her own vomit (204). Cranston, as well as the studio and the network, argued that this plot development was going too far and would cause the audience to lose all sympathy for Walt. As Cranston explains, Gilligan "listened and came to agree. He devised a slightly less damning way for Walt to be involved in Jane's death" (205)—by jostling Jesse in an effort to wake him up, Walt inadvertently causes Jane to turn over on her back. This is an excellent example of how much careful thought went into the creation of *Breaking Bad* and how much it was a collaborative process—and all the better for it. As Cranston writes: "Studios and networks have a reputation for diluting the creative process with their notes. Decision by committee. . . . But extra eyes on a story line can actually be useful and generative, and throughout the run of *Breaking Bad* our studio and our network helped us make the story better" (205). Gilligan initially wanted to portray Jane's death in a way that would paint Walt as a much darker character, but by persuading him to change the story, Cranston and others retained the ambiguity and complexity of the character. For alternate accounts of this matter, see Sepinwall, *Revolution Was Televised*, 358; and Bianculli, *Platinum Age*, who quotes Gilligan saying: "the original version was, [Walt]

actually shoots [Jane] up with more [heroin]. He was more active in his culpability . . . and I'm glad that I got talked out of that one." Stache, *Breaking Bad*, 25, supports this account. For a balanced assessment of Walt's culpability in Jane's death, see David R. Koepsell and Vanessa Gonzalez, "Walt's Rap Sheet," in *Breaking Bad and Philosophy*, ed. Koepsell and Arp, 7–9. On this scene, see also Sepinwall, *Breaking Bad 101*, 87–90. The scene of Jane's death is one of the most discussed and disputed moments in *Breaking Bad*, and viewers will undoubtedly never agree about it.

51. See Guffey and Koontz, *Wanna Cook?*, 398.

52. Bryan Cranston accurately describes Hank as a "dickish, emasculating brother-in-law bragging about his exploits as a DEA agent" (*Life in Parts*, 192).

53. Once again I find myself in disagreement with Vince Gilligan, who admires Hank: "Hank is a very good DEA agent. In my mind, that's what Hank is: he's very good at his job and he's very much a straight arrow" (interview in Thompson, *Breaking Bad*, 54). For a defense of Hank, see Guffey and Koontz, *Wanna Cook?*, 167–68; and Stache, *Breaking Bad*, 141–45.

54. For a similar interpretation, see Guffey and Koontz, *Wanna Cook?*, 107.

55. Sepinwall does a good job of summarizing how morally ambiguous many of the characters in *Breaking Bad* are. See his *Breaking Bad 101*, 175–76: "Gus has a tragic origin story that makes him seem both human and more like Walt and/or Jesse, but he's also been responsible for many deaths. . . . Skyler has on some level been trapped by circumstances, but also has chosen to go deeper and deeper into Walt's world. Jesse has been manipulated and used by Walt from the beginning of their professional relationship, but he tried to use a twelve-step group as a drug client base. Hank is obsessed with Gus as much out of his own sense of ego as of any desire for justice. The good guys have deep flaws, and the villains have moments of abundant humanity." This is excellent analysis, but one wonders why, after all this, Sepinwall continues to divide the world of *Breaking Bad* simplistically into "good guys" and "villains." The truth is: all the major characters in *Breaking Bad* are in some ways presented sympathetically as human beings, but all of them are also deeply flawed and do morally dubious things at one point or another. This is what makes *Breaking Bad* a work of art and not a run-of-the-mill TV series. I sense that habits viewers developed, perhaps over decades, watching television when it was a morally simplistic medium have carried over to the new era, when television has developed the moral complexity of great literature of the past, such as Shakespeare's plays and Dostoevsky's novels. Viewers nostalgically cling to the time when television characters did divide easily into "good guys" and "bad guys." Although Dostoevsky does make careful moral distinctions among his characters, would one ever go through *The Brothers Karamazov* trying to distinguish the "good guys" from the "bad guys"?

56. In 3/12, Skyler formulates another version of Achilles's choice: "I'll tell you what, Walt, I'd rather have them think I'm Bonnie What's-Her-Name than some complete idiot." Skyler thinks it is worse to be viewed as a fool than as a criminal.

57. For this phrase, see book 4, section 283, of Nietzsche's *The Gay Science*.

58. Once again, Cranston shows insight into the character he brought to life. He grasps the difference between judging Walt morally and appreciating the challenge he

faces: "Walter White was more alive in the last year of his life than he had been in the previous fifty. He went from utter failure to great power. . . . I don't agree with the decisions Walt made or the actions he took, of course. But I feel for him. If you have two years to live, you don't let them cut your balls off. You go out fighting" (*Life in Parts*, 233). Here Cranston catches the essence of a tragic hero, as he also does in his *Inside the Actor's Studio* interview, when he says of Walt: "He went out on his terms." From comments such as these, we can tell why Bryan Cranston was able to do such a great job of playing Walter White. It seems that he was better able than Vince Gilligan to identify with the character.

59. In 5/16, a neighbor says of Walt, "He looked exactly like the Unabomber." Marie tells the police: "He's going to blow up City Hall. He has some kind of manifesto he wants to see on the 6 o'clock news."

60. In fact, David Bianculli reports of an interview with Gilligan: "Alternative endings were considered, in which Walter White would be carried off to jail in handcuffs, or, perhaps worse, get away with all his crimes. [Gilligan said:] 'We even had thought of ending the series with everyone else that he loves dying all around him, and he is the only one, perversely, that survives. Like a cockroach, and his hell, his torment, is that everyone else dies. But that seemed a little too consciously ironic to go in that direction'" (Bianculli, *Platinum Age*, 205). When an interviewer asked Gilligan whether he considered having Walt die of his cancer, Gilligan replied: "When it came down to it, it seemed most fitting for Walt's end that it wasn't the cancer that got him, but a death of his own making. It seemed appropriate for the character, and the journey we had taken him on, for Walt to have an active hand in his mortality" (Thompson, *Breaking Bad*, 62). Gilligan does not say it, but he is talking about what is "fitting" and "appropriate" for a tragic hero—who should be active in his own fate.

61. On the aptness of the ending, see Sepinwall, *Breaking Bad 101*, 264–70, for a thoughtful and provocative discussion; he considers whether either of the prior two episodes would have made better finales.

62. Stache astutely observes, "The fact that the bad guys at the end of Season 5 were unlikable, morally repugnant animals provides one reason why so many fans remained Team Walt until the end" (*Breaking Bad*, 130).

63. On this point, see Guffey and Koontz, *Wanna Cook?*, 308.

64. Unlike many analysts of the show, I do not believe that Walt's final confession that he enjoyed being Heisenberg utterly negates his earlier claims that he did what he did for his family's sake. *Breaking Bad* is fundamentally about *mixed motives* in human beings. Much of what he does in the last few episodes clearly shows that Walt is still concerned about his family.

65. Oddly enough, Gilligan does choose to invoke the tragic when he speaks of *Better Call Saul*: "We've realized more and more, that this show is a tragedy. And the tragedy comes when Jimmy McGill disappears and Saul Goodman appears" (Bianculli, *Platinum Age*, 207). In fact, Jimmy McGill/Saul Goodman is the opposite of a tragic figure—he is the quintessential survivor; he has no principles for which he would risk his life. That is why he is still alive at the end of *Breaking Bad*.

66. Gilligan has admitted that in the end, much to his surprise, Walt redeemed himself: "Walt found surprising ways—surprising to me at least—to redeem himself, at least a little bit. That's not to say he completely redeemed himself. He couldn't come back from the decisions he made; he's more villain than hero in the end. But, it surprised me he came back even partially. He found heartfelt ways of making amends and made a start back from the place he'd gone to. I was so down on him for the last season or so because he'd become such a bastard. It was a happy occurrence that he turned the corner toward redemption. If he never had the time to make it there, he made some solid steps—and that's something" (Thompson, *Breaking Bad*, 64). Once again, Gilligan is trapped in the conventional categories of "hero" versus "villain" and does not allow for the possibility of a "tragic hero." In fact, he gives an excellent description of the way a tragic hero dies, especially in Shakespeare's plays. Walt does a lot more to redeem himself than Macbeth does. One has to wonder whether Shakespeare was ever "down" on Macbeth. Gilligan made another revealing comment in his interview with David Thompson: "It's an odd thing, but the longer the show went with Walter White, the less sympathy I had for him. It was an irony that I had been so worried in those early days about him being *likable*, but at the end of it all I honestly believe I liked him less than the average viewer of *Breaking Bad*. I talked to my own mother and my longtime girlfriend, and they'd say, 'I was so sad to see Walter die' and I think, 'Really? He got off easy!' He was going to die from episode 1 on—we're all going to die—and he died on his own terms; he went out more or less as a hero." Here I can finally agree with Gilligan—he gets the force of the show's ending exactly right. He also said of the great "Ozymandias" episode (5/14): "It really wrapped things up very tragically" (qtd. in Sepinwall, *Breaking Bad 101*, 258).

67. The satisfying nature of the show's genuinely tragic ending is one reason why many have judged *Breaking Bad* the best television series of all time (see, for example, Stache, *Breaking Bad*, xv–xvi).

68. Aristotle, *The Poetics*, trans. W. Hamilton Fyfe (Cambridge: Harvard University Press, 1932), 15, 31 (chaps. 4 and 7, 43b25 and 50b30).

69. In 1/4, Hank announces, "Albuquerque just might have a new kingpin," only to have the camera cut to a shirtless Walt shaving in his tighty-whities and looking somewhat less than regal. Invoking aristocratic imagery in 2/7, Jesse tells his criminal crew: "We're going to be kings. Well, I'm going to be king. You guys will be princes and dukes." Suddenly, we are back in the world of the fraudulent king and duke of *Huckleberry Finn*. Even average Americans crave these aristocratic titles.

70. For a discussion of the more general theme of disability in *Breaking Bad*, see Jami L. Anderson, "A Life Not Worth Living," in *Breaking Bad*, ed. Pierson, 103–18.

71. For a fuller discussion of the portrayal of Latino characters in *Breaking Bad*, see Andrew Howe, "Not Your Average Mexican: *Breaking Bad* and the Destruction of Latino Stereotypes," in *Breaking Bad*, ed. Pierson, 87–102.

72. The many references to and quotations from films like *The Godfather* and *Scarface* in *Breaking Bad* create the impression that for many characters in the series, gang violence and the masculine aggressiveness that produces it are a thing of the past—something

that ordinary Americans like the White family see only in old movies on television. With a long history in film already, the gangster appears as a belated figure in *Breaking Bad*.

73. There are a number of Western-style gunfights in *Breaking Bad*; see, for example, 3/12 and 5/2. Episode 5/5, "Dead Freight," is an homage to Edison's 1903 *The Great Train Robbery* (dir. Edwin Porter), often regarded as the first film Western. On *Breaking Bad* as a "modern Western," see Thompson, *Breaking Bad*, 78–79.

74. For the importance of the desert in *Breaking Bad*, see Ensley F. Guffey, "Buying the House: Place in *Breaking Bad*," in *Breaking Bad*, ed. Pierson, 169–70.

75. In another geographic comparison, Sicily is to New York in the *Godfather* films as Mexico is to Albuquerque in *Breaking Bad*.

76. On this point, see Thompson, *Breaking Bad*, 71.

77. Michael Corleone is subject to similar psychological pressures in the *Godfather* films.

78. See Stache, *Breaking Bad*, 116: "Vince Gilligan comments that perhaps viewers like the bad guys because they are good at their jobs, arguing, 'What is it people like about Darth Vader? Is it that he's so evil, or that he's so good at his job? I think it might be the latter.'"

79. Cleaning is an important motif in *Breaking Bad*. Walt's obsessive efforts to clean his body, his house, and his pool (not to mention laundering his money) reflect his growing sense of his own corruption and the moral pollution that surrounds him. The motif of obsessive cleaning in *Breaking Bad* calls to mind Lady Macbeth's famous words: "Out, damn'd spot! . . . What, will these hands ne'er be clean?" (5.1.35, 43).

80. If we knew the full backstories of all the characters in *Breaking Bad*, we might sympathize with more of them. In Walt's encounter with Krazy-8 in 1/3, we learn that this vicious criminal once took classes in business administration at UNM. He wanted to become a musician, but his father told him that there was no money in it. In these respects, Krazy-8's story resembles Walt's. We get the barest hints of Gus's backstory and must wonder what really happened in Chile. Gus seems at first to be doing everything out of purely financial motives, but we gradually learn that he is seeking revenge on the Salamanca clan and the drug cartel for having killed a dear friend. The *Breaking Bad* prequel, *Better Call Saul*, is slowly filling us in on the backstories of its characters.

81. In search of some form of nobility in *Breaking Bad*, one might be tempted, since there is so much law-breaking in the series, to turn to the majesty of the law, that great bulwark against the forces of criminality that threaten to destroy civilized society. The problem with this approach is that the chief representative of the law in *Breaking Bad* is Saul Goodman. The inflatable Statue of Liberty sitting atop his strip-mall law office provides a wry comment on the American dream. In *The Godfather I*, we see the real Statue of Liberty several times—still a symbol of America's promise to its immigrants. In *Breaking Bad*, we see only a cheap simulacrum of the Statue of Liberty, perhaps a symbol of how the American dream has declined in the twenty-first century. Similarly, the mock-up of the United States Constitution in Saul's office makes a mockery of the document, as he often does in court when defending his criminal clients.

82. See David P. Pierson, "Breaking Neoliberal? Contemporary Neoliberal Discourses and Politics in AMC's *Breaking Bad*," in *Breaking Bad*, ed. Pierson, 26.

83. In 2/5, we learn that Hank would have made a fine bootlegger; he brews his own beer, called Schraderbräu. This episode pointedly juxtaposes Hank's legal beer making with Walt's illegal meth making, hinting at some form of equivalence between the two activities.

84. In fact, Hank underestimates the point about the government's varying attitudes toward meth—the US government was once a meth pusher itself. The development and industrial production of meth was actively promoted by governments on both sides during World War II; countries including Germany, Japan, and the United States distributed the drug to their soldiers to fight combat fatigue and to spark combat performance (see Guffey and Koontz, *Wanna Cook?*, 50).

85. For a positive view of the marriage of Hank and Marie, see Guffey and Koontz, *Wanna Cook?*, 172, 183.

86. Jesse refers to Skyler as a "ballbuster" in 1/4. In 3/5, Hank asks his partner, "Did you leave your balls in your wife's purse?" Fear of emasculation by women is endemic among the men in the series.

87. Therapeutic culture seems to play the role in Walter White's tragedy that Christianity does in Macbeth's. The values promoted by therapeutic culture—niceness, kindness, affability, the absence of anger—are inherited from Christianity. As we have seen, Macbeth believes that men in Scotland have lost their manliness because they have been "gospelled." Similarly in *Breaking Bad*, the various twelve-step programs are designed to neutralize the masculinity in anyone who deviates from social norms. If Macbeth had lived in twenty-first-century Albuquerque, his friends might have organized an intervention so that he could learn to deal with his "vaulting ambition" problem. If one sees that "criminality" has replaced "martial heroism" and "therapy" has replaced "Christianity" in Walter White's life, one gets a measure of the ignobility of the modern world.

88. In 4/12, Jesse and Gus meet in an empty chapel.

89. For a critique of contemporary notions of masculinity and a defense of traditional notions of manliness, see Harvey C. Mansfield, *Manliness* (New Haven: Yale University Press, 2006).

5. The Apocalyptic Strain in Popular Culture

Epigraph: These words appear on the back cover of the graphic novel on which the TV series is based—*The Walking Dead: Compendium One* (Berkeley, CA: Image Comics, 2015).

1. For discussions of this period, see Lawrence R. Samuel, *The American Dream: A Cultural History* (Syracuse, NY: Syracuse University Press, 2012), 42–71; and Jim Cullen, *The American Dream: A Short History of an Idea That Shaped a Nation* (New York: Oxford University Press, 2003), 133–57.

2. On the importance of Whyte's book, see Cullen, *American Dream*, 153. As Cullen notes, David Riesman's *The Lonely Crowd* was also important for the way it criticized conformism in America.

3. See Samuel, *American Dream*, 61, for the way "the dark side of the American dream" began to surface in popular culture as early as the 1950s.

4. Among such busy overachievers are the people who work in the entertainment industry itself. These apocalyptic fantasies, in which professionals are in effect reunited with their families, may reflect the guilt feelings of a Hollywood community in which the broken family is the norm rather than the exception.

5. *Revolution* rests on the same parallel. Co-executive producer Jon Favreau says in an interview: "We call the show *Revolution* because it harkens back to a time when we were colonists under an oppressive monarchy. It's about a new kind of revolutionary war, where the people must rise up and build a nation all over again" (*TV Guide*, September 17–23, 2012), 33.

6. Robert Kirkman (the creator of the graphic novel series) has revealed that he originally conceived of the story as an alien invasion narrative: "The whole story was hinging upon a later reveal that it was aliens that caused the zombies and that this was part of a massive alien takeover" (qtd. in Paul Ruditis, *The Walking Dead Chronicles: The Official Companion Book* [New York: Abrams, 2011], 16). For the record, I have read a good deal of the graphic novel series, but my analysis in this chapter is based almost entirely on the TV series. The show's creators have deliberately chosen *not* to follow the exact plotline of the graphic novels, in order to maintain suspense and keep their options open.

7. On zombies and globalization, see Daniel W. Drenzer, *Theory of International Politics and Zombies* (Princeton: Princeton University Press, 2011), esp. 15.

8. In American popular culture, zombies originally functioned as a symbol of slavery. Zombie films were typically set in the American South or the Caribbean, and the zombies were generally black; often some kind of plantation owner commanded them. A good example is Val Lewton's 1943 *I Walked with a Zombie*. In films like this, the chief feature of zombies is their subjugation to the will of a master. This background lends plausibility to the idea that, in contemporary pop culture, zombies may symbolize slavery to modern institutions. George Romero's pioneering zombie films have been interpreted as portraying the slavery of the American people to their consumerist fantasies. In his second zombie film, *Dawn of the Dead* (1978), the zombies are irresistibly drawn to a suburban shopping mall (see Camilla Fojas, *Zombies, Migrants, and Queers: Race and Crisis Capitalism in Pop Culture* [Urbana: University of Illinois Press, 2017], 68). Fojas develops an interpretation of the significance of zombies in American popular culture, including in *The Walking Dead*, that offers an alternative to the view advanced in this chapter.

9. See Fojas, *Zombies, Migrants, and Queers*, 68–69.

10. On the use of the CDC in *The Walking Dead*, see Ruditis, *Walking Dead Chronicles*, 173–74. On the look of the CDC interiors in the show, production designer Alex Hajdu had this to say: "When I read the script it felt very Cold War to me, in a Kubrick kind of way. . . . Of course the image of the war room in *Dr. Strangelove* came to mind. I felt nothing better illustrated the futility of a powerful government institution faced with an unresolvable dilemma than that symbolic reference" (*Chronicles,* 174). Anyone

who still thinks that American television shows are produced by people who have no idea what they are doing should ponder Hadju's comments. He is clearly thinking in political terms, and he is drawing upon cinematic tradition in the process. And he is only the production designer! Yet even he is consciously making a "symbolic film reference." As I have often argued, the people who create the best of American television are a good deal more sophisticated than most academics think.

11. See www.cdc.gov/phpr/zombies. For further commentary on the CDC website, see a series of three articles I wrote: (1) "Zombie Apocalypse in a 'DC' Comic," www .lewrockwell.com/2013/09/paul-cantor/zombie-apocalypse/; (2) "The Walking Dead and a Refuge from the Modern State," www.lewrockwell.com/2013/09/paul-cantor/the-walking-dead-2/; and (3) "The Economics of Apocalypse: A Tale of Two CDC's," www .lewrockwell.com/2013/10/paul-cantor/the-economics-of-apocalypse/.

12. In Maureen Dowd's column on the movie *World War Z*, "A Zombie Scare with a Zombie Chaser" (*New York Times*, June 22, 2013), she quotes Dr. Ali S. Khan, director of the CDC Office of Public Health Preparedness and Response, saying with regard to *Zombie Pandemic*: "You may laugh now, but when it happens you'll be happy you read this, and hey, maybe you'll even learn a thing or two about how to prepare for a *real* emergency."

13. *World War Z* is a libel on the competence of the human species. The film consists of one scene of mass panic after another. Women in particular are repeatedly shown to be utterly incapable of dealing with a crisis (unless they are in the Israeli army). The film's central symbol for humanity is a pair of frightened little girls who cannot be left alone for a minute without tears and screams coming on (the film takes the notion of "helicopter parents" literally). In *World War Z*, the military is shown to be the only source of order among human beings. The UN's navy is at the center of coordinating humanity's response to the zombie outbreak, which tells us something about the film, because the UN does not have a navy. Evidently the creators of the film have never met an authoritarian regime they do not like. North Korea comes in for special praise from a rogue CIA agent for its approach to the zombie plague: "They pulled the teeth of all 23 million in less than twenty-four hours—the greatest feat of social engineering in history. Brilliant—no teeth, no bite, no great spread." Social engineering by governments, the more totalitarian the better, is the film's answer to all human problems. Rather than the CDC, it is the WHO that miraculously comes up with a countermeasure against the zombies in *World War Z*. On the film, see Fojas, *Zombies, Migrants, and Queers*, 73–77; John Podhoretz, "Zombies in the Mineshaft," *Weekly Standard*, July 8/July 15, 2013: 47; and Ryan McMaken, "Horror Film as Neocon Fantasy," http:lewrockwell.com/mcmaken/mcmaken158.html.

14. Ruditis, *Walking Dead Chronicles*, 11. The way the government herds people in cities into various forms of holding facilities or concentration camps is actually portrayed in season 1 of the spinoff from *The Walking Dead, Fear the Walking Dead*.

15. This discussion of fictional zombie plagues may seem purely academic, but such imaginary disasters do have genuine parallels in the real world. For example, critics of the federal government's response to Hurricane Katrina have dwelled on the way the

government's insistence on concentrating people in centers such as the New Orleans Superdome made matters worse, while spontaneous and improvised solutions offered by ordinary citizens and local volunteer organizations succeeded in saving lives and improving conditions. On this subject, see my book *The Invisible Hand in Popular Culture: Liberty vs. Authority in American Film and TV* (Lexington: University Press of Kentucky, 2012), 423–24n33; as well as Neille Ilel, "A Healthy Dose of Anarchy," *Reason* 38, no. 7 (December 2006): 48–56; and Rebecca Solnit, *A Paradise Built in Hell: The Extraordinary Communities That Arise in Disaster* (New York: Penguin, 2010), 231–304. As these studies show, the government approach to disaster relies on a top-down model of order, a generalized and therefore abstract view of the problem that often turns out to be blind to local needs and concerns. As we will see, *The Walking Dead* portrays individual people dealing with their immediate, personal problems in concrete circumstances with which they are intimately familiar—a bottom-up response that may well be better adapted to survival in a catastrophic situation.

16. *Walking Dead* executive producer Gale Anne Hurd comments on the danger that looms "whenever you put all your eggs in one basket—especially when it's the fate of humanity" (*TV Guide,* December 8–21, 2014, 18).

17. See Nassim Nicholas Taleb, *Antifragile: Things That Gain from Disorder* (New York: Random House, 2012).

18. Mobility has always been a vital component of the American dream. Consider the importance in *Breaking Bad* of the RV in which Walt and Jesse initially cook their meth. Albert Brooks's film *Lost in America* offers a hilarious send-up of the mobile home version of the American dream.

19. The same pattern develops in what amounts to the first "zombie" novel, Daniel Defoe's *A Journal of the Plague Year* (1722), one of the earliest "walking dead" narratives (in fact it is an account of the great London plague of 1665). Defoe contrasts the government's plan to fix the population of London in place through quarantines monitored by an elaborate system of panoptical surveillance, with the hastily improvised schemes of ordinary citizens to evade the municipal lockdown by fleeing the city and dispersing into the countryside. It is not clear which approach Defoe endorses; he shows the advantages and disadvantages of both. In particular, he repeatedly praises municipal officials in London for their draconian efforts to contain the plague by turning the city effectively into a gigantic prison, while at the same time pointing out how often this policy backfired; as in *The Walking Dead,* concentrating the population in the city only spread the plague faster and made matters worse. At other points in the book, Defoe shows that escaping the city to the countryside was the most effective survival strategy, even at the risk of spreading the plague further.

20. A helpful framework for thinking about *The Walking Dead* is provided by the brilliant work of political scientist and anthropologist James C. Scott. Challenging the generally unexamined assumption that living in states is the norm for human existence, Scott has shown in a series of remarkable books that humanity has typically alternated between nomadism and settlement, between barbarism and civilization, just as the characters in *The Walking Dead* do. Human beings are attracted to large settlements

by the security they provide and their abundance of food. But these settlements are governed autocratically, and eventually, if not immediately, they oppress their subjects, burdening them with ruinous taxes, backbreaking work requirements, and regimented lifestyles, thereby denying them the freedom and independence of nomadic existence. When the burden of the state's demands—such as slaving away on useless projects like building pyramids—becomes too great, the oppressed people just pick up and leave, heading back for the hills or slipping back into the jungle from whence they originally came. Historians are traditionally mystified by the sudden collapse of pyramid-building civilizations. Scott makes us wonder how they ever survived as long as they did when they made such brutal and insane demands upon their citizens. As Scott documents, for most of human history—before the comparatively recent emergence of the modern nation-state with its sophisticated means of bureaucratic surveillance and control—the situation that so-called civilized people stigmatize as "barbarism" was a genuine and perennially attractive alternative for human beings. The narrative rhythm of settlement and flight in *The Walking Dead* reflects Scott's understanding of the human condition. In analyzing strategies for evading and escaping oppressive state control, Scott comes up with the concept of "shatter zones"—interstices between state spaces that occupy the permeable boundary line between civilization and barbarism. Scott's concept of "shatter zones" is an apt way of characterizing the territory *The Walking Dead* explores. Among Scott's books, see especially *The Art of Not Being Governed: An Anarchistic History of Upland Southeast Asia* (New Haven: Yale University Press, 2009); and *Against the Grain: A Deep History of the Earliest States* (New Haven: Yale University Press, 2017). Without intending to, these books read like a commentary on the world of *The Walking Dead*.

21. In season 5, Grady Memorial Hospital in Atlanta becomes another potential deathtrap for our heroes and heroines.

22. In the fifteenth episode of season 3, Grimes repudiates his repudiation of democracy and claims to be reestablishing majority rule in the band of survivors. All quotations from television shows in this chapter have been transcribed from the DVD versions.

23. Robert Kirkman has actually said of the entire TV series: "*The Walking Dead* is a soap opera," and "I'm really just doing a soap opera about survival" (Ruditis, *Walking Dead Chronicles*, 10, 23).

24. *TV Guide*, October 16–29, 2017, 20. See Michael J. Totten, "*The Walking Dead* in an Age of Anxiety: Why We're Obsessed with Zombies," *City Journal*, Autumn 2015, 3: "The last people on earth can reinvent themselves into something better, or more powerful. Glenn, a pizza-delivery driver before the zombie plague, becomes, postapocalypse, a vital strategist and skillful navigator of deadly terrain. Philip Blake was an office drone in the old, normal world; in the dark new world, he's the Governor, the feared and charismatic ruler of Woodbury, a walled-off town of survivors. Carol was a cringing victim of domestic violence before the end of civilization; after, she chops her zombified husband's body into pieces with an ax and transforms herself into a hardened, capable survivor."

25. Ruditis, *Walking Dead Chronicles*, 24.

26. See Jack Cashill, "Alexis de Tocqueville and the Walking Dead," *American Thinker*, December 26, 2013.

27. *Revolution* adds an interesting twist—its characters are forced to resort to swords and bows-and-arrows because the reconstituted government forces have outlawed firearms among the general populace. *Revolution* presents gun control in a sinister light, as does another series, *Under the Dome*. Given the Hollywood community's seemingly universal support for gun control, it is surprising how many of the television shows it produces offer arguments against gun control.

28. The CDC's *Zombie Pandemic* contains instructions for putting together supplies for an emergency. It recommends "games and activities for children," as well as a "manual can opener." It says nothing about weapons. The characters in *The Walking Dead* do not make this mistake. Being more realistic, they load up on guns and ammunition whenever they have the opportunity.

29. This development provokes some negative comments from the women in the third episode of season 1. One says, "I'm beginning to question the division of labor here." This situation triggers nostalgia among the women for the work-saving devices in pre-apocalypse civilization: "Scrubbin' on a washboard ain't half as good as my old Maytag back home." Another woman says, "I miss my coffee maker." Modernity has some advocates in *The Walking Dead*, especially among the women. On women in the series, see Fojas, *Zombies, Migrants, and Queers*, 77.

30. It occurred to me that the way Carl is torn in season 1 between his real father (a good guy) and a substitute father (a bad guy) is reminiscent of the situation of the young boy in the classic Western *Shane*. Then it occurred to me that the substitute father in *The Walking Dead* is named Shane. The creators of the show were way ahead of me on this point.

31. The creators of *The Walking Dead* are well aware of its connections to Westerns. Production designer Alex Hajdu said of one of the Atlanta scenes: "It was like a Sergio Leone spaghetti Western, like *Once Upon a Time in the West*. You expected to see the silhouettes of bandits on the roof. The courtyard became like the street of an old western town where the showdown takes place" (Ruditis, *Walking Dead Chronicles*, 162). Director of photography David Boyd compared the way *The Walking Dead* is shot to John Ford's method in *The Searchers* (Ruditis, *Walking Dead Chronicles*, 165).

32. The symbolic value of this moment was not lost on the show's executive producer, Gale Anne Hurd, who commented, "There is almost a western sensibility to it; that lone sheriff riding into town, riding into hostile territory" (Ruditis, *Walking Dead Chronicles*, 190).

33. In a brief chapter, I have been able to discuss only a few examples of the patterns I am identifying in contemporary popular culture. In *Invisible Hand in Popular Culture*, I discuss *Falling Skies* at greater length (341–44) in a chapter devoted to alien invasion narratives, which includes analyses of *The X-Files, Invasion, The Event, V, Fringe*, and several other examples of the genre. I discuss the convergence of science fiction and the Western at a number of points in the book (see, for example, 87–90 and 342–44) and also the way that apocalyptic disasters propel characters back into the state of nature (see, for example, 144–45, and 423–24n33). I devote a chapter to showing how state-of-nature thinking can be applied to understanding Westerns in the case of *Deadwood* (97–127, 381–88).

34. On the way zombie narratives reflect anxieties about the increasingly urbanized nature of the modern world, see Totten, "Age of Anxiety," 5.

35. On this development, see the chapter "The Original Frontier" in Cantor, *Invisible Hand,* esp. 91–94, where I discuss the negative portrait of the South encrypted in the TV Western *Have Gun—Will Travel.*

36. I am aware that Alaska, the site of several of these series, is not in the South; the point of all these shows, however, is that they offer alternatives to the conventional urban settings that now dominate American television. *God, Guns, and Automobiles* deals with a car dealership in the rural town of Butler, in Bates County, Missouri. The title of this show is probably a reference to a famous speech that then presidential candidate Barack Obama gave in San Francisco on April 11, 2008, in which he said of people in small towns in the Midwest: "They cling to their guns, or religion" (for further discussion of this speech, see Cantor, *Invisible Hand,* 154, 392n42). For an excellent discussion of this group of reality TV shows, see Victor Davis Hanson, "Good Ol' Boy, Inc.," on National Review Online, December 31, 2013, www.nationalreview.com/article/367231/good-ol-boy-inc-victor-davis-hanson.

37. Totten, "Age of Anxiety," 5: "A mechanic fixes my car. I couldn't raise enough food to sustain me, solve a serious engine problem, or get water to my house, except by bucket from a stream or river. Nor can I set broken bones, put out large house fires, or build a refrigerator to keep my produce from rotting. . . . Ironically, people who lived 200 years ago were better prepared to survive in a postapocalyptic environment, and, on some level, we all know it."

38. *The Walking Dead* was not picked up as a series by any of the major networks, either broadcast or cable. Instead the series was developed by AMC, at the time known only for scheduling old movies (Ruditis, *Walking Dead Chronicles,* 46, 51). AMC became a major player precisely by developing shows that no other network at the time would touch, including *Breaking Bad.*

39. Their trek to Washington is originally inspired by a character named Eugene, who claims to be a government scientist with a cure for the zombie plague—he just needs to get to DC to implement it. It is characteristic of the series that the man claiming to be a scientific expert turns out to be a complete fraud.

40. To reinforce this point, later (in season 5, episode 16), Deanna says that she "would like to share something in the spirit of transparency."

41. Totten describes Daryl as "precisely the sort of man you'd want to cover your back" (4). The Alexandria sequence is an excellent example of how *The Walking Dead* TV series is much more complex and sophisticated than the graphic novel on which it is based. Almost all the telling details we have analyzed in this sequence—the transparency, the ecobase sewage filtration, the gourmet recipes, the white wine, the ten-speed bike—are not present in the graphic novel. There Alexandria is presided over by a male leader, Douglas Monroe, and although he is identified as the Democratic representative of the Second District of Ohio, he has none of the characteristics that make Deanna such a perfect emblem in the TV series of the DC elite. The only details about Alexandria the TV series takes from the graphic novel are the facts that it runs on a solar power grid,

it practices gun control, and it contains a gay couple named Aaron and Eric. The entire theme of culture clash so richly developed in the TV series is absent from the graphic novel. The Alexandria sequence appears in chapters 12 and 13 in *The Walking Dead: Compendium Two* (Berkeley, CA: Image Comics, 2012). The corresponding moments in the TV series are roughly season 5, episodes 11–16.

42. For a brief but insightful article that brings together *Revolution, Falling Skies, The Walking Dead,* and *Last Resort* along the lines I have been discussing, see Alessandra Stanley, "A Future with Swords, Not iPhones," *New York Times,* September 16, 2012. Stanley concludes: "Fighting back is a theme that has special resonance these days."

ACKNOWLEDGMENTS

Among the many friends, colleagues, and students with whom I have profitably discussed the material covered in this book, I would like especially to thank Brooks Welden Anderson, Mark Conard, Andrea Dvorak, Mark Edmundson, Peter Hufnagel, Bill Irwin, Michael Valdez Moses, and Timothy Schott. My brother, Donald Ochacher, who introduced me to the delights of talking about film and television many years ago, was especially helpful with comments on the *Godfather* films and *Breaking Bad*. I owe the book's epigraph from Raymond Chandler to Adam Schulman. Bill Kristol and Andy Zwick have done a great deal to promote and disseminate my work on popular culture through several episodes of *Conversations with Bill Kristol*, including one devoted specifically to this book.

I have benefited greatly from the opportunity to present my ideas on the subjects covered in this book on a number of public occasions. For that I would like to thank the following institutions: Ashland University, Duke University, George Mason University, Hampden-Sydney College, Harvard University, Lee University, North Carolina State University, Rhodes College, UCLA, and the University of Houston. I specifically thank the many people at these institutions who worked behind the scenes to invite me to lecture and who made sure that the events went smoothly. The give-and-take at these sessions helped me to formulate my ideas more crisply and also suggested new ideas to me. For example, the point about the relation of reality TV shows to *The Walking Dead* that I discuss in chapter 5 was first suggested to me by a student questioner at Hampden-Sydney College.

I must as always thank the godfather of my work on popular culture, Steve Wrinn, who has had a hand as editor and publisher in all three of my books on the subject. He was still at University Press of Kentucky when this book was accepted for publication. It has been a pleasure to work again with all the people at Kentucky, and I want to thank especially Anne Dean Dotson and David Cobb, as well as the anonymous readers of my manuscript for the press, who made many useful suggestions about how to improve this book. Susan Murray has been an ideal copyeditor.

An earlier version of chapter 1 was published under the title "Aristocracy in America," in *Claremont Review of Books* 13, no. 2 (Spring 2013): 44–49. An earlier version of chapter 2 was published under the title "Being Claude Dukenfield: W. C. Fields and the American Dream," in *Perspectives on Political Science* 31, no. 2 (Spring 2002): 71–76. Another portion of chapter 2 was published under the title "Fields of Glory: The Absurdist Anti-Politics of W. C. Fields," in *Reason*, May 2000: 47–48. An earlier version of chapter 5 was published under the same title in the *Hedgehog Review* 15, no. 2 (Summer 2013): 23–33. All these essays have been substantially revised and expanded for publication in this book.

INDEX

Achilles, 96, 116, 119, 123

Adventures of Huckleberry Finn, The
(Twain): con men and con games
in, 20–23; dark portrayal of the
American dream and, 4; identity
construction and, 4, 19–20; as a
meditation on aristocracy versus
democracy, 18–19, 29–30; paradox
of innocence and darkness in,
17–18; portrayal of aristocratic
feuds in, 28–29; portrayal of the
southern aristocratic ideal in,
25–27; significance in American
popular culture, 3, 17; theme
of sham aristocracy in, 23–25;
Twain's treatment of the South and
aristocratic literature in, 27–28

aesthetic judgment: versus moral
judgment, 14–15

Al Capone: Icon (PBS documentary), 13

Alger, Horatio, 1, 16

alien invasion narrative, 11

Alpert, David, 146

AMC network, 91–92, 193n38

American dream: apocalyptic narratives
in popular culture and, 136–37;
danger of domestication, 11–12;
dark portrayals of and the vitality
of American popular culture, 16;
embodiment in material terms,
133–35; W. C. Fields and the comic
debunking of, 39–43, 47; W. C.
Fields's life and, 4–5, 47; film and
the fantasy of being someone else,
32–33; *Huckleberry Finn* and the
dark portrayal of, 4; as interrogated
by *Breaking Bad*, 2–3, 6–8, 88–93,
103–8, 131–32 (*see also* Breaking
Bad); as interrogated by the *Godfather*
films, 2–3, 5–6, 48–53, 72, 73, 82–83
(*see also* Godfather films); issue of
gambling and, 74; mid-twentieth
century anxiety and disenchantment
concerning, 135–36; outlaw heroes
and, 15–16; overview of portrayals
of the dark side of, 2–3; return of an
older conception of in apocalyptic
narratives, 139; traditional version of,
3; trust in American institutions and,
134–35; Mark Twain's life and, 3–4,
161n6; *The Walking Dead* and the
dark portrayal of, 8–9

Americanization: tragedy of in the
Godfather films, 52–53, 72–83

American popular culture: crime
narratives as an alternative
to domestic existence, 12–13;
embodiment of Middle American
values in reality TV and apocalyptic
narratives, 152–57; outlaw heroes,